# ANTHROPOLOGY
in CHINA

# 中
# CHINESE STUDIES ■ ON ■ CHINA

**THE CHINESE COMMUNIST PARTY'S NOMENKLATURA SYSTEM**
*Edited by John P. Burns*

**THE ASIATIC MODE OF PRODUCTION IN CHINA**
*Edited by Timothy Brook*

**BASIC PRINCIPLES OF CIVIL LAW IN CHINA**
*Edited by William C. Jones*

**MAO ZEDONG ON DIALECTICAL MATERIALISM**
*Edited by Nick Knight*

**ZHU WEIZHENG**
**COMING OUT OF THE MIDDLE AGES**
*Translated and edited by Ruth Hayhoe*

**YAN JIAQI AND CHINA'S STRUGGLE FOR DEMOCRACY**
*Translated and edited by Dali L. Yang*

**ANTHROPOLOGY IN CHINA**
**Defining the Discipline**
*Edited by Gregory Eliyu Guldin*

# ANTHROPOLOGY in CHINA
## Defining the Discipline

### Edited by **GREGORY ELIYU GULDIN**

**M.E. Sharpe, Inc.**
Armonk, New York   London, England

Copyright © 1990 by M. E. Sharpe, Inc.

All rights reserved. No part of this book may be reproduced in any form without written permission from the publisher, M. E. Sharpe, Inc., 80 Business Park Drive, Armonk, New York 10504.

Available in the United Kingdom and Europe from M. E. Sharpe, Publishers, 3 Henrietta Street, London WC2E 8LU.

Previously published as Vol. 20, No. 4 and Vol. 21, No. 1 of *Chinese Sociology and Anthropology*.

**Library of Congress Cataloging-in-Publication Data**

Anthropology in China : defining the discipline / edited by Gregory Eliyu Guldin.
    p.    cm.—(Chinese studies on China)
  Selected articles from Chinese scholarly journals.
  Includes bibliographical references and index.
  ISBN 0-87332-833-7
  1. Ethnology—China. 2. China—Social life and customs. I. Guldin, Gregory Eliyu. II. Series.
GN635.C5A58   1991
301'.0951—dc20                                            90-21710
                                                                                  CIP

Printed in the United States of America

MV  10  9  8  7  6  5  4  3  2  1

# Contents

Contributors     vii
Introduction     ix

**Part I. Overview and Historical Background**

1
Chinese Anthropologies
*Gregory Eliyu Guldin*     3

**Part II. The Argument for a Four-Fields Anthropology**

2
The Scope and Function of Anthropology
*Liang Zhaotao*     33

3
The Chinese People Need Anthropology
*Chen Guoqiang*     42

**Part III. What Is Archaeology?**

4
What Is Archaeology?
*Xia Nai*     59

5
New Issues in Archaeological Typology
*Su Bingqi*     68

6
Characteristics and Sequence of Development of Neolithic Cultures in China
*Zeng Qi*     73

7
On "Ethnoarchaeology"
*Liang Zhaotao and Zhang Shouqi*     91

## Part IV. Paleoanthropology and Neoanthropology

**8**
Paleoanthropology and Neoanthropology
*Wu Rukang* — 111

**9**
The Impact of Physical Anthropology on Construction of the "Two Civilizations"
*Huang Xinmei* — 114

**10**
Modernization Requires Anthropometry
*Zhang Zhenbiao* — 121

**11**
Paleolithic Research in China, 1980–1984
*Zhang Senshui* — 127

## Part V. Developing Ethnology

**12**
New China's Ethnology: Research and Prospects
*Lin Yaohua* — 141

**13**
Developing Ethnology in Our Country Is What the Construction of Socialism Needs
*Huang Shuping* — 162

## Part VI. Ethnolinguistics

**14**
Developments in the Scientific Study of Nationality Languages in the Thirty-five Years Since Our Nation Was Founded
*Fu Maoji* — 177

**15**
Language and Nationality
*Ma Xueliang and Dai Qingxia* — 189

Index — 211

# Contributors

**Gregory Eliyu Guldin** is an associate professor at Pacific Lutheran University in Tacoma, Washington.

**Chen Guoqiang** is founder and professor of the Anthropology Department at Xiamen University.

**Dai Qingxia** is affiliated with the Department of Minority Languages, Central Institute of Nationalities, Beijing.

**Fu Maoji** is affiliated with the Department of Minority Languages, Central Institute of Nationalities, Beijing.

**Huang Shuping** was with the Department of Ethnology of the Central Institute of Nationalities, Beijing, until 1988, when she was transferred to Zhongshan University's Anthropology Department.

**Huang Xinmei** is with the Anthropology Department of Zhongshan University in Guangzhou.

**Liang Zhaotao** was founder and professor of the Anthropology Department at Zhongshan University before his death in 1987.

**Ma Xueliang** is affiliated with the Department of Minority Languages, Central Institute of Nationalities, Beijing.

**Su Bingqi** is professor in Beijing University's Archaeology Department and a prominent leader in CASS's Institute of Archaeology.

**Wu Rukang** is affiliated with the Institute of Vertebrate Paleontology and Paleoanthropology, CAS, Beijing.

**Xia Nai** was the head of CASS's Institute of Archaeology before his death in 1986.

**Zeng Qi** is associate professor in Zhongshan University's Anthropology Department.

**Zhang Shenshui** is an associate researcher at the Institute of Vertebrate Paleontology and Paleoanthropology, CAS, Beijing.

**Zhang Shouqi** is a professor at Zhongshan University.

**Zhang Zhenbiao** is an associate researcher at the Institute of Vertebrate Paleontology and Paleoanthropology, CAS, Beijing.

GREGORY ELIYU GULDIN

# Introduction

CHINESE today do not agree on the fundamental parameters of the field of anthropology in the People's Republic of China. For this reason, I refer to "Chinese anthropologies" or the "anthropological sciences in China" so as not to anticipate the Chinese answer to this question. In the background piece, "Chinese Anthropologies," the history of the introduction of anthropology to China is traced to provide a context for the contemporary discussion over the nature of the anthropological sciences in China today and their contribution to the country's development. Underlying much of the discussion by Chinese contributors is the question of the sinification of the disciplines and its relation to the importation of foreign models of anthropology.

The first two Chinese selections focus on the argument for the establishment in China of a four-fields anthropology, the original inspiration for which clearly derived from the United States. The essays by the founders of China's first anthropology departments, Liang Zhaotao and Chen Guoqiang, seek to convince social scientific colleagues of the validity of a science banned from the PRC for over thirty years. The repeated reference in these and other essays to the opinions and experience of foreigners is quite striking, considering the near total absence of such Western referents in the pre-1979 period.

By contrast, the essays by archaologists, paleoanthropologists, ethnologists, and linguists all are based on very different assumptions of the independence and institutional distinctiveness of each of the anthropological sciences. Following the Soviet model's separation (or elimination) of their approaches, these disciplines define their intellectual niche in the academic world in quite different terms from that of the four-fields approach. The archaeologists, for example, present an academic world view that stresses the independent nature of the field of archaeology. Xia

Nai and Su Bingqi, the elders of the field, give classical definitions of its theoretical orientation and methodology as adapted to meet Chinese circumstances, while Zeng Qi summarizes some recent work on the Neolithic representative of the development of archaeology as a whole in the country.[1] Finally, Liang Zhaotao and Zhang Shouqi—two authors raised in the four-fields approach—combine to show the validity of the integrated application of ethnology and archaeology to solve problems of mutual interest. Here, too, one notes a systematic appeal to the experience of the non-Chinese anthropological world.

The other three disciplines are then briefly presented. Wu Rukang, one of the foremost paleoanthropologists in China and the world, calls for the establishment of a new discipline, "neoanthropology" (*jinrenleixue*), which would parallel paleoanthropology but deal with the physical anthropological study of contemporary Homo sapiens. Huang Xinmei, a medical doctor who has taken up physical anthropology (partially under the tutelage of Wu Rukang), presents the case for China to make better use of its new discipline in the construction of the "two civilizations," that is, what the Chinese refer to as "spiritual civilization" and "material civilization." These terms may be interpreted as referring to the ideological and material aspects of Chinese culture.

The selection by Zhang Zhenbiao deals with a subfield that is disparaged today in the West. Anthropometry is largely on the ash-heap of anthropological history in the United States, but in China it has been shorn of the racist functions it served earlier in this century and, as the author points out, can be made to serve a socialist society. The final physical anthropological selection reviews paleolithic research in China during the first half of the 1980s. Readers should note the repeated reference to Beijing (Peking) Man's use of fire; simultaneous with the publication of this article (and others) has been the continuing controversy surrounding Lewis Binford's remarks casting doubt on the use of fire by Homo erectus pekinensis.

The essays on ethnology present this field's clear insistence that it should have an existence and life of its own. Lin Yaohua, who some consider to be the dean of ethnology in post-Liberation China, shows in

[1]One might also take note here of the parallel discovery in both Neolithic and Paleolithic research (as indicated in the essays by Zeng Qi and Zhang Senshui), of the far more widespread geographic extent of early cultural complexes beyond the Yellow River plain, the area long held to be the sole "cradle" of Chinese cultural development.

his essay the continuing impact of Marxist-Leninist formulations as well as Stalin's theories on Chinese ethnology. Yet at the same time, his piece also shows us how Chinese ethnologists, with fierce pride, have not blindly followed these foreign masters, but have skillfully adapted their ideas to Chinese needs and desires. One might also note parenthetically that the ethnology museum that Lin calls for is now under construction in Beijing.

Huang Shuping, a generation younger and a student of Lin's, like Lin makes the point that Marxism-Leninism cannot substitute for ethnology. Ethnology may take certain insights into the historical and cultural process from Marx, Engels, Lenin, Stalin, and Mao, but these theorists only set the general picture. Ethnology is needed for the details of individual societies and situations, and especially for the practical application of these general insights. Here again, the author argues that China should take advantage of the field's insights.

Although anthropological linguistics does not exist in the PRC, there has been a long history of specialists studying the languages of minority nationalities. Here Fu Maoji reviews work done since the early 1950s. What is striking to the observer is how much continuity there has been in this work over a thirty-year span (always remembering the disruption of the Cultural Revolution years, of course). In this essay, as well as the one by Ma Xueliang and Dai Qingxia, one again finds the strong emphasis on integrating academic work with practical application. In the latter selection, moreover, we are treated to the insights Chinese language specialists have garnered into the nature of the interaction between language and nationality from their work on the national minorities. In both pieces, the reader should be advised that references to "Han script" and the "Han language" might be more recognizable as "Chinese characters" and the "Chinese language (Mandarin)." The authors are being careful not to abrogate the term "Chinese" to designate the Han, only one of China's fifty-six recognized nationalities (albeit the majority, with 93 percent of the population).

## Acknowledgments

A year's stay in China during 1986 to research this topic and to teach anthropology there was made possible by sabbatical year support from Pacific Lutheran University. My host *danwei* in China was the anthropology department of Zhongshan University, and I am indebted to the faculty and students there for their aid in helping me better understand China and anthropology. Interviews and observations were conducted there as well as at Xiamen and Beijing Universities, the Central Institute of Nationalities, CASS's Archaeological and Nationalities Institutes, the Guangdong Institute of Nationalities, the CAS Institute of Vertebrate Paleontology and Paleoanthropology, and the Guangdong Minzu Xueyuan. I especially thank the faculty at Zhongshan for helping me select the articles used in this book.

An abbreviated version of the essay on "Chinese Anthropologies" appeared in *Social Research* 54, 4 (Winter 1987): 757–78.

# Part I

# Overview and Historical Background

GREGORY ELIYU GULDIN

# 1 | Chinese Anthropologies

WHEN SPEAKING of anthropology in the Peoples' Republic of China (PRC), it is often best to refer to the anthropological sciences rather than to anthropology. Unlike the situation in the United States, there is no widespread consensus even among its practitioners as to the fundamental nature of the field. In its American version, anthropology has traditionally been seen as an integrated and holistic discipline composed of four subfields: archaeology, physical (biological) anthropology, cultural anthropology, and linguistics. In today's People's Republic of China, most of the scientists working in these four "subfields" would themselves vigorously protest their inclusion in any such overarching frame. The essays appearing in this volume reflect just such a fundamental disagreement.

China, of course, is not unique in formulating its anthropology along lines other than those laid down in the United States; Great Britain, France, and the Soviet Union, among others, have all developed their own definitions and set their own parameters for the "science of man," to use Clyde Kluckhohn's phrase. There is indeed something inherently anthropological about this realization that every culture has had its special impact on the structure, function, and use of the social sciences in its own land. This insight, however, raises the old bugaboo of cultural relativism in a new metacontext, for if the social sciences as practiced in a particular country are the product of the unique social forces in that country, how can we speak of a *universal* anthropology (or any other social science) when each version of anthropology (or whatever) will be hopelessly mired in the particularities of particular times and places?

Leaving aside for the time being such a global question, let us explore the contemporary Chinese anthropological landscape and contrast its contours with its American counterpart. Two university departments, with their attached museums and research institutes, designate themselves anthropology departments and are both located in the south of the country. Zhongshan University in Guangzhou (Canton) and Xiamen (Amoy) University in Fujian province both adhere to the "four fields" approach which is standard in the United States (see the essays by Liang and Chen). Their students are thus exposed to a gamut of courses broadly similar to those of most undergraduate anthropology curricula in America. Undergraduates may major in either archaeology or ethnology at Zhongshan and in archaeology or anthropology at Xiamen. Graduate degrees are offered in archaeology and cultural anthropology; China's first Ph.D. in anthropology was awarded to China's first Tibetan doctoral degree holder, Gelek, in July 1986 at Zhongshan.

In the north and much the rest of the country, however, anthropology clearly has another referent, one more in the European and Soviet mode. There anthropology clearly refers to *physical* anthropology and encompasses mainly the study of human paleontology as well as the study of contemporary human physical variation. The preeminent locus for such studies is the Chinese Academy of Sciences' Institute of Vertebrate Paleontology and Paleoanthropology (IVPP). This research institute is the descendant of the Cenozoic Research Laboratory of Peking Man fame and today oversees on a national basis investigations into China's paleolithic and protohominid past.

Oft-ridiculed in the West, anthropometry is a respected component of this version of anthropology. The careful and precise measurement of human variations, from skull size to waistline to posture, is not tainted with racism as it was (and is) in the United States and is seen as a valuable aid to industry and commodity production; it is applied anthropology par excellence. Fudan University's biology department houses an anthropology section doing just this and other types of physical anthropological research. Zhongshan University also teaches anthropometry to its students as do many biology departments and medical schools throughout the country. The latter two types of institutions are also the loci for what is often another subbranch of physical anthropology in the United States, human genetics. So too are primate studies placed in biology departments, with the most advanced work being conducted in Yunnan.[1]

Of all the four subfields of the American version, archaeology and

---

[1] The Kunming Zoological Institute is the one academic institution in China (outside of biology departments) currently focusing on primatology.

ethnology are the most developed as independent disciplines in China. Archaeologists have their own research institutes, university majors,[2] and government excavation teams. Of all the anthropologically related disciplines, theirs is the one with the widest popular recognition and the strongest level of university and governmental support. Unlike their American counterparts, however, Chinese archaeologists do not draw a sharp theoretical or organizational distinction between historic and prehistoric archaeology and excavate sites from the Neolithic to the Qing dynasty.

The other key component of American anthropology, cultural anthropology, finds its closest equivalent in ethnology in the PRC. Most ethnologists there are specialists on the non-Han minorities of China who make up 7 percent of the total population; this disciplinary division of labor thus leaves sociology with a clear field to study the Han majority.[3] A network of Institutes of Nationalities, sometimes attached to local branches of the Chinese Academy of Social Sciences (CASS), is found throughout areas of the country with significant minority populations. Scholars at these institutions carry out ethnographic investigations as needed by the authorities or as dictated by their own research interests. Similarly, one will also find ethnologists in Beijing and elsewhere at local *minzu xueyuan*, universities for minority nationality students. For both types of institutions, their Beijing affiliates (CASS-Beijing and the Central Institute of Nationalities) are the most prestigious and important locales of scholarship and influence.

As for the last of the American four fields, anthropological linguistics, this subdiscipline is in China similar to ethnology in being mostly encompassed within the realm of minority studies. Each of the departments and research institutes of anthropology as well as the CASS Institutes of Nationalities and the *minzu xueyuan* all have their ethnolinguistic specialists on the languages of the local minorities. Other

---

[2] All in history departments save for the sole archaeology department at Beijing University and the two archaeology specialties in anthropology departments at Zhongshan and Xiamen universities.

[3] Ethnologists have recently been wrestling with the question of whether or not their field should encompass the study of the Han majority population or be restricted to the national minorities. Many feel that although the Han should ideally be included in their investigative scope, their priority should remain the minorities because of the pressing needs of these populations and of the government for an informed nationalities policy. As for sociology, three recent studies do much to shed light on its post-1949 developments: see Arkush (1981), Chu (1984), and Wong (1979).

aspects of the linguistics domain, such as semantics, transformative grammars, and the like, are found in the completely separate academic world of linguistics and language study.

The following portrait of anthropology in China of the mid-1980s can thus be drawn: four-fields anthropology established in the south while ethnology, physical anthropology, archaeology, and linguistics go their separate ways elsewhere in the country. Nationwide scholarly associations reflect these divisions so that separate organizations exist for anthropologists, ethnologists, archaeologists, linguists, and paleoanthropologists.

**West Wind**

Given the plethora of institutes, journals, and scholars that now comprise the world of these anthropological sciences, it is hard to imagine that sixty years ago they were in their infancy. Today, Chinese social scientists point to Cai Yuanpei's 1926 article "On Ethnology" as the first article written by a Chinese advocating anthropology or ethnology. Cai himself, one of the foremost intellectuals of his day, had learned of anthropology from the Japanese, and indeed it was the Japanese who were the first conduit for things anthropological to reach China. By the 1930s, however, European and American influences began to outweigh Japanese as Western works were translated into Chinese, Chinese students went abroad to study, and Western social scientists came to teach and do research in China.

The 1930s, then, saw the emergence of the anthropological sciences in China, but these were disciplines clearly formed in a Western mold. Visitors from abroad—from A. R. Radcliffe-Brown to Sergei Shirokogorov (the White Russian tutor of Fei Xiaotong before Malinowski) to Davidson Black—taught and propagandized their theoretical perspectives in China. German diffusionism, English functionalism, American historical-particularism, and Japanese classical evolutionary theories all found the academic equivalent of the Open Door in China. No one foreign school dominated, but most significant is the fact that there were no *Chinese* schools to compete with them. Moreover, in the period before 1949 there was never a Chinese full professor of anthropology; Westerners held all senior posts and Chinese served as junior faculty.

For all of the four fields of anthropological interest the situation in the years before the triumph of the revolutionary forces was basically the same. Chinese absorbed the foreign theories, methodologies, and outlooks of their Western mentors either in China or abroad at their mentors' home institutions. Those fortunate enough to go overseas would return home to trumpet the perspectives of the particular school they trained in. These returned scholars, people like Liu Han, Wu Dingliang, Fei Xiaotong, Lin Yaohua,[4] Yang Kun, Pan Guangdan, Ling Chunsheng, Yang Chengzhi, and Wu Wenzao, were to become the leaders of their field in the late prerevolutionary and early postrevolutionary periods and thus comprise the founding generation of Chinese anthropological scientists.

In linguistics, Chao Yuanren, Li Fangkwei, and Luo Changpei introduced Western linguistic methods and theories (basically structuralism) and were heavily influenced by Bloomfield, Sapir, and other anthropological linguists. The American emphases on American Indian languages and the problems encountered in the study of unwritten languages were seen as applicable parallels to the study of China's minority populations. The Chinese sought to apply similar analyses and methodologies to their work in China.

Foreign influences were also great in physical anthropology and archaeology, as the few great excavations of the prerevolutionary period were all conducted under the leadership of foreigners. Davidson Black, Johann Andersson, Pierre Teilhard de Chardin, and others trained the first generation of Chinese scholars in these fields. Many of these—Wu Dingliang, Pei Wenzhong, Jia Lanpo—got their start at the famous Peking Man site of Zhoukoudian (Choukoutien).

In the pre-1949 period sociocultural anthropology was not well distinguished from the allied fields of sociology and social work. Wu Wenzao in the north and Yang Chengzhi in the south are thus known as the founders of both Chinese sociology and social anthropology. Wu followed Malinowski and so did his students at Yanjing and Qinghua universities, thereby establishing a British perspective in North China. In the south Yang influenced generations of students with a more American definition of anthropology, a definition derived from foreign instructors at the American-run Lingnan University in Guangzhou. Alongside Lin Huixiang of Xiamen University and the University of Manila (also American-run), Yang tutored the future founder of the first anthropology department in post-Liberation China, Liang Zhaotao of

---

[4]Best known in the West as Lin Yueh-hwa, the author of The Golden Wing. He is also well known in China for On the History of Primitive Society.

Zhongshan University, while Lin had a decisive impact on the founder of China's second department, Chen Guoqiang of Xiamen University.

Although Radcliffe-Brown did lecture in Beijing for a spell, and although Malinowski is well known as the mentor of Fei Xiaotong, the American influence was also quite strong on early Chinese ethnologists/sociologists, even those in the north. Chinese ethnologists now in their seventies and eighties mention Franz Boas, more than anyone else, as having had the most significant impact on their anthropological development. Lowie and Kroeber were also important influences; one can still see their works today on those bookshelves that survived the Red Guard ravages of the mid-1960s.

War with the Japanese moved the academic centers of China to the interior and the southwest and gave these anthropologists an opportunity to have intensive interaction with China's own minorities. With war's end came a flowering of the discipline as new courses, majors, and even a handful of departments were set up (at Qinghua and Zhongshan universities). Research was reform-oriented and sought to aid the national efforts first of defense and then of reconstruction. Although schools from the Boasian historical-particularist to evolutionism all found their adherents, functionalism was probably the preeminent orientation (Chen 1982). With the Guomindang collapse in 1948-49, scholars were forced to choose their futures. Many noted social scientists such as Ruey I-fu, Wei Huilin, and Ling Chunsheng departed for Taiwan to rebuild the institutions and the discipline they had left behind in the new "People's China" being constructed on the mainland.

**North Wind**

While some scholars were fleeing New China, others were anxiously wending their way back to the homeland to help build the new society. The majority watched and waited for signs from the triumphant Communist Party. For social scientists, the wait was not long.

Anthropology immediately came under suspicion. After barely a year in existence, Zhongshan University's anthropology department was suspended in November 1949 and moved as a unit into the sociology department. Other nascent anthropology departments or majors suffered the same fate as the discipline as a whole fell under a cloud. Anthropology in China in 1949 had just begun to take root, to mature, but it had not yet shown its worth (or even what it was) to the public, to the politically progressive forces in China, or even to academia. Having collaborated with colonialism elsewhere, associated with the great imperialist powers of the United States, Great Britain, and France, it is no wonder anthropology was distrusted by the Communists. That functionalism was its preeminent theoretical orientation in China did not help either (Chen 1982).

In 1951 criticism of sociology intensified: it was reactionary, foreign, imperialistic. By 1952 Yanjing's sociology department was abolished along with its embedded anthropology section. Likewise the fate of Qinghua's and Zhongshan's sociology-anthropology programs as the country's entire higher educational system underwent a massive reorganization. Following the Soviet model, the "bourgeois" social sciences of sociology and anthropology (and others) were proscribed and their adherents scattered to other departments or fields.

For many ethnologists a key decision affecting their futures was the 1951 State Council directive that all scholars in "minority studies" (i.e., those erstwhile anthropologists-sociologists) move to the newly formed Central Institute of Nationalities (CIN)[5] in Beijing. Fei Xiaotong, Lin Yaohua, Pan Guangdan, Li Youyi, and other top scholars came over from Yanjing and Qinghua universities that autumn. The Central Institute of Nationalities thus came to house most of China's trained ethnologist-anthropologists, and by the mid-1950s it had become *the* center for ethnological teaching and theorizing in the People's Republic. The largest group of students were minority nationality cadres who attended the institute to study nationality policies and nationality theory from a Marxist perspective before returning to their home districts to serve as government and/or party officials.

After the revolution linguistics had also been declared useless and linguistic departments in Zhongshan and Beijing universities abolished. Many linguists at these institution moved to history and Chinese language departments. In 1956, however, the government recognized the need for trained linguists when it established a minority languages institute under the Chinese Academy of Sciences and transferred a number of linguists to this new unit.[6] When a new Nationalities Institute was also established under CAS in 1958, both linguists and ethnologists

[5] Also known as the Central Academy of Nationalities or the Central Institute of Minorities.

[6] The unit (*danwei*) is the key organizational unit of Chinese life from university to factory to cooperative.

found a new institutional home there as well.

The two institutes were merged in 1961 to function as a centralized research and policy center for the government. Key tasks undertaken at this Nationalities Institute were: (1) the formulation of nationalities policy recommendations for the government based on Marxist-Leninist ethnological theory and practice. A major recipient of such advice would be the national, provincial, and local *minwei*, or governmental nationalities policy committees, on which ethnologists would sometimes serve in an advisory or support capacity. (2) Research on the minorities' history prior to 1840 (but also sometimes including late nineteenth and early twentieth century developments). (3) Establishing a library and materials archive for nationality studies. Today the Nationalities Institute, boasting 218 researchers, is the largest component of the autonomous (since 1978) Chinese Academy of Social Sciences.

The reorganization in 1952, by contrast, did not do away with archaeology and physical anthropology. On the contrary, archaeology began to thrive with official government support and encouragement. Since the pre-Liberation archaeological institutes and their directors had mostly left for Taiwan, a new institutional frame for archaeology was necessary, and the Institute of Archaeology was established under the Academy of Sciences. On the university campuses, archaeology continued to be taught as part of history department curricula. Physical anthropology, meanwhile, with twin bases in the Institute of Vertebrate Paleontology and Paleoanthropology under CAS and in an anthropological unit in Fudan University's biology department in Shanghai, laid sole claim to the title "anthropology" as per the Soviet model. Other than at these two units, people dropped their identification as anthropologists and called themselves archaeologists or ethnologists or minority specialists.

Another key difference before and after Liberation was that ethnologists and others now found themselves involved en masse in nationwide government projects. Whenever the nation embarked on projects or campaigns that could utilize their skills, these intellectuals were willy-nilly involved for better or worse. In the early 1950s it was mostly for the better as a number of projects were undertaken that demanded the talents of China's erstwhile anthropologists.

Between 1950 and 1952 *minzu fangwen tuan* (visit the minorities teams) were sent out by the central government to determine how many nationalities there actually were in China. The Han majority had traditionally exploited and oppressed the minorities (6 percent of the population in the 1950s), and the CPC itself did not have extensive experience with the minorities. The goals of the teams that fanned out over China's border and minority areas were to establish friendly relations with the minority peoples on a people-to-people basis and to determine the needs of the people and help secure whatever supplies they needed urgently, such as medicines or food.

A parallel project was a special investigation into the languages of the national minorities. This of course helped with the classification effort, but it also involved linguists in the practical task of devising scripts for those peoples without one. Of the fifty-odd officially recognized minorities, fewer than twenty had scripts prior to 1949, and linguists were quickly impressed into this applied linguistic field. Another key task that linguists worked on dealt with the languages (the so-called dialects) of the Han majority. Problems of "interdialectical" communication and illiteracy were tackled and simplified scripts devised. This great linguistic field laboratory experience also stimulated much academic discussion on the classification of Chinese languages: Is there one Chinese language family or many? Is Sino-Tibetan a real family and with what branches? Is Miao-Yao a proper Sino-Tibetan offshoot?

These linguistic investigations became part of an even more encompassing series of investigations begun in 1956. For the next few years Minority Nationalities Social Research Teams fanned out across the country in response to the desire of Chairman Mao and the Nationality Commission of the Standing Committee of the National People's Congress to record and understand the minorities' situation. One question the teams investigated was to determine how many of the hundreds of groups claiming to be nationalities should actually be accorded such status. After years of investigation the list would be winnowed down to fifty-two (including the Han majority), but later revisions would bring the number back up to fifty-six. An even more pressing avenue of research the teams had to deal with, however, was the question of what types of policies to apply to the minority areas became central as the rest of China collectivized and moved boldly into the new socialist consciousness of the Great Leap Forward period of the late 1950s.

Armed with an outline of research topics, research teams would move into a village for two or three months at a time. One or two researchers would share living quarters with a local family but would not burden them with their cooking or other needs. They usually relied on interpreters and after their stay would move on to another village in the district deemed representative, eventually to compile district or countywide comparative reports on the nationality. At the time these reports were all considered *neibu* (for internal circulation only), but materials collected then served as the basis for scholarly articles in the early 1960s and during the last decade as well.

These structural reorganizations and nationwide projects of the 1950s were undertaken in a context of successive political campaigns, for politics had made a major impact on Chinese academic life. Soon after Liberation some intellectuals had participated in thought reform, but widespread thought reform propaganda campaigns only began in earnest a few years later. By 1952 and 1953 such campaigns, lasting for a few months at a time, had hit most educational and research institutes. Intellectuals were encouraged to criticize thinking and attitudes that overevaluated the West as well as China's "feudal past." Marxism was introduced into the curriculum, and study sessions of universities and research units and scholars were strongly urged to integrate this new perspective into their work. A few intellectuals became dispirited under the pressure, especially those on campus denounced for the first time by their eighteen-year-old students.

Others reacted differently and began seriously to integrate Marxist-Leninism into their intellectual frames. Some were deeply affected by their participation in the early 1950s' "visit the minorities teams"; party policies stressing the equality and unity of China's nationalities favorably impressed those familiar with the sorry tale of pre-1949 Han-minority relations. They were inspired to begin the study of dialectical materialism, historical materialism, and that touchstone of Marxist ethnology, Friedrich Engels' *Origin of the Family, Private Property, and the State.*

When the Anti-Rightist campaign hit in the summer of 1957 following the Hundred Flowers period, a chill descended over all intellectual circles. For many, though, there was little interruption or effect on their research; those in the natural sciences were affected far less than social scientists, so life at many units of the Chinese Academy of Sciences continued almost uninterrupted, especially for those in archaeology and paleoanthropology. Many of the most prominent of the newly minted ethnologists, however, were severely criticized. Wu Wenzao, Fei Xiaotong, Pan Guangdan, and Wu Zelin were singled out for particular attention and relieved of their leadership positions.

Although the ongoing Social Research teams continued their fieldwork investigations during and after the Anti-Rightist campaign, the atmosphere in which they worked had changed. After the first year of full-scale fieldwork, the results so far were reviewed and criticized. Evidence in the teams' work of bourgeois theories and approaches like those of the above three scholars was sought and found. One key error of the early fieldwork was held to be an overemphasis on the superstructure (religion, ideology, myths) as opposed to the economic base of the society in question. Since one of the government's major goals in pursuing the fieldwork was to clarify the nature of the social structure and the class relationships among minorities, such a superstructural emphasis was seen as a diversion that would harm the investigations.

"Hunting for exotica" (*lieh qi*) was another chief accusation brought against field researchers. The anthropological-ethnological passion for recording the whole gamut of customs and beliefs of a people seemed a dubious use of time when there was so much more important work to be done. "Hunting for exotica" furthermore insulted the national minorities by holding them up to ridicule by the Han and thus harmed national unity as well; this was thus quite a serious accusation, and from this time on many people preferred to investigate safer topics such as the economic base and class stand of the villages they studied.

Yet even when they did so, researchers could be faulted. Some were criticized for failing to report bad class relations in their areas, even when the researchers felt class relations were not a problem. The dogmatic application of the class struggle principle distorted the data and made fieldworkers even more cautious in their reportage. When the Great Leap Forward caught up with the villages under study, the researchers were often involved in these changes as well. Ideologically, class struggle was even further emphasized, and the slogan in the field in 1958 was *hou jin, bo gu* (stress the present and slight the past). In the effort to build communism all people, including ethnologists, were to concentrate on the coming millennium and not dawdle peripherally researching grandma's nearly forgotten taboos.

In response to such criticisms, research over the next decade or two fairly ignored religion, old customs, myths, kinship structures, and the rest of the "superstructure." Those combining ethnology with physical anthropological investigations in the field also had to drop their research when they likewise came under criticism, and again it was for insulting the national minorities. Researchers like Yang Chengzhi, doing anthropometrical studies of the minorities, were bitterly attacked by local people who had been required to take off their clothes! This "shocking" request of the outside Han scholars was compounded by the (unfounded) suspicion of many that such studies were meant to prove racist ideas of minority inferiority.

The universities meanwhile had moved away from their early 1950s' slogan of "Respect the teacher; love the student." The honeymoon many intellectuals had with the new regime meant that for most the early thought reform campaigns had fallen lightly on them. The situation only gradually changed throughout the mid-1950s. Ethnology courses continued in history departments, but as campaigns waxed and waned they left their mark on curricula. Ethnology courses were forced to add material on primitive societies (à la Engels' *Origin*), on current Soviet theories, and on Marxism. Western theorists from Margaret Mead to Radcliffe-Brown were criticized and their works dropped from class discussion. When ethnology as a field succumbed to all the criticisms and was proscribed as a discipline in 1958, nationalities studies became the final refuge of the anthropologists cum ethnologists.

Despite the official ban on the term ethnology, however, work and research in minority studies continued on much the same lines before and after the formal semantic taboo. As the 1950s wore on, though, there was increasingly only one channel of learning about ethnology, especially foreign ethnology, and that was from the USSR. Books, articles, and experts all arrived from the Soviet Union to influence profoundly the definition and conduct of the field. Although a handful of PRC students and researchers went to the USSR, contacts during the heyday of Soviet-Chinese cooperation occurred mostly in the PRC itself.

Between 1954 and 1959 about ten Soviet scholars in ethnology and linguistics came to the Central Institute of Nationalities. Nikolai Cheboksarov had arguably the greatest influence of the Soviet guests by dint of the training classes he held for graduate students. The first postgraduate training classes ever held for ethnology students at CIN provided the budding minority specialists with their first systematic training in fieldwork techniques. From the institute most of these students went into the field on the Social History Research investigation teams to apply what Cheboksarov had taught them. A teacher with great prestige as the head of the ethnology section in Moscow University's history department, Cheboksarov commanded respect both then and now among his students for his scholarship and teaching.

Cheboksarov also introduced to his Chinese colleagues and students the then current theoretical frame of economic-cultural patterns, which postulated a Steward-like ecological base to different cultural patterns but coupled it to certain economic factors. A number of Chinese scholars worked with Soviet theorists to apply this approach to China. Thirty years later, Chinese ethnologists are still finding this theory useful (see Lin and Cheboksarov 1984).

Perhaps the most significant Soviet impact on Chinese theoretical developments in ethnology was the emphasis on viewing the history of "primitive societies" from a Marxist-Leninist perspective. The importance of Engels' *Origin* was crucial in this. Most Chinese ethnologists today, however, are quick to point out that neither this work nor Lewis Henry Morgan's *Ancient Society*, the book that informed much of Engels' ideas on the subject, can or should be considered gospel. Morgan was not a dialectical materialist, and both he and Engels are acknowledged to have made significant ethnographic errors.

Another key Soviet influence is to be seen on the definition of nationality. More than merely an academic debate over terminology, this question involved major decisions on which groups would be designated as national minorities and which groups denied such status. Although input on this question was taken from Marx, Engels, and Lenin, the definition operationally used from the 1950s on was basically Stalin's. To Stalin, a nationality had to have a common territory, language, economic form, and psychological characteristics. Stalin's theoretical influence was also felt in linguistics, and it was largely due to his articles on language policy that linguistics in China was split off from literature studies.

In contrast to ethnology and language studies, Soviet influence on paleoanthropology and archaeology was much more limited. The Western-educated leadership of the IVPP did not think much of Soviet scholarship in this area and fairly ignored it, although there were some cooperative projects in the 1950s. Archaeologists and paleoanthropologists were involved in at least one major controversy inspired by Soviet contact, regarding Engels' formulation that "labor created man." To Engels, labor began with the making of tools, and so the first human beings were the first toolmakers. This was fine for archaeologists who were used to defining human cultures as beginning with Paleolithic tool manufacture. Physical anthropologists, though, had a traditional preference for using bipedalism as a hominid diagnostic and thus came into conflict with Engels' formulation. If one did not accept Engels' view of the matter and insert his "labor created man" into one's articles, could one really claim to be a Marxist-Leninist scholar?

By the time of the Great Leap Forward in 1958, pressures were also being felt in archaeological circles to use Marx as a general guide, especially in the analysis of material culture (Yen 1985:21). Archaeologists had spent the early 1950s setting up their new organizations and training a new generation of specialists. The mid-1950s saw work begin in earnest. Significant excavations included the Neolithic site of Banpo and other locations in the Yellow River valley. Work also expanded into the Yangzi River valley, and by the mid-1960s the Neolithic Yangshao culture was beginning to form a prominent part of a new conception of the Chinese past. (See Zeng Qi's essay for an overview of Neolithic finds and cultural sequences.)

Beginning in 1960, however, a new conception of the Chinese present was being constructed as what the Russians felt and wrote about scholarly matters began to decline in importance. With the break in relations with the Soviets, those who had studied Russian as their only foreign language found themselves increasingly cut off from developments abroad as subscriptions to Soviet periodicals gradually lapsed in the 1960s. Scholars in Beijing were probably more affected by the Sino-Soviet split than those elsewhere in China, for few of the Soviet experts had spent extended time away from their Beijing host institutions. Soviet influence in the south and elsewhere was thus comparatively weak.

By the time of the split, most of the research of the Minorities Social History Project had been completed and analysis and publication of the results began. When the Four Cleanups campaign came to the countryside in 1964, most researchers went home and the investigation teams were disbanded. Other teachers and researchers, however, were sent to the countryside for a year or two as part of the Four Cleanups, and some ethnologists used these stints to live with minority families and take field notes on what they observed before they too returned to their urban homes. Many of them would soon return to the countryside under more trying circumstances.

## Typhoon

"The Red Guards were terrible! And the older scholars were the ones who were hurt the most—mostly by being locked up. All of us had to go to May

7 Cadre Schools for labor reform for a few years." Older scholars whose positions of power and training abroad had supposedly exposed them most to the bureaucratic and imperialist viruses were indeed the ones most bitterly criticized during the Great Proletarian Cultural Revolution's peak years of 1966–69. Subjected to long criticism sessions, screamed at by their juniors for hours on end, and vilified as *chou lao jiu* (stinking old nine; an epithet for intellectuals), these and many other researchers also had to suffer Red Guard rampages in their homes during searches for incriminating materials. Many lost their books, research notes, and other data gathered over decades. Efforts years later after the storm had passed to relocate these materials were usually fruitless.

As with scholars in other fields, those in the anthropological sciences also were sent down to the countryside to labor for a few years. Sometimes separately, sometimes together, most researchers spent the years following 1968 far away from their home units. Universities and research institutes closed, subscriptions to foreign and domestic publications halted, and most research came to an end. Yet not all of the anthropologically relevant units were put on hold, and not all units experienced Red Guard horror scenes: both the Institute of Archaeology and the IVPP kept their doors open and saw mostly pro forma criticism sessions.[7] Nevertheless, most excavations were halted for the decade 1966-1976, and many sites were ruined (Yen 1985:21). All museums closed, but the Zhoukoudian Museum was reopened in 1972.

By 1972 things had indeed begun to improve, with schools and institutes tentatively reopening. Archaeology journals reappeared that year and fieldwork recommenced. At the universities, however, the new "worker-peasant-soldier" students helped maintain a properly proletarian, Marxist, and xenophobic Cultural Revolutionary atmosphere by closely monitoring intellectuals returning from the countryside. Party member faculty sat in on the classes of suspect instructors and reported errors to the authorities or confronted the offending teacher directly. Most of those criticized would have to wait till the end of the decade before they could answer back.

[7] Scholars report that at small units this was quite common. Those who were being criticized were rarely hit or physically abused; people knew them well and would have to work with them after the current campaign was over. People would interrupt their work for a criticism session, go get criticized, and then return to their desks. At larger, more impersonal units one was at greater risk of being belted by someone known only marginally, if at all, and who would probably be assigned elsewhere to work in the future.

The anti-intellectual atmosphere of the Cultural Revolution continued and was renewed during the early and mid-1970s by such periodic campaigns as the "Criticize Lin, Criticize Confucius" campaign. Theoretical treatments of problems were considered "bourgeois academics"; emphasis had to be placed on practical applications. Students were thus trained without theory in archaeology and nationalities work, and all research and activities were supposed to be done collectively to avoid bourgeois individualist biases.

The returned intellectuals naturally remained cautious in their newly revived units, and even a prominent paleoanthropologist, IVPP Director Wu Rukang, felt it politic to write, at the end of this period, that he and his fellow researchers in paleoanthropology conducted their studies not only to understand human origins "but also to propagandize historical materialism among the workers, peasants, and soldiers" (Wu 1980:7). Intellectuals remained on figurative tenterhooks well into the late 1970s and began to lower their guard only after the fateful 1978 Central Committee session of the CPC committed China to an "open door" policy and a policy of reform.

## Spring Breeze

In 1980 the first foreign language materials began to arrive again at Zhongshan University's anthropology department library. Subscriptions suspended since 1965 or so began to flow again, with *Current Anthropology* and *Netherlands Bulletin* joining other foreign publications from Eastern and Western Europe, the United States, the USSR, and Japan in the "materials rooms" of this and other anthropological units.

The 1980s also saw a relative explosion of domestic scholarly publications ranging from *Minzu yuyan* (Nationality Languages) to *Renleixue xuebao* (Acta Anthropologica Sinica) to *Kaogu* (Archaeology). This was a startling reversal not only of the situation during the Cultural Revolution but of China's prerevolutionary past. Prior to 1949 there were few anthropological materials in Chinese; English was the language of anthropological scholarship. After 1950, however, reading in English became a suspect activity and, especially after the Anti-Rightist campaign, English-language materials were consulted only at home. Russian was approved of for a while, but even so there was not that much available. Even had there been, few scholars could have used Russian-language materials for academic purposes as most spoke and read English, not

Russian. With the Cultural Revolution all foreign language publications were taboo, and even when the atmosphere lightened during the mid-1970s, foreign publications remained scarce.

With the open door policy of the 1980s there has been a relative flood of foreign-language publications, with the overwhelming majority in English, followed by Japanese and Russian. The old and young can read English, the middle-aged Russian (perhaps), but almost no one can read Japanese. Unlike forty years ago, however, one need not be able to read foreign languages to keep abreast of developments abroad. Compared to 1949, there is a plethora of social science-friendly publishing houses and journals of translation, so that there is now a relative abundance of materials in Chinese.

There has likewise been a great expansion in the number of academic associations formed. The Chinese Anthropological Society has already held a number of nationwide conferences which have attempted to define the field as it is and should be in China.[8] The reestablishment of the Ethnology Association in 1980 symbolized the reemergence of the field of ethnology from political and academic purgatory, and it was soon joined by many other national, provincial, and local associations of ethnologists, archaeologists, and linguists. Recently the physical anthropologists have banded together in their own society as well.

In 1980 Zhongshan University received permission to reestablish an anthropology department; within four years Xiamen University became the site of China's second anthropology department. The heads of the new departments, Liang Zhaotao and Chen Guoqiang, had both been students of Lin Huixiang (one of the lights of pre-Liberation anthropology) at Xiamen University, and they had kept intact the anthropological perspective during the many years when the discipline, its theories, and approaches were condemned, vilified, and banished. Liang had labored for over forty years in anthropology's service and was recognized throughout China as a superb organizer and partisan of anthropology when he was feted on his seventieth birthday by his colleagues and students just one year before his death in 1987.

Other universities may have people desirous of developing anthropology departments, but none has as yet done so. Neither have ethnology departments been established at any university in China so far. CIN once more houses an ethnology department, and ethnology has indeed re-

---

[8]See Guldin (1987) for the results of these conferences.

emerged throughout the national system of *minzu xueyuan*. The Chinese Academy of Social Sciences has split off from the Chinese Academy of Science, and its Nationalities Institute in Beijing boasts over two hundred researchers, primarily ethnologists. Ethnologists are also housed at provincial and local CASS Nationalities Institutes and at *minwei* at all levels.

The intellectual climate since the 1978 Central Committee session has been the most hospitable in the history of the People's Republic despite the temporary clouds of the Spiritual Pollution campaign and the Anti-Bourgeois Liberalization campaign. Intellectuals report that they are given more respect than before, that they are asked to take on national tasks by the country's leadership and the State Education Committee, and that they are allowed to pursue their own research and can publish its results without submitting manuscripts for prior party approval. "Thinking is liberated; we now seek truth from facts and do not just repeat what Mao or Marx said" was the way one Beijing ethnographer put it.

True, perhaps, but as the campaign against "bourgeois liberalization" underlined, this intellectual freedom is limited and must remain within the socialist frame by following the "Four Cardinal Principles." To those outside the country, this insistence on the Marxist parameters of scholarship may seem insufferable, but it is perhaps not quite so chafing to many intellectuals in the PRC. By now, the majority of Chinese teachers, researchers, and students have grown up with a Marxist-Leninist world view and take it for granted as the proper theoretical frame.

The older generation, educated and politically socialized before the revolution, is the one that has had the most problems with Marxism and whose thinking by and large was not fundamentally changed despite the interminable meetings and hardships they suffered and despite even their own statements (self-criticisms) to the contrary. Some ideological and theoretical reorientations did come about, but it proved difficult to shift the intellectual frames of large numbers of mature academics. By contrast, although many of the younger generation may indeed criticize "party sticks" and some professors for their narrow insistence on ideological formulas, it appears that few of even these Chinese "Young Turks" want to abandon Marxism. They want to "unite the best of the North and West," that is, to combine Marxism and the Soviet approach with Western scientific methodology and technology to create a uniquely Chinese discipline.

The new openness of the 1980s has allowed a number of controversies to air, some in pursuit of this uniquely Chinese perspective and some that address the goals and definition of the anthropological fields themselves. In ethnology, for example, researchers are asking (see the Huang and Lin essays) what should be the object of today's ethnological study. Should it be to investigate and classify the evolutionary stages of minority nationality groups à la Morgan and Engels, or to look at the "contemporary situation of minorities and speak to their economic and cultural development"? Much of the minorities work in the 1950s and later blindly followed Morganian guidelines on the stages of societal development, and some writers still engage in such exercises. Increasingly, however, criticisms and "exceptions" to Morgan's scheme are being found, and there is now a substantial minority of ethnologists who question much of the hitherto sacrosanct assumptions about "primitive society," Morgan's kinship classifications, and Stalin's nationality definition.

On the latter question a critical majority may have already emerged. Recently a nationwide conference was held that discussed this very topic. Most speakers disagreed with some aspect of Stalin's definition, and one even went so far as to declare: "According to his [Stalin's] criteria, even the Han wouldn't count as a nationality!" The conference consensus was that ethnology should fit Chinese conditions and not blindly apply formulas designed for other countries.

Overall, however, Chinese ethnologists are just beginning to apply this insight. Many theoretical questions are arising in the aftermath of the institutional revivals of the last few years and as much of the material gathered during the Social History investigations of the 1950s and 1960s is being published openly for the first time. One can argue, furthermore, that most Chinese ethnologists are pursuing what in the West would be dubbed ethnography, the detailed study of a particular ethnic group or nationality, rather than ethnology, which relies on systematic comparison of different peoples to form theoretical statements about some aspect of human life. Rich in ethnographic materials but relatively unformed theoretically (besides a Marxist-Leninist and evolutionary base), Chinese ethnology is in the formative stage.

Archaeology, by contrast, is more well defined. The late Xia Nai, chief molder of modern China's archaeology, has described the period since 1949 as "China's Golden Age of Archaeology" (1984:1). Pointing to the wealth of discoveries, the revolution in technology, the increasing number of interdisciplinary connections (with history, sociology, ethnology, and geology), and the expansion in the location of sites to encompass the entire breadth of China (from south to west to northeast), Xia felt that archaeology as a discipline was doing very well indeed in China (See also CASS 1984).

In 1986, for example, a good year for the study of the past, 572 sites were active across the nation. At Wushan in the Yangzi River delta, teeth and bone fragments have led to "one of the most important paleolithic Asian finds in recent years": the discovery of perhaps a new species of human ancestor dating to 1.8 million years ago (*Renmin ribao* 1987). With the continuing reports and analyses of Ramapithecus, Sivapithecus, and Dryopithecus remains in China, world paleoanthropology must increasingly take note of the fossil evidence from the East Asian land mass.

Work on the Neolithic has if anything been even more prolific. Indeed, since 1949 over seven thousand new Neolithic sites have been found, and more than four hundred of these excavated (Yen 1985:20). Work in 1986 on the early Neolithic Peiligang culture and the late Neolithic Longshan culture has raised questions of the link between the two and spurred theoretical reinterpretations of the importance of areas in China other than the Yellow River for Neolithic origins. In 1985 and 1986 work in the Xiling Gorge area led researchers to conclude that the Yangzi River valley not only witnessed the development of a Neolithic culture over seven thousand years ago but was just as much a cradle of Chinese civilization as was the Yellow River valley (*China Daily* 1987).

The revived archaeology associations and journals have also focused on this and related questions, and annual archaeology conferences have been dedicated to these controversies. The origin of civilization in China has once again become the focus of reinterpretations of the Shang dynasty on the heels of new excavations like the 1983 work on a Shang city in Yanshi county. Controversies have also swirled around the questions of the origins of cities, the importance of foreign contacts in the development of Chinese civilization and culture, and the relative impact of non-Han peoples on Han culture and society in ancient times.

The importance of these theoretical controversies also points to a major facet of archaeology in the PRC in the 1980s. Archaeology today has a new goal in addition to the old one of simply salvaging sites before they make way for construction projects. Research questions and the reformulation of prehistorical and historical synopses have become much more central to archaeological life. Marxism-Leninism and Mao Zedong

Thought remain the guides to basic theory in both paleoanthropology and archaeology, but many archaeologists still maintain a theoretical stance heavily influenced by Western and especially French perspectives. The West's "New Archaeology," however, is not yet widely appreciated in China.

Of the anthropologically related sciences, linguistics has probably revived the least. There is still no university with a linguistics department (although CIN or Beijing University may eventually set one up), and even today little work is being done in language and culture studies. Yet journals and societies have revived or been set up anew, and contact once again made with foreign linguists and their works. China's third generation of linguists, people now in their fifties who were educated in the 1950s, have maintained continuity in approach and methodology with their predecessor generations, with scholars like Ma Xueliang and Fu Maoji, but they have also begun to explore the generative and transformative grammars of the Chomskian approach.

This new exposure was hard going at first. When China's linguists reconnected with foreign theoretical developments in the 1970s, they found it difficult to understand much of what was written. They had missed out on the rise and decline of an entirely new paradigm in linguistics; as one linguist sardonically put it, "When America had the Chomskian revolution, we had the Cultural Revolution." The upshot of this has been that the Chomskian impact has been much less than the structuralist on the development of Chinese linguistics.

**One Discipline or Many?**

The revival of anthropology, ethnology, and linguistics coupled with the reinvigoration of archaeology and paleoanthropology, means that there is not one, but many, anthropological disciplines in China. Anthropology departments trumpet the idea that there is a basic unity in these fields that could best be served by their close integration (if not amalgamation), but there is strong resistance elsewhere to this line of thinking. As mentioned, in the north the four-fields model of anthropology was never as firmly established as in the south, and the Soviet model had a greater impact in the north. In Beijing what might be considered anthropological "subdisciplines"—ethnology and paleoanthropology, for instance—were set up in separate institutional frames and given independent raisons d'etre. Without such preestablished, rival institutional structures to deal with, would-be anthropologists in the south could set up four-fields anthropology departments and institutes with far less resistance. Zhongshan and Xiamen universities have done so.

Reestablishing these departments picked up the historical threads severed in the early 1950s and directly tied today's scholars and students to the pioneer generations of Chinese anthropology. Liang Zhaotao and Chen Guoqiang, founding chairs of the revived departments, were students of Yang Chengzhi and Lin Huixiang, who in turn were greatly influenced by Cai Yuanpei and Sergei Shirokogorov. Leadership outside the university departments has followed similar generational lines: the IVPP's deputy department head, Wu Xinzhi, is a student of Wu Rukang, who in turn carries on the legacy of Pei Wenzhong, Jia Lanpo, and Wu Dingliang. One could follow similar generational chains for linguistics and archaeology; for them as well, a basic continuity of theoretical and disciplinary approach exists between teacher and student.

Yet there is also change within that continuity. China is now experiencing the gradual assumption of leadership by the first generation of scholars educated in the post-Liberation era. Mostly in their fifties, members of this generation came of age during the 1950s and are part of the nationwide phenomenon of the Soviet-influenced generation taking its turn in positions of power.[9]

This generation of leadership, newly ensconced in power, is of course not eager to yield its control of disciplines and institutions to somebody's vision of a united and holistic anthropology. Archaeologists have defined themselves (see Xia and Su essays) either as part of history (the Soviet view) or, increasingly, as an independent science. Noted archaeologists such as An Zhimin view anthropology as primarily ethnology and speak of the great difficulties of doing ethnoarchaeology, not to mention uniting archaeology with anthropology. Ethnologists also view anthropology as having a distinctly different perspective from ethnology and mostly maintain that the disciplines should retain their own identities.

What is the prognosis, then, for anthropology as an integrated, four-

[9] "New Cold War"–influenced commentators have seen something suspicious in the replacement of senior officials in their seventies and eighties by people in their fifties who were educated in the Soviet Union or by visiting Soviet scholars. It is hard to see, however, who else the elders could be replaced by or who else the younger scholars could have been influenced by given the nature of the PRC situation in the 1950s. Also doubtful is the assumption that a "Soviet-influenced education" necessarily makes one pro-Soviet; some of the most virulently anti-Soviet Chinese one encounters today in the PRC were "Soviet-educated."

fields discipline in China? Such an anthropology's devouring or replacement of the other anthropological sciences is quite unlikely. Most ethnologists and archaeologists prefer to continue as they have, and neither anthropological linguistics nor physical anthropology per se yet exists as a discrete field or subfield. They continue instead as subsets of ethnology or linguistics or of biology or paleontology.

Some influential social scientists and decision makers like Fei Xiaotong view anthropology itself as unnecessary in China, as a duplication of the already extant fields of archaeology, ethnology, and sociology. Although they do not oppose anthropology's right to exist in China, they "don't really understand what the anthropology departments do" (Fei: personal communication). In light of such high-placed opposition, it is a testimony to the "hundred flowers" opening of the post-1978 period that anthropology was allowed to be reestablished in the early 1980s. For the foreseeable future, then, anthropology and its sister four-fields disciplines, will all coexist as parallel and independent fields in the People's Republic.

Another factor mitigating against the development of a united discipline, is the dearth of people in China today who call themselves anthropologists. All of the faculty and researchers in the anthropological sciences educated since 1949 have been trained as specialists in something other than anthropology (mostly in ethnology or archaeology), and given the nature of the compartmentalized Soviet-model educational system, they have had little cross-disciplinary exposure during their years of study. Reconstituting four-fields anthropology departments and institutes, primarily with specialists from separate disciplinary perspectives, means either reliance on the pre-1949 crop of scholars to import the sense of what the integrated field is like, or reeducating younger scholars to this perspective (anthropological thought reform?).

It is not easy, then, to revive a discipline after a ban of thirty years. It is necessary to recreate the definition, goals, and consciousness that sustain the field, all above and beyond securing the institutional support and political alliances needed to obtain the approval of higher levels and to establish physically an anthropological unit. A battle must be fought to create a space for the department and discipline in an already extant academic universe of defined territories and budgets, and outside units must be convinced to give jobs to graduates. (Titling a student's major the vague-sounding "anthropology" [*renleixue*, the study of humans] is not as helpful in this latter task compared to the more easily recognized fields of *minzuxue* [nationalities study, i.e., ethnology] or archaeology.)

China's first generation of "anthropology" students in forty years is thus only now in formation, and it will be up to them to come to grips with the role of anthropology in the China of the future. Having seen their field previously influenced by both the West and North, and viewing both influences alone as inadequate, will the new students help create a new Chinese anthropology that creatively blends the best of both West and North into a distinctly sinified anthropology?

This is an important question, for unlike the situation in the 1940s, anthropology must now show that there is a place for it in socialist China, that it can be shorn of its capitalist and imperialist assumptions and functions and instead serve China in its drive for socialist modernization. This socialist sinification of anthropology is indeed precisely the mandate of both party and government; one cannot simply copy the form and substance of foreign anthropologies and mechanically apply them to China. Using Marxist-Leninism as a guide, ethnology and the other anthropological sciences must be molded to serve China's modernization effort.[10]

To do so calls first for an objective evaluation of the good and bad points of foreign anthropologies. Lin Yaohua, one of the most influential ethnologists of the postrevolutionary period, has made such an evaluation (personal communication). The West he credits with giving ethnology a holistic understanding of humanity, but he criticizes Western anthropology for the inherent ethnocentrism and racism derived from its origins in colonialism. By contrast, the USSR scores well in this area for its "objective and unbiased theoretical treatment of primitive societies." Lin also regards Soviet economic-cultural classification theory[11] highly although he, like others, faults Stalin's nationality definition and some other Soviet formulations. As for Chinese ethnology, although blessed by a plethora of potential fieldwork sites and fieldworkers, the key weakness, to Lin and others, is a lack of foreign materials and exposure.

To combat this, many scholars in the anthropological sciences have these past few years attempted to summarize foreign theoretical and substantive approaches in short journal articles. The Liang and Zhang selections appearing in this volume are prime examples of this and the related attempt to bring foreign material to bear on Chinese academic

---

[10] Conferences have already been held in China to discuss this very question. See Guldin (1987) for their published results.

[11] See Lin and Cheboksarov (1984) for an application of this theory to China.

debate. Increasing contact with these foreign materials has thus raised the question of how to absorb selectively the theories and data from the outside. Chinese scholars are very careful to talk about the West's disciplines serving not as *models* for China but rather as *referents*. Neither Soviet nor American nor any other anthropology should be adopted blindly. China should develop an autonomous anthropology and ethnology that are uniquely Chinese.

Two alternative perspectives on implementing the latter have begun to gel. The first feels that anthropology must be sinified, and that from China's experience and needs a Chinese and Marxist ethnology-anthropology should emerge. The other view holds that there should evolve in China and elsewhere an ethnology-anthropology that is neither Western nor Soviet nor Chinese but is guided by Marxism in theoretical and methodological terms. The Marxist frame is assumed in both models, as befits anthropology and ethnology in a socialist society. Beyond this common ideological underpinning, Chinese scholars are not yet certain how the sinification of these social sciences would proceed. In the natural sciences, in paleoanthropology and archaeology, by contrast, people never talk of sinifying their fields; the universalism of these fields is now assumed.

This returns us to the global question of the universality of anthropology, of one anthropology or many in today's world, that was touched on earlier. Ethnologist-anthropologist Chen Yongling of CIN gave me his perspective: "There is indeed a general anthropology of theory and methodology. But every country has its own characteristics and contributions. The more such contributions from more countries, the more fruitful world anthropology. We in China don't aim to separate Chinese anthropology from the outside world but instead want to 'digest' others' anthropologies and apply them selectively to our own situation."

## Chinese and World Anthropology: A Personal Comment

We should thus expect and indeed welcome differences between national versions of anthropology. Two such differences in the Chinese and American anthropological scenes forcefully struck this observer. One was the extensive use of team fieldwork in all of the Chinese anthropological sciences,[12] and the other was the relative respectability there of

[12]Salzman's (1986) critique of American anthropology and especially ethnology for ignoring the benefits of the team approach seems quite relevant here.

the applied aspects of the craft. In China pressure is on theoretical academics to prove their work worthwhile, while those involved in applied work are assured of public approval and support. The government's strong role in academia ensures that the talents of anthropological scientists are used in matters as varied as bilingual education policy, helmet size specifications for the People's Liberation Army, and tourist control at archaeological sites. In the United States, by contrast, applied anthropologists have been the ones struggling for recognition and support.

It is in these areas, perhaps, that Chinese anthropology can begin to make its contribution to world anthropology. Anthropologists abroad have much to learn from the Chinese team approach to research and from the Chinese attempt to make their academic disciplines fit human needs; it would be particularly fitting for a socialist country's anthropology to make that contribution. When one also considers China's richness in prehistoric sites, its abundance of languages and dialects, and its incredible regional and ethnic diversity, it is not difficult to foresee the future necessity to test all anthropological theories of human origins and behavior against the experience of one billion Chinese and their ancestors. Now that China's anthropological scientists have emerged from the lost two decades of 1957-1978, perhaps they can call forth a Chinese "East Wind" to join with the already extant North and West winds to influence the flow of global anthropological currents.

## References Cited

Arkush, R. David (1981). *Fei Xiaotong and Sociology in Revolutionary China*. Cambridge: Harvard University Press.
Cai Yuanpei (1926). "Shuo minzuxue" (On ethnology), *Yi ban* (December).
CASS Archaeology Institute (1984). "Zhongguo kaoguxuede huangjin shidai" (Chinese archaeology's golden age), *Kaogu* 10:865-71.
Chen Yongling (1982). "Xifang Minzuxue zhi Chunru Zhongguo" (The introduction of Western ethnology into China), *Minzu tuanjie* 9:36–37.
China Daily (1987). "Ancient Sites Found on Yangtze," January 23, 1987:3.
Chu, David S. K., ed. (1984). *Sociology and Society in Contemporary China 1979–1983*. Armonk, N.Y.: M. E. Sharpe.
Engels, Friedrich (1972 [1884]). *Origin of the Family, Private Property and the State*. New York: International Publishers.
Guldin, Gregory Eliyu (1987). "Anthropology in the People's Republic of China," *Anthropology Newsletter* 28, 5 (May): 34.
Lin Yaohua and Nikolai Cheboksarov (1984). "Zhongguode jingji wenhua leixing" (China's Economic-Cultural Types), *Minzu yanjiu lunwenji* 3:10–53. Beijing:

Nationalities Institute, Central Institute of Nationalities.
Morgan, Lewis Henry (1877). *Ancient Society*. New York: Holt.
*Renmin ribao* (Overseas Edition) (1987). "Woguo qunian jinxing 572 xiang kaogu fajue" (China carried out 572 archaeological digs last year), March 18, 1987:6.
Salzman, Philip Carl (1986). "Is Traditional Fieldwork Outmoded?" *Current Anthropology* 27, 5 (December):528–30.
Wong Siu-lun (1979). *Sociology and Socialism in Contemporary China*. London: Routledge and Kegan Paul.
Wu Rukang (1980). "Zhongguo gurenleixue sanshi nian, 1949–1979" (Thirty years of Chinese paleoanthropology, 1949-1979), *Gujizhui dongwu yu gurenlei* 18, 1 (January): 1–8.
Xia Nai (1984). "Qianyan" (Foreword), in *Xin Zhongguode kaogu faxian he yanjiu* (New China's archaeological discoveries and research). Beijing: Cultural Relics Press, pp. 1–3.
Yen Wenming (1985). "Xinshiqi shidai kaogu yanjiude huigu yu qianzhan" (Reminiscences and a look ahead at Neolithic archaeological research), *Wenwu* 85, 3:20–27.

# Part II

# The Argument for a Four-Fields Anthropology

LIANG ZHAOTAO

## 2 The Scope and Function of Anthropology

THROUGHOUT the world, every country, school of thought, and scholar has its own definition of "anthropology." The simplest, however, and the one most broadly acknowledged, is that it is "the science of the study of Man." Nevertheless, there are just too many sciences that are involved in the study of people, such as medical science, biology, history, economics, and sociology, and all are in one way or another studies of human beings. Moreover, each field of science has its own scientific system [of inquiry]. If anthropology is to be so elective and all-inclusive, then it is inevitable that it would become tantamount to not having anthropology at all. Moreover, such an all-embracing definition would perhaps not be acceptable to scholars in those many fields and sciences. Therefore, we need to be clear on the connotations of anthropology itself, on the objectives and subject matter of its study, its scope, and where its emphases lie. Otherwise we will create confusion and perhaps even find ourselves in a situation in which anthropology does not even exist. Anthropology, we believe, has its own parameters or boundaries. These boundaries allow it to include the scientific study of the origins and the development of the human species itself, and the origins and the laws that govern the development and evolution of the material civilization and mental and spiritual cultures created by the human race. On this basis, anthropology also studies the physical and cultural relationships among various human species, ethnic divisions, nations, and other forms of human commonalities. Furthermore, the science applies the theories and methods of anthropology to the study and resolution of practical problems related to contemporary human societies.

"Renleixue de yanjiu neirong yu zuoyong," in *Renleixue yanjiu* (Anthropological studies) (Beijing: Chinese Academy of Social Sciences Press, 1984), pp. 11–16.

The study of the origin and development of humanity itself is called physical anthropology. The study of the origin and development of the material and spiritual cultures created by human beings is called cultural anthropology. These are the two major subdisciplines in anthropology.

Physical anthropology is the comparative study of the physical characteristics of modern human races, populations, and nationalities and their categorization, as well as formation of the physical attributes of communities among the human beings that inhabit the world in modern times and the historical relationships that lead to the production of the mixtures of ethnic identities—attributes that are expressed outwardly in physical form, such as skin pigmentation, hair formation, skull formation, physique, and blood type. This area of anthropology is generally known as physical anthropology, or, more precisely, the physical anthropology of modern humans (homo sapiens). On the other hand, owing to the fact that physical anthropology studies the origin of the human species and the evolution of early humans, it also takes the fossils of ancient humans that are excavated from geological strata as objects of its study. It studies these relics in comparison with ancient apes as well as modern apes. This is known as paleoanthropology, a branch of physical anthropology. That is to say, the first area studies modern or contemporary man, while the second deals with ancient man, but both belong to physical anthropology.

Humanity's emergence from the state of animal-ness cannot be separated from a dialectical relationship with the human creation of culture. Anthropology must study human culture, for there is no such thing as "anthropology" apart from and independent of human culture. When we speak of culture or civilization we are referring to the term "culture" in the broad, generalized sense it is employed in anthropology. It includes the forces and relations of production as well as the economic base and the superstructure. Because cultural anthropology studies the origin and development of culture, in addition to studying the ancient civilizations that human beings have "left behind" and that are excavated by archaeologists, it also searches for the survivals of ancient cultures among modern cultures of both relatively backward peoples and people in civilized societies, for what is referred to in Marxism as "cultural fossils" and "social fossils." Owing to the fact that one of the primary objects of cultural anthropological study is nationalities that retain relatively large measures of such "cultural fossils," it is often taken to be equivalent to ethnology. In fact, there are still some distinctions between the two. In the realm of cultural anthropology, in terms of field of study, archaeology covers the past while ethnology is contemporary. We should therefore say that ethnology is a subdiscipline of cultural anthropology, and so the two are not entirely equivalent.

In some countries, such as among some British and American scholars, since they feel that the connotations of the term "culture" in cultural anthropology are too broad, they prefer to focus their study on a narrower group of areas, such as social organizations, social systems, or marriage forms, and they call this social anthropology. As such, it is a part of cultural anthropology. If we take this to be modern ethnological studies, we can also consider it to be part of ethnology.

Some scholars, furthermore, focus entirely on the study of modern social systems and the laws that regulate and govern people's social lives. They also employ the theories of anthropology and its method of social survey to study the social life and psychological conditions of rural peasants, urban workers or people in other strata of society among minority nationalities and among so-called civilized societies, applying the results of such studies to resolve, it is hoped, certain practical social problems. Or they may, in physical anthropology, study problems of practical application to modern human life. All these are known under the rubric of applied anthropology.

Human spiritual culture includes such things as religious beliefs, myths, tales, folk songs, aphorisms and sayings, dance, paintings and drawings, sculpture, and customs and mores. Some scholars in anthropology devote themselves entirely to the study of these areas, and their subfield is known as folklore studies. In the realm of cultural anthropology, folklore emphasizes on-the-spot field investigations. As a study of history and the relationships among local nationality groups, this study is obliged to reflect the material honestly and to conduct its analysis faithfully. Therefore, folklore also differs somewhat from the study of "folk literature," which is taken as a branch of literary studies. Some scholars mistakenly assume that ethnology is confined to the study of alien nationalities that are culturally backward, while folklore refers to the science of studying the lore and mores of one's own country or nationality. Such a distinction is erroneous and absurd. We should say, instead, that folklore is a branch of ethnology. This strict distinction between folklore and ethnology is only rarely made, however. For example, in some European continental countries, especially in Germany, folklore and ethnology are considered as one discipline, whose contents include such things as social systems. The German journal of folklore studies, for instance, uses the term "Volkskunde" as its title. This term is equivalent to the term "folklore" in English, and its contents include ethnology. In German, the term "ethnology" is rendered as "Volkerkunde," which has the same etymological root as the English word "folk."

Archaeology, too, has its own scientific system. In most countries, however, the discipline of archaeology is subsumed under anthropology. This is true for anthropology departments in colleges and universities and also for the organizational structure of the international associations and conferences of anthropology. The reason for this is that archaeology's chief task lies also in the study of the origin and development of human culture. The role it plays in anthropology is even more important than its role in history as a science. It is in anthropology that the greatest use for archaeology's theories can be put into play, for there is an intimate linkage among archaeology, ethnology, and physical anthropology. In terms of theory they are interconnected and consistent with one another, and when we put the three together in an integrated study, the theoretical results that emerge as scientific laws will serve as the theoretical system undergirding the discipline of anthropology as a whole.

Human language is an integral part of human culture because language is innate to humanity. When people study the origin of the human race, they very often attempt to derive from fossil skull fragments observations concerning the development of language zones. At the same time, ethnologists also use such items in the study of linguistics as syntax patterns and glossaries to distinguish the peculiar attributes of what they call a nationality's "common language." They also discover, from linguistic material, traces of the processes of social development and the interaction and relationship among certain nationalities. When someone studies the languages of contemporary peoples, the study belongs to what can be called modern linguistics. When, on the other hand, someone studies the historical vestiges of such languages, the study would belong to historical linguistics. The discipline of linguistics certainly has its own independent system [of inquiry and study], but when one studies the origins of language and the relationships between the languages of certain nationalities, then one is in the realm of anthropology, and the study ought to be conducted in coordination with the disciplines of paleoanthropology and ethnology. The study would essentially be comparative and therefore is generally known as comparative linguistics. Between linguistics and anthropology there is thus a close link. In many international conferences of anthropologists, linguistics is often placed within the scientific system of anthropology. Modern anthropologists are able to extrapolate from the structure of languages explanations of phenomena in the structure of human societies. This is known as "structural anthropology." In November 1980 at the First Seminar of Chinese Ethnologists in Guiyang, Professor Yang Kun made a critical introduction of this latest development of anthropological theory in a paper entitled "On Levi-Strauss's School of Structural Anthropology." In terms of the relationship between anthropology and linguistics, we can affirm that, in the realm of anthropology itself, comparative linguistics is a very important department.

The growth and development of anthropology has itself led to more detailed and specialized divisions and subdivisions. At the same time, however, there has been increasing reinforcement of integrated and comprehensive studies. Among the various universities, colleges, and research organizations on anthropology in the world, there are many different patterns of structural development, with some dividing into many subfields and some into few, each dependent on local conditions. We also note, however, that the three major components—physical anthropology, ethnology, and archaeology—are indispensable. In the United States, and in some other countries that have lost their colonies, ethnology has become not quite as popular as it had been, for since the Second World War these countries no longer have the freedom to study the nationalities in their erstwhile colonies. Instead, they seem to have switched their focus to the study of social or applied anthropology. China, on the other hand, is a multinationality country. We have broad vistas to open up in the area of ethnology. Therefore, for us, ethnology remains an indispensable department in anthropology.

Internationally, anthropology is an important scientific discipline. In all countries, any university or college of some renown has a department of anthropology and perhaps an anthropological museum.

Since Liberation, under the correct leadership of the Communist Party, we have discovered in China fossils of ancient apes that lived over 10 million years ago, as well as other fossils from as early as the Yuanmou ape-man, which lived 1.7 million years ago, to modern homo sapiens dating back some 10 thousand years. This series of scientific discoveries on what may be the earliest origins of the human race and its evolution, and on the development of human culture in the Paleolithic age, puts us in the foremost rank in the world in this particular area. We are also in the front rank with regard to the excavation of Neolithic archaeological material and material from the period of the earliest human transition, after the Neolithic age, into a class society. We have discovered such material in many places in our country, and it provides extremely rich scientific data for theorizing about the forms of human social development and the laws governing development. As of now there are fifty-six nationalities in China. Our nationality cultures flourish and together make up a colorful tapestry [of cultural influences]. In our effort to gather anthropological data from these nationalities, we have accumulated raw research and investigative material to the tune of several tens of million words, including investigative reports on the languages of the various nationalities. This treasure trove of scientific data is something foreign scholars would gladly give their eyeteeth for, but they do not have ready access to it as we do. This, too, puts us in the number-one spot in the world. Our country is extremely large in size and scope, and we have a tremendously long history of continuous cultural development. There are many major differences among our various nationalities. Since Liberation China has implemented a socialist nationalities policy, and this has brought about a great transformation in the nationalities' societies. From here on, especially in the process of implementing and realizing the four modernizations, there is bound to be an even greater transformation. All these practical social problems need to be studied further, and we can do that best only on the basis of having a deep knowledge about the conditions of the various nationalities, on the basis of ethnological studies.

Even though ethnology, archaeology, and physical anthropology workers in China have, in the last thirty years, traced a circuitous path of development, they have, nonetheless, under the party's leadership, made great efforts to learn Marxism and have enhanced their theoretical foundations. Moreover, since they possessed a massive trove of rich material for research, they have begun to form an independent, Marxism-guided system of scholarship. There are flaws, however. In the past, we have generally assumed, in a biased way, that anthropology referred only to physical anthropology and have ignored the real substance of its linkage with culture. Therefore archaeology, ethnology, and physical anthropology have become separate from one another, and consequently the combative power of each, in terms of a scientific system or academic organization, has been weakened. From now on we must establish a solid structure for the study of anthropology as a whole in terms of teaching and research organizations as well as scholarly associations, in which these three fields may be integrated into one focused force. We must establish, therefore, China's own scientific system in the area of anthropology and employ the massive amounts of scientific data we have, to explain and develop the philosophical ideas of dialectic and historical materialism. At the same time, we can also use these philosophical ideas to guide us in enhancing the philosophical underpinning of our nation's anthropological studies, to establish thereby our own brand of anthropological science, to enrich the treasure chest of Marxist theory, and to direct us in our resolution of related, practical social problems.

For over a century there has been a struggle between the idealist school and the materialist school in anthropology. No matter how complex the ideas, theories, and methodologies in the field of anthropology may be, and how many different schools there are, they can all be summed up in two major categories. One maintains that the origin of human beings can be found in labor and production, that human civilization begins in material production and develops along the lines of the objective laws governing social development. This is the materialist school. The other category is the idealist thought that maintains exactly the opposite and holds that all has origin in the mental world and psychological conditions of the human race and denies that human society is governed by objectively existing laws of development. Undoubtedly, anthropology has a class nature. Under the differing guidance of a proletarian world view and a bourgeois world view, there will naturally be differing explanations of the origins and development of the human race and of its culture.

Marx and Engels indefatigably carried out a polemical battle against the bourgeois anthropologists of their own day. At the same time, they laid down a basis for a scientific theory of anthropology based on dialectic materialism. The two famous essays, "The Role of Labor in the Transformation Process of Ape to Man" and *Origin of the Family, Private Property, and the State* are the theoretical writings that represent the proletariat's world view in anthropological studies. The former creatively expressed and proved the brilliant theory that labor created the human race. Marxism describes and studies the birth of humanity in intimate conjunction with the appearance of material culture (including the tools of labor production) created by human beings, the appearance of their society, and the generation and development of their language.

Therefore, Marx and Engels are the founders of the school of anthropology that combines the physical attributes of humans and their cultures in an integrated study. The latter work is the first Marxist study in cultural anthropology. In it, archaeology and ethnology are integrated. This essay laid the foundation for a theory of cultural anthropology that rests on the importance of the socioeconomic base. It argued and proved that the development of the forces of production is the motivating force that propels human society forward. It is a work that established the theoretical system of historical materialism in anthropology, a system that sees such things as culture and social systems as the superstructure built upon the economic base. Back when Marx and Engels set pen to paper and wrote this magnificent essay, they carefully studied many bourgeois writings of the time related to this branch of science. They criticized these writings, made synopses of them, and filled many of the gaps in them. In other words, they critically inherited the viewpoints and methods in these writings; employing the philosophical method of "dividing one into two," they absorbed from these bourgeois viewpoints the useful parts that conformed to objective realities and criticized their erroneous viewpoints. Thus they established their own independent system of theory.

So, too, should we take Marx and Engels as our example in establishing our own school of anthropology. We should take their dialectical and historical materialism as our guiding thought and, in close conjunction with the material in our country, critically inherit the legacy of the bourgeois writings on anthropology that have appeared since the passing of Marx and Engels. In the same spirit we must study the history of the teachings on anthropology in the world at large, criticize but also lay claim to the legacy of the theories, viewpoints, and methods of foreign schools of anthropology, and thereby enrich the contents of Marxist anthropology. We must also use the rich material available to us to develop further the Marxist doctrine concerning the labor creation of the human race and the objective laws of the development of human society. We must, furthermore, develop the ancient and continuously resplendent cultural tradition of the Chinese people. We must, on the one hand, analyze the cultural differences among our many nationalities, recognizing the existence of the minority nationalities, and, on the other hand, achieve an integrated understanding of the common characteristics and attributes of the various cultures of the nationalities, and explain clearly the history of the union and unity of the people of all nationalities. Finally, then, we will be able to employ our country's own theory of anthropology in the service of the party's nationalities policy, in the service of enhancing the lives of our people in the countryside as well as urban areas, in the service of industrial and agricultural production, and make a contribution to the nation's four modernizations endeavor.

CHEN GUOQIANG

# 3 The Chinese People Need Anthropology

ANTHROPOLOGY is an important discipline. It is a discipline that belongs to the natural sciences and also to the social sciences. In our country, for many years anthropology has been mistakenly understood to be just a natural science, that is, as physical anthropology, or was even further confined to paleoanthropology, the discipline that studies human fossils. In fact, prior to Liberation, anthropological studies in our country included both physical and cultural anthropology, and anthropology was respected as a very important social science whose objects, content, and materials of study were extremely rich and abundant.

In recent years in foreign countries there has been an increasingly intimate link between the science of anthropology and the social life of the people. The scope of the study of anthropology has been continuously expanded and a number of derivative branch sciences have been developed. All this indicates that anthropology occupies a most significant place in the realm of science. In the last few years, there has been a recovery of anthropological studies in our country.

We believe that when we look back at the objects and contents of anthropology in the past and compare them with current conditions, we will be able to clarify the status and role of its study, and if we conduct the investigation with a close linkage with the needs of our people, we will be able, all the better, to clarify the significance and the meaning of the study of anthropology. We will discuss these various questions below.

"Wuoguo renmin xuyao renleixue," in *Renleixue yanjiu* (Anthropological studies) (Beijing: Chinese Academy of Social Sciences, 1984), pp. 1–10.

## Anthropology Is a Science that Studies the Physical and Cultural Aspects of Humanity

The term "anthropology" comes from the Greek and means "human (anthropos)" added to "science (logos)." Thus it refers to a science that studies people.

As Engels pointed out in *Natural Dialectics*, "every science is an analysis of either a single form and state of motion or a series of mutually related and mutually transforming forms and states of motions." As a science, anthropology takes as the object of its study the form of motion that makes up the generation and development of the human race. The human race is a part of Nature and therefore has its natural properties. But humans also live among a certain set of social relationships, and thus humanity also has social properties. Anthropology studies both the physical properties and the cultural properties of humanity. It therefore belongs to both the natural sciences and the social sciences. Engels furthermore said that anthropology "is the bridge that crosses over from the study of the morphology and the physiology of human beings and human races to the study of history. This is a bridge that has yet to be studied and explained in a continuous way and in detail." This statement clearly points out that anthropology is a transitional science that lies between the natural sciences and the social sciences. The object of the study of anthropology is the defined mode of motion in the generation and development of the human species, motion that has a natural aspect and also ought to have a societal aspect. In other words, anthropology ought to be a science that studies the laws that govern the generation and development of the physical and cultural properties of humanity.

Many well-known modern anthropologists believe that in addition to the study of the physical properties of human beings, anthropology should also study human culture. The American, [Clark] Wissler, said: "Anthropology is the science that studies Man. It includes the study of all questions that relate to human beings as social animals." England's [Bronislaw] Malinowski also said: "Anthropology is a science that studies the human race and its culture in all degrees and levels of development. It includes the study of the physical nature of human beings, the racial differences among them, civilization, and societal formation as well as questions related to Man's mental and spiritual responses to the environment." We can easily perceive from these discussions and statements that anthropology is a social science that studies both human physique and human culture.

Anthropology Professor Lin Huixiang of Xiamen University summed up the positions of various schools of anthropology and proposed a definition that set out its contents and scope of study. He said: "Anthropology is a science that employs a historical perspective in studying humanity and its culture. It includes the study of the origins of human species, the separation and differentiation of races, and the study of the primitive conditions of material life, societal structure, spiritual responses, etc. In other words, anthropology is a natural history of the human race that encompasses the study of humans in both prehistoric and historic times, barbaric peoples and civilized peoples; however, its focus is on the prehistoric era and on barbaric peoples." Here he proposed that anthropology should be the study of both the physical properties and the cultural conditions of the human race, but with emphasis placed on the primitive age.

In the past, people in some countries, such as Britain and the United States, took the broader view of anthropology and felt that it should include both physical and cultural anthropology. On the other hand, in the Soviet Union and a number of other European countries, anthropology has been generally confined to the study of the physical properties of the human species alone. As for China, prior to Liberation we employed both of these approaches to anthropology. However, in the series known as *Daxue congshu* (Miscellaneous texts for use in universities), published by the Commercial Press, the broader definition appears to have been adopted. This series published as a special monograph Lin Huixiang's *Wenhua renleixue* (Cultural anthropology) to be used as the textbook and reference material for universities and colleges in the country.

Lin believed that in addition to physical anthropology, anthropology ought to include the following subfields: cultural anthropology (including social anthropology and ethnology), prehistoric archaeology, and ethnography. Furthermore, he held that the contents of cultural anthropology ought to be made up of seven parts, namely, a general theory of anthropology, the history of cultural anthropology, primitive material culture, primitive social organization, primitive religions, primitive art, and primitive languages and writing. In this way it would be a science that synthesizes the material on all peoples with an emphasis on the investigation of the generation and development of primitive cultures.

Somewhat similar to this view were ideas contained in the book *Xiandai renleixue* (Contemporary anthropology) written by Zhang Liyuan in 1933. This view was based, with some slight modification, on the categorization adopted by the Anthropology Research Laboratory of London University. Zhang proposed that anthropology ought to include the subfields of physical anthropology (including such subjects as zoology, paleontology, physiology, psychology, and raciology) and cultural anthropology (including archaeology, folk arts and crafts, sociology, linguistics, and folklore). Thus while particular subfields selected may differ, all of these scholars point out that anthropology ought to encompass the area of culture.

Professor Lin explained specifically that in his opinion, among the four subfields of anthropology, cultural anthropology had the distinction of being most integrated, comprehensive, and theoretical; its emphasis is on exploring the fundamental principles of the field. In contrast, prehistoric archaeology and ethnography are more concrete and specific, with a much more narrative character; they focus on the narration of "facts." All these subfields are coordinated with one another. Prehistoric archaeology and ethnography contribute specific material to the study of cultural anthropology, whereas cultural anthropology provides explanatory theories for prehistoric archaeology and ethnography. Prior to Liberation, there was in our academic circles a very intimate relationship between anthropology and sociology. Even so, however, there was little likelihood that the two could have been confused with each other. This was because the primary focus of sociology was to study the practical and contemporary problems of human society and to discuss the fundamental underlying principles of society. Professor Lin pointed out that there were three basic distinctions between anthropology and sociology: (1) The character of anthropology is historical whereas that of sociology is theoretical. (2) The subject matter and nature of anthropology is not connected to that of sociology. Anthropology focuses on the primitive or primal conditions of human society whereas sociology focuses on contemporary social life. (3) What anthropology studies is, for the most part, primitive society, whereas sociology for the most part discusses contemporary society.

Prior to Liberation, there was an extremely close linkage between cultural anthropology and archaeology and ethnography. Anthropology, at that time, included not only cultural anthropology but also the subfields of prehistoric archaeology and ethnography. There was, among these subfields, a sense of cooperation as well as of division of labor. Each had its emphasis, and there was no repetition or unnecessary overlap. Prehistoric archaeology and ethnography conducted concrete archaeological excavations and studies of ethnic groups, and they provided concrete material for cultural anthropology to study. For its part, cultural anthropology provided explanatory principles and theories for the study of prehistoric archaeology and ethnography. These were compatibly coordinated and mutually enhancing. Together they deepened our understanding of the laws that governed the origins and development of human culture. Therefore, at that time there were no questions raised as to whether with the existence of archaeology and ethnography it was possible to dispense with cultural anthropology. Even though in a number of countries ethnology came to be another name for cultural anthropology, it is clear that with anthropology including ethnology, ethnography, folklore, mythology, and so forth, the object and contents of the study of cultural anthropology are broader and more expansive than those of ethnology.

## With the Development of Society, Anthropology Grows in Breadth and Number of Subdisciplines

For the last thirty years, anthropology in China has been treated in the same vein as sociology, ethnology, legal studies, and religious studies, as a bourgeois science, and as such has not been promoted publicly and its development adversely affected. And yet some subfields that were included under the rubric of anthropology in the past (for instance, in physical anthropology, the study of paleoanthropology or fossil anthropology, and in the area of cultural anthropology, prehistoric archaeology and ethnography) have flourished and developed in China. In paleoanthropology, for example, under the leadership of such organizations as the Institute of Vertebrate Paleontology and Paleoanthropology of the Chinese Academy of Sciences, there have been discoveries and research results of major significance on the fossils of ancient human beings. In prehistoric archaeology, under the leadership of such organizations as the Institute of Archaeology of the Chinese Academy of Social Sciences, many Stone Age sites and relics have been discovered and excavated. In ethnography, under the leadership of the Nationalities Affairs Commission of the State Council and the Institute of Nationalities Studies of the Chinese Academy of Social Sciences, we have launched several nationwide surveys of the social histories of minorities in China and have accumulated data on this subject to the tune of several tens of millions words. This, too, has been a magnificently fruitful research undertaking.

On the other hand, owing to the fact that anthropology as a general subject has not been fully promoted, there has come to be a state of near blankness in some subfields of anthropology. For example, there has been a hiatus for many years in archeometry, raciology, and folklore studies, and there has not yet been in the entire country a single organization devoted to the specialized study of anthropology. Although we do have anthropology research groups or teams in the Beijing Museum of Natural History and the Shanghai Museum of Natural History, and we do have an Anthropology Research Room in the biology department of Fudan University and a Museum of Anthropology at Xiamen University, all these do not add up to a sizable number of researchers, and our strength in this area is weak. Although after Liberation Professor Lin Huixiang did propose to set up at Xiamen University an anthropology department and laboratory, nevertheless, for a long time there has not been a single department of anthropology in all of the higher education institutions in the country. In April 1981, an anthropology department was formed at Zhongshan University [in Guangzhou], which included two fields of specialization, archaeology and ethnology. At Xiamen University, too, opinions are brewing for the establishment of an anthropology department, which will include two fields of specialization, anthropology and archaeology. All this serves as a new point of departure for the development of anthropology in China.

In other countries anthropology has been developing with a great flourish in recent years. Following the progress of social life in general, the content, number, and designation of subfields have expanded. In the course of its own development, anthropology has made linkages with many related fields of study, and, consequently many cross-disciplines have been developed. In physical anthropology, for example, new subdisciplines such as eugenics, psychological anthropology, medical anthropology, nutritional anthropology, geriatric anthropology, and action anthropology have emerged. In cultural anthropology, subfields such as political anthropology, economic anthropology, educational anthropology, anthropological studies of human labor-efficiency, rural anthropology, and urban anthropology have also come forth. In terms of the general trend, it appears that the field of anthropology has gradually expanded in institutions of higher education and in some cases has even subsumed history as a field. Therefore, in the United States, for instance, there are more departments of anthropology than history departments.

On December 11, 1980, Dr. Gonzales, vice-president of the University of Maryland, was invited jointly by the Institute of Nationality Studies of the Chinese Academy of Social Sciences and the Institute of Nationality Studies of the Central Institute of Nationalities to address a Chinese audience on the general conditions and trends of anthropological studies in the United States. He said that today in America anthropology is deemed a science that studies Man in general. It includes four branches of learning, namely, physical anthropology (the study of the physique and special features of the physical formations of ancient and contemporary human beings), archaeology (the study of the modes of life of ancient human beings in all places), social anthropology (which some call ethnology, the study of the various aspects of life of contemporary ethnic groups), and linguistics (comparative linguistics). He said that while the division of subfields of anthropology has become more detailed, it is a matter of great achievement for an anthropologist to be well versed in one or two or three of these subdisciplines. The American anthropologist, Professor Arthur Wolf of Stanford University, also presented a report at Xiamen University on January 19, 1981, entitled "On the Significance of Contemporary Anthropological Studies." He, too, mentioned that anthropology is made up of four divisions: physical anthropology, anthropological archaeology, social anthropology, and anthropological linguistics. He suggested that an anthropologist should probably know something about each of these four subfields but should focus his attention on studying one of them. He reaffirmed that anthropology is a branch of both the natural sciences and the humanities.

In addition, Professor Fawkes, chairman of the anthropology department of Australian National University, visited Xiamen University on September 19, 1980. In a seminar discussion with students and colleagues at the university, he introduced the situation in his department at ANU. He mentioned that they had a curriculum covering three aspects, that is, human ecology, archaeology, and social anthropology. He pointed out that because the discipline of anthropology has developed in a very complex way, it is possible and feasible for an anthropologist to become expert in only one of these many complicated areas. We are told that the situation in the Philippines is quite similar. Anthropology Professor Shi Zhenmin of Lassal University informed us through a letter that in his department anthropology included both physical and cultural anthropology. Furthermore, according to the information provided by Anthropology Professor Chie Nakane of Nihon Daigaku (Japan University) of Japan, who is also vice-president of the International Association of Anthropologists, as a science, cultural anthropology achieved independent status as a discipline in Japan only in the post–World War II period. He says that in some Japanese universities, departments of cultural (social) anthropology have been established. He also informs us that in 1971, a new scholarly publication, *Jinruigaku senkan* (Special bulletin on anthropology) was published, which was a journal devoted to the introduction of scholarly work on cultural anthropology. Finally, we know that in such places in our country as Taiwan and Hong Kong, universities also have anthropology departments where studies on both physical and cultural anthropology are included.

From the above-mentioned reports concerning the conditions and experiences in foreign countries and in Taiwan and Hong Kong, we can see that the field of anthropology still very much includes both a physical and a cultural aspect, as it did before Liberation. In physical anthropology we should study not just ancient human beings (human fossils) but also the physical features—and the calibration of such features—of contemporary human species. In cultural anthropology, we find, in addition to conventional archaeology and social anthropology, an outstanding proposal that language studies should be included. From the general trends, we have found that there seems to be a continuous expansion of the realm of anthropological studies to the extent that in some cases, history as a discipline has been subsumed or included. In other cases we find an integration of anthropology with related disciplines and the generation of branches of peripheral disciplines. The examples cited above—the development, in physical anthropology of such studies as eugenics, psychological anthropology, medical anthropology, nutritional anthropology, geriatric anthropology, and action anthropology, and, in cultural anthropology, of such studies as political anthropology, economic anthropology, agricultural anthropology, educational anthropology, urban anthropology, and anthropological studies of human labor efficiency—have all emerged in response to the needs of contemporary society and the evolution and development of the fields of study. Because anthropology as a discipline has expanded to have an impact on contemporary social life, its relationship with sociology has become all the more intimate, and there is today the phenomenon of partial cross-disciplinary connections and overlapping among these two fields.

We also note, however, that the study and teaching of both sociology and anthropology are very common in such places as the United States, Australia, and the Philippines, to name a few. The relationship between these two fields in those places is intimate, and they are well coordinated with each other. At the same time, each discipline has its own emphases and is distinguished from the others. Professor Wolf had the following to say in response to a question posed to him during his visit on the distinction between and relationship of anthropology and sociology. He said that one distinction is that anthropology is the study of the culture of other peoples, whereas sociology tends to be the study of one's own nation. Another distinction is in terms of methodology. He said that in sociology, one has to gather information through conversations with a large number of people, whereas in anthropology the researcher has to live for some period among the people being studied, and the work is conducted primarily as field study. He said that in the United States, anthropology and sociology are separate. The same opinion is confirmed by Professor Huang Shumin of the sociology and anthropology department of Northwestern University in the United States. Professor Huang attended the celebrations of the sixtieth anniversary of the founding of Xiamen University in April 1981, and I had an opportunity to discuss the subject with him. Professor Huang mentioned that in some American universities and colleges, sociology and anthropology are combined in a single department, but this is largely for the purpose of reducing the number of people involved in bureaucratic administration; in terms of research and teaching the two disciplines are still separated. This, he said, is because the subjects being studied in anthropology cannot be replaced by sociology. At Australian National University the departments of anthropology and sociology are separate. There the scope of the anthropology department is broader; its focus is on field work and on-the-spot investigation. It is considered a comprehensive, integrated discipline. On the other hand, the sociology department focuses on the problems and the demographics of contemporary society. In terms of the geographic foci of the departments, the anthropology department focuses on the Pacific and Southeast Asian regions, whereas the sociology department focuses on contemporary Australian society.

From the above we can see that in recent years, the study of anthropology in the United States, Australia, and other countries has expanded considerably in scope in response to the needs of society and the development of science. In all these places, people have continued to follow a pattern that includes physical anthropology, archaeology, social anthropology, and anthropological linguistics within the general boundaries of science, and, in teaching, to educate students first in a general foundation and then proceed to demand of them specialization and expertise in some part of the field. We can learn much from these methods and examples.

## The Study of Anthropology Is Compatible with China's Needs; We Should Strenuously Develop Anthropology

Even prior to Liberation, anthropology as a field of study included both physical and cultural anthropology. Even though there has not been any overall comprehensive promotion of anthropology since Liberation, there have been developments and advances in some of its subfields. During the ten years of catastrophe, all scientific undertakings suffered from the trampling by the "Gang of Four." Since the Gang's downfall, the party's Central Committee has brought about a new springtime for the sciences. One after another, sciences that had had a weak foundation in the past or that had been suspended for many years have been restored. These include disciplines such as sociology, ethnology, law, and religious studies. Anthropology, too, has received attention from the leadership in this area. The reason those of us engaged in anthropology are so anxious to see its restoration and development is that the contents of its study are conducive to the socialist construction of our homeland, to the four modernizations program, and to the building of both the material and spiritual cultures of socialism.

We can, from the following angles, perceive the urgent need among our people for the study of anthropology:

First, as a science that studies the origin and development of humanity and its civilization, anthropology first takes up the study of the physical characteristics of human beings. The study of ancient human beings sheds light on questions regarding the roots and origin of the human species as well as on the "labor created Man" question. This helps us to learn dialectical and historical materialism, thus aiding us in constructing a correct world view and philosophy of life. Furthermore, the study of the physical properties of modern human beings and racial variations will help us in our understanding of the current lives that we lead and the racial composition of the human species in the world. In the past we mistakenly took the measurements and calibration of human physical properties to be a "bourgeois thing" and decided that we had no need to study them. Now we have come to realize that the measurement of physical properties of human beings is of great use in forming the nation's economic plans and policies regarding the people's livelihood. In particular, it is indispensable for the design of products in aeronautics, automobiles, medicine, public health, sports, construction, and light industries. Furthermore, the study of races helps us in our criticism of theories advocating racial superiority and helps promote mutual understanding among and friendly coexistence of the various nationalities in the world. On top of that, the study of eugenics, for instance, can help us cultivate and nurture people with strong and sound minds and physiques, people who are important for the construction of the four modernizations and who can bear upon their shoulders that awesome responsibility. Recent discoveries such as the phenomenon of the radiation of fire-like heat from the human body, known as *qi-gong* (breath exercise) and the aura that emanates from the human body, are also things that need to be studied in conjunction with anthropology. All these are needed in our nation's current endeavor for the four modernizations.

Second, in anthropology there is the study of cultural anthropology, which investigates the origins and development of human cultures. In the broad sense of the term, this includes archaeology, ethnology, ethnography, folklore, and mythology. In our country, the significance of the study of archaeology and ethnography have been generally acknowledged. However, we should be mindful that there is more than just that. Cultural anthropology is not merely a general and theoretical study, and the principles and theories it provides contribute to the study of archaeology and ethnography. They also contribute to the study of ethnology, folklore, and mythology. These are also very necessary in the realm of scholarship. In particular, we need to integrate all the different aspects of the science and carry out special topical studies and explanations. Through the study of the origin and development of human culture we can find help for the understanding of the development of humanity, for only when we know the past and have a grasp of the laws that govern development can we effectively create the future. This, too, is an urgent need for our endeavor to build the material and spiritual cultures of socialism.

Third, the new subfields and the peripheral, cross-disciplinary subjects of study generated on the fringes of anthropology are all deeply connected with the designing of national plans and the livelihood of the people. As Engels said in *Natural Dialectics* when he emphasized the immense significance of the "marginal sciences," "It is precisely on these points that we should anticipate the greatest results." Whether it is in sciences connected to physical anthropology, namely, eugenics, psychological anthropology, medical anthropology, nutritional anthropology, and action anthropology, or in sciences connected to cultural anthropology, such as political anthropology, economic anthropology, educational anthropology, anthropological linguistics, rural anthropology, and urban anthropology, the current studies of the lives and culture of contemporary human beings, the study of these in the various realms of politics, economics, ideology, and the construction and improvement of rural areas and cities and towns all involve problems that are the very same ones that our people today encounter in their efforts to realize the socialist four modernizations. If we do not study them, we will suffer setbacks in our work. If, on the other hand, we take brisk steps to study them and to grasp the laws that govern them, we will be able to serve the cause of building up our socialist homeland all the better and faster.

Fourth, we can look at the matter from the angle of nurturing talent and international scholarly interchange. Since anthropology is an important science, we should take steps to speed up the nurturing of talents in this field. Developing the study of anthropology will also allow us to develop greater international cultural exchange with other countries. We should consult anthropological studies in such countries as the United States, Japan, Australia, and the Southeast Asian countries. We should absorb from them the essentials and rid ourselves of the dross, and, under the guidance of Marxism and in connection with the needs of our people, gradually establish a system of anthropological study in our country. In 1978, the Tenth International Congress of the Anthropological and Ethnological Sciences was convened in India. Over two thousand scientists from more than seventy countries attended the conference. Yet we did not send a delegation. To foster greater international cultural exchange from now on, we should develop and promote the study of anthropology to create the necessary conditions for our participation in these conferences.

Even before Liberation, the distinctions between anthropology and sociology were quite clear in our country, and in recent years, in international circles, these distinctions have been clarified even more. For many years sociology, as much as anthropology, was wiped out in our country. After the "Gang of Four" was crushed, with the concern and care of the party's Central Committee, the Institute of Sociology was established under the Chinese Academy of Social Sciences in 1979. The article "On the Relationship of Historical Materialism and Sociology," published in journal *Zhexue yanjiu* (Philosophical studies), pointed out that "In order to study and understand more deeply and concretely life in our society, we must have sociology." Regarding the objectives and subject matter of sociology, Wang Kang wrote in "Sociology: Now and in the Past" that "Sociology is a science that studies social life, social relationships, the transformation of society, and social problems in general" (*Shehui kexue zhanxian* [Social sciences battlefront], no. 1, 1980). In the study of social problems, sociology places its emphasis on the problems of present social existence. While it may have some relationship and interpenetration with some of the aforementioned marginal subfields of anthropology, it cannot by any means take the place of anthropology, especially in terms of covering the two major subfields of anthropology, namely, physical and cultural anthropology. We acknowledge that there is an intimate relationship between anthropology and sociology and that the two can be coordinated and mutually enhancing, but we do not feel that the two can be combined. We do not think that sociology can take the place of anthropology.

Now for the question of whether it is necessary for anthropology to include so many subdisciplines, and will there not be some overlapping and redundancy? As discussed earlier, physical anthropology and cultural anthropology each includes a number of subfields, and each, in response to society's needs and the development of science, has given rise to a number of branch disciplines. These have all been determined by the needs and demands of society. The division of labor and the mutual reinforcement between cultural anthropology and some related sciences such as archaeology and ethnology that have already existed in their own right are also not affected adversely by individual and independent developments. At the moment, in foreign countries where there is an active nurturing of talents in the study of anthropology, the emphasis is on making sure that scholars in the field put down a solid foundation in the four major areas, namely, physical anthropology, archaeology, social anthropology, and linguistics, before they focus on any one of them. This method of training has its merits. If a broad foundation is firmly established and then one goes beyond that to concentrate on a particular subfield, the foundation will be all the more solid and firm. Furthermore, the scholar will have stronger adaptability in his future work and will not, as a consequence of being too specialized, damage the nation's use of talent by not being able to find proper job placement after graduation, resulting in having no application for what they have learned.

Anthropology has not been promoted for quite a few years. We need it. After the crushing of the "Gang of Four," the Central Committee brought about a springtime for sciences. In this springtime of knowledge we must, under the guidance of Marxism and Mao Zedong Thought, put our greatest efforts behind the promotion of anthropology. We must establish more anthropology-related research organizations to bring about more and greater academic fruits. We must establish more departments of anthropology in our universities and colleges and nurture more talent in the field of anthropology. We must set up more anthropology museums to popularize anthropological knowledge. Let us allow anthropology to contribute to our nation's endeavor to realize the socialist four modernizations.

# Part III

# What Is Archaeology?

# XIA NAI

# 4 | What Is Archaeology?

ANCIENT things are the subject of study of archaeology, but as a scientific discipline, archaeology is a very new field. Its origins, though, are very early because once a society has developed to a certain stage, and once the ideas and consciousness of its members have developed to a certain stage, they generate an interest in their own historical past and in the relics and traces left behind by their ancient ancestors. For all sorts of reasons they collect and investigate ancient objects and traces of ancient life, and some even go further to record their findings and explore their meaning, undertaking specific research on individual items. All this, however, merely foreshadows archaeology; it is not yet what scholastic circles today would call scientific, modern archaeology.

The concept of "archaeology" and its boundaries as a subject of study are not always the same over time, and they are also different, even in the same time period, in the minds and interpretations of different people. So, it is incumbent upon us to explain our own current understanding of the meaning of archaeology as a discipline.

The Chinese term for archaeology, *kaoguxue*, is translated from European languages, and the common etymological root of the term "archaeology" in these European languages is the word "archaiologia." This word in Greek comes from the combination of two terms, one meaning ancient times or things of ancient days, and the other meaning science. In ancient Greece, this noun generally referred to the study of ancient history; this was Plato's meaning when he used the term back in the fourth century B.C. After a long period of disuse, the term was revived in the seventeenth century to refer to the study of ancient things and ancient relics. At first (i.e., in the seventeenth and eighteenth centu-

"Shenme shi kaoguxue." *Kaogu* (Archaeology) 10 (1984): 931–35, 948.

ries) it referred primarily to objects of art, and it was not until the nineteenth century that the meaning of the term was broadened to refer to all ancient things and ancient relics.

In China, as far back as the Eastern Han dynasty (first to second century), there already appeared the term *guxue* (ancient studies). For example, the *Hou Han shu* (History of the Latter Han dynasty) claimed that Zheng Xing was strong in *guxue* and that he had a liking for *guxue*. The same book also said: "Ma Rong was a transmitter of ancient studies; Jia Kuei plied ancient studies; Huan Tan liked ancient studies." All these were broad references to the subject of learning that took ancient times as its subject of study. Then, in the middle of the Northern Song dynasty (the eleventh century), the study of inscriptions on bronzes and stone tablets, known as *jinshixue* or epigraphy, was born, and this was the forerunner of archaeology. In the beginning, this study was restricted to objects known as *ji jin* (sacrificial bronzes) and instruments of the past known as *yiqi*, as well as ancient stone engravings. Also at this time, however, there was already the linking together of the two words *kao* and *gu* [which together make up the term *kaoguxue* for archaeology in modern usage] in writing. For example, the Northern Song scholar Lu Dalin finished a book in 1092 entitled *Kaogutu* (An illustrated study of ancient things), in which he recorded and described bronze and jade objects of ancient times that were in private as well as governmental collections; here the author was using the term *kaogu* precisely to mean the study of ancient artifacts or objects. Somewhat later, in the Southern Song dynasty, Cheng Dachang titled his book *Kaogu bian* and Ye Daqing titled his *Kaogu zhi yi*. In these two books, however, although the term *kaogu* appears in both titles and in the texts, the contents of the books were primarily on the exegetical criticism and verification of [ancient] literary works and writings, and so here we must make allowance for a different usage of the term *kaogu*. By the later Qing dynasty, the boundaries of the study of *jinshixue* (epigraphy) had become vastly expanded. Some people, such as Luo Zhenyu, proposed that the name of the field should be changed to *guqiwuxue* (The study of antiquities). Quite naturally, this *guqiwuxue*, from the Qing to the period of Republican China, was much closer to the "archaeology" (*kaoguxue*) of modern and contemporary times. Therefore, some people have translated the Western term "archaeology" as *guwuxue*, or the study of antiquities (for example, in the *Bai ke ming hui* [Glossary of names of all disciplines], Commercial Press, 1931, p. 28). Although *guqiwuxue*, after being systematized, may yet become part of archaeology in China, we feel that it is not, in and of itself, the same as archaeology. Moreover, the term *kaoguxue* or archaeology has already become a general name for a field of scientific study, and so we should simply adopt it. Japan imported this field of study from Europe and in the beginning used both *kaoguxue* and *guwuxue* interchangeably. Since 1887, however (i.e., the twentieth year of the Meiji reign), Japanese have used the term *kaoguxue* (*kokogaku*) exclusively (see *Kokogaku minaru*, comp. Egami Namio, 1976, p. 2).

As for the definition of the field of archaeology, in the past there have indeed been many different and almost irreconcilable opinions and interpretations. At the moment, however, even though there may not be total unanimity, it can be said that there is a general understanding and interpretation among scholars. We can say that *kaoguxue*, or archaeology, is a science that seeks to understand the conditions of ancient human beings based on the study of the actual physical objects left behind by the activities of these ancient human beings.''

This definition calls for some explanation. Archaeology is a department of the science of history. Its object is the ancient past, which connotes a specific period of time in the past. Therefore, modern and contemporary history would not belong to the realm of archaeology. For example, for Britain, the lower chronological boundary for the study of archaeology is the Norman invasion (A.D. 1066); for France, it is the fall of the Carolingian Empire (A.D. 987); for the various countries in the American continents it is the discovery of the continents by Columbus (A.D. 1492). In China at present, the lower chronological boundary is the fall of the Ming dynasty (A.D. 1644). In recent years, a field of study has emerged in Britain known as "medieval archaeology," which has pushed the lower boundary to the revolution by the bourgeoisie, namely, A.D. 1640. Also there is "industrial archaeology," which studies the relics and traces of the beginning of modern industry. Some countries in the Americas have so-called historical archaeology or archaeology of the colonial period, which refers to the archaeological study of the history between 1492 and the times at which these countries variously achieved independence (which would mean the late eighteenth century and early nineteenth century). Naturally, with the passage of time, the lower boundaries of "ancient times" and "archaeology" would move downward also. The field of "industrial archaeology," however, which is actually a study of the relics and traces of industry in the early part of modern history, and the "historical archaeology" of modern America are all, in our opinion, merely fields that utilize the methods of archaeology to study a particular facet of modern history. It appears that they cannot be counted as departments of archaeology itself. On the other hand, some people believe that archaeology is exclusively focused on the study of relics and objects of the prehistoric era (e.g., this is the third definition provided for the term "archaeology" in the *Oxford English Dictionary*). This opinion is to discard the absolute age of a period as a criterion, and to adopt instead the [relative] age of a stage of cultural development. In that case, the archaeological study of the historical periods of those countries that have very ancient civilizations would be eliminated from the study of archaeology. That, we feel, is not right. At the moment, generally speaking, we have adopted a broader set of connotations for the term. We include, in the field of archaeology, three periods—prehistorical, early historical, and historical. Naturally, the older the history is, the rarer the written record and the more important the study of archaeology would be. When we get to the prehistoric period, where there are simply no written records, the study of prehistoric history would be almost entirely dependent on archaeology. Therefore, prehistoric history is tantamount to prehistoric archaeology.

The object of archaeology is things, or concrete objects. Some people have a tendency to make out their own ideas from the surface meaning of terms, and here they place undue emphasis on the word "*gu*" (ancient), and they think that archaeology is simply the investigation of things of ancient times, whether they be historical events, systems, or objects. In fact, the object of the study of archaeology is just the material remains, including both relics as objects and relics as traces. For this reason it is different from history in the narrow sense, which uses written documentary records. Although both archaeology and history in the narrow sense have the restoration of the shape of human history as it was as their goal, and both are the two major components of the science of history (i.e., history in the broad sense) and are like the two wheels of a cart or the two wings of a bird so that neither is dispensable, nevertheless, the two are independent, albeit closely related, departments of the science of history. Both take the study of the ancient history of humanity (in the broad sense) as their goals, but they employ different methods and use different materials. One studies the concrete objects that reflect the activities of ancient human beings, and the other studies the written records (documents) that record those human activities. Some people also consider the study of ancient history, which relies exclusively on documentary records, as archaeology. This does not conform with the interpretation commonly held of modern archaeology.

The concrete objects of the study of archaeology, that is, the material remains, should be the remains of the activities of ancient humans. Archaeology is a department of the science of history. In *The Holy Family*, Marx and Engels said: "History is nothing more than the activity of Man in the pursuit of his own goals." (See *The Complete Works of Karl Marx and Frederich Engels* [People's Press, 1957], 2:119.) Therefore, the ancient objects that archaeology studies are, in general, objects that had been processed or finished, in a deliberate or conscious way, by ancient humans. If they are objects of nature that have not been worked on by human hands, they still must at least be those objects that can be determined to have been related to human activity and reflect the activity of ancient humans. Thus rocks, minerals, and fossil animals or vegetation in geological strata from ages prior to the emergence of human beings cannot be placed within the boundaries of the study of archaeology even though they are much older than the human race. In fact, even material remains from the period since the appearance of the human race, if they are unrelated to human activity, would also be excluded from archaeological studies. Therefore, archaeology is a science of history belonging to the realm of the humanistic sciences, and not to the realm of the natural sciences. On the other hand, as long as it is a concrete object that reflects the activities of ancient human beings, such a thing would become the object of archaeology. This means that we are not confined to the instruments and tools of ancient times (or "ancient things," including tools, weapons, instruments and vessels of daily use, and decorations) but should also include the remnant traces of human abodes and other activities (for example, religious or artistic activities). These would include all buildings or relics of buildings such as temples, shrines, palaces, domiciles, workplaces, mines, fortresses, or city walls, and, in addition, natural objects that reflect the activities of ancient human beings (e.g., agricultural products, the remains of domesticated animals, products of fishing and hunting). Because the objects of archaeology are material remains, in the Soviet Union after the October Revolution the name "archaeology" was changed to "material culture history." Although this did serve to single out the special characteristic of the field of archaeology, and indeed the material used by archaeologists is undeniably [primarily] material remains and relics, when we remember that archaeology's objective is to reconstruct ancient human history, we must acknowledge that archaeology is inclusive of all aspects and is not confined to material culture alone. Archaeology is capable of bringing about, through the study of material relics, an understanding of the structure and evolution of ancient societies. This is so-called *shehui kaoguxue* (social archaeology), which encompasses the history of mental or spiritual cultures, including artistic views and religious beliefs. That is why, in 1957, after almost thirty years of using the name "Institute of the History of Material Culture," [the central institution of archaeological studies] in the Soviet Union went back to calling itself the "Institute of Archaeology." Another reason for this is that the name "archaeology" is the one commonly used throughout the world. However, we should still make the major object of our study the tools that were the means of human labor. Marx once said: "In order for us to understand the organic composition of animals that have perished, we must study the structure of the skeletal remains. The same significance holds for the study of objects that remain as evidence of the means of labor in order for us to be able to determine socioeconomic forms that also have perished" (*Das Kapital* [People's Press, 1957], 1:195–95).

Although ancient humans engaged in all types of activities, the chief aspect of such activities is that of being a member of a society. Humanity's specialty is that we are social animals. All objects humans have worked on (including tools) and all the cultures created by human beings invariably reflect the commonly held traditions of the society in which those human beings existed. Even the creations and inventions of an individual have, as their foundation, the cultural tradition that is cumulatively built up by the society in which he or she exists, and it is only by being accepted and disseminated by other members of the society that the creations or inventions of any individual can become a component of the cultural tradition of the society. The chief objects of the study of archaeology, therefore, are these concrete objects with a societal character. Archaeologists study the objects as types, and not singular, isolated objects. The latter refer to antiques, and these do not serve as scientific specimens for the study of archaeology. Even if [among these latter objects] we find ones that have outstanding artistic value, they would serve as good specimens for the study of the history of art, and they stand as evidence of the artistic talents of particular persons or individuals. On the other hand, what archaeology studies are the attributes and traditions of a society or an archaeological culture, not the creations of any individual person. This would be the distinction between the archaeology of art and the study of art history. In other words, the two differ in emphasis. It also appears that there should not be a question of evaluating [specific] historical figures in the study of archaeology. This is not only because the actual, concrete objects studied in archaeology, for the most part, could not be connected to specific historical figures; even more important is that the responsibilities are different for these two types of study—the goal of archaeology is to study the ancient conditions of the human race [as a whole]. In a horizontal [synchronic] sense, we [in archaeology] must study the conditions under which all types of human activities took place in any given period, and also the interrelationship among these activities. In a vertical sense, we study the [diachronic] processes of evolution and change in these various types of human activities over time. Finally, we seek to explain the laws that govern these historical processes.

As a field of historical science, archaeology should not be confined to the description and systematic classification of objects and relics of ancient times, or to the verification of their age and the determination of their usage. A historical science should explain the laws that govern historical processes. Of course, there are some bourgeois historical scientists, including archaeologists, who do not acknowledge that historical processes are governed by objective laws. Therefore, it is their belief that aside from historical facts themselves, there is only the study of the authenticity of historical material and the compiling of historical narratives. They do not believe that there is history, or historiography, which deals with explaining the laws governing historical processes. Then there are those who, while acknowledging that there are objective laws, nonetheless, equate them with the laws of natural science, and lump the two together. For example, the "New Archaeology" school in the United States in the 1960s had precisely this problem. They thought that the primary goal of archaeology was to search for the "law of cultural dynamics." They yapped on for more than twenty years. "New Archaeology" has become "old archaeology," but they still have not been able to produce a single new law that is generally recognized. Marxism recognizes not only that there are such laws for historical processes, but also that the [principle of] historical materialism of Marxism is the most fundamental of these laws. The difference between historical phenomena and natural phenomena is determined from the former's element of "Social Man." To a greater or lesser extent, the law of cause and effect, which governs the transformation processes of natural phenomena, is a mechanical one; the law that governs the processes of history, on the other hand, is a dialectical one. Engels once said: "It is Man that brings about effects in the realm of society and history. Man possesses awareness. Man acts after having given careful and deliberate thought to the action, or he may act out of the impulse of passion, and his actions carry with them anticipation of goals and results." Naturally, "[we acknowledge that] this [human role] cannot, in the slightest sense, alter the fact that historical processes must obey the dictates of general, intrinsic laws." Nonetheless, it remains a very important thing "for the study of history, especially for the study of a particular age or a particular development of events." (See F. Engels, *Feuerbach and the End of German Classical Philosophy* [People's Press, 1960], pp. 36–38.) We cannot write Chinese history (including China's archaeology) as a simple description of the history of social development. Instead we must explore the general laws of historical processes, and that means in doing so we must also explore the points of difference that lie between the historical processes of different countries and nations, and also the objective reasons [for these differences]. This, for instance, is true of the study of the many types of archaeological cultures in the field of prehistoric archaeology. Even though there are myriad forms of archaeological cultures, and even though they have undergone many changes, there are some common general laws that govern and explain the overall historical processes from their emergence to their peak of development and finally to their destruction and extinction, either in the form of merging with another culture or in the form of undergoing a qualitative change and becoming another culture altogether. At the same time, owing to differences in natural environmental conditions, sociohistorical backgrounds, and human activities, other laws come into play and generate the various attributes and processes of transformation peculiar to each of many different archaeological cultures. This type of differentiation makes research colorful and attractive and so intrigues the scholar. This is also true of the archaeology of the historical period of all countries—there are commonalities and also an individuality according to the national attributes that they possess. If we were to only discuss the general laws of social development and ignored the peculiarities of the developmental processes in each nation, we would be studying sociology, a social science, and not archaeology, a science of history.

In short, archaeology is an historical science. In terms of the goals of its study, what it studies, and the perspectives from which the study is undertaken, it is similar to the science of history in the strict sense—that which, basically, is founded on the study of documentation. The major difference between the two—and this is the special characteristic of archaeology—lies in two things. First, the historical material on which the study of archaeology is based comprises relics left behind from ancient times. It may be integrated with documentation, but for all intents and purposes, archaeology does not principally rely on documentary material. Second, the period that archaeology deals with is the age of antiquity, not the contemporary period. Although the meaning of the term "ancient times" or "antiquity" may differ from country to country and nationality to nationality, it is clear that the subject of archaeological study has to be at a considerable distance, in the sense of time, from the present age.

It is only when we have correctly comprehended the nature of the discipline of archaeology that we can begin to discuss what methods we ought to adopt in undertaking research in this discipline. As for the problems of methodology, then, I hope in the future to write another essay discussing them.

SU BINGQI

# 5 New Issues in Archaeological Typology

*A Lecture Outline for Archaeology Majors of the [Entering] Classes of 1977 and 1978 at Beijing University*

1. The establishment of the systematic structure of modern archaeology as an academic discipline with field archaeology as its foundation took place within a short few decades from the last half of the nineteenth century to the early twentieth century.

Geology and paleontology are its "brother" sciences. The history of the formation of the system of these two academic disciplines is, in each case, very similar to that of modern archaeology. This fact alone suffices to demonstrate the close relationship that exists among these disciplines.

a. Although the objects of study of the three disciplines are different, they all belong to the category of historical science in the broad sense of the term.

b. The major subjects and lessons to be studied in each of the three disciplines include the problems of periodization, characteristic identification, distribution, and regionalization, within their respective parameters.

c. The principal research methods such as stratigraphy and typology (also known as taxonomy) are [the same for] the three disciplines. Although different in concrete application, they are common and correspondent in principle and have a similar character in that they form the theoretical foundation for their respective systems.

d. The publication of Darwin's *Origin of Species* in 1859 propelled the theory of evolution to a new stage, and this became one of the three

"Kaogu leixingxue de xin keti." In *Su Bingqi kaoguxue lunshu xuanji* (Selected archaeological works of Su Bingqi) (Beijing: Cultural Relics Publishing House, 1984), pp. 235–38.

greatest discoveries in the natural sciences of the nineteenth century. The premise of its theoretical foundation is similar to the cited examples. Furthermore, the several major research projects that achieved tremendous results and were epochal in the history of archaeology in terms of the strict application of the methods of stratigraphy and typology in carrying out field archaeological studies took place in the period shortly after this momentous discovery.

e. From the above, we can see that modern archaeology is most closely related to paleontology in terms of theoretical foundations, and its development is intimately linked to the historical development of biology. This is by no means an accident; the roots for such intimacy can only be traced through the historical conditions of society.

2. The development of modern biological sciences has moved in two directions, the macroscopic and the microscopic. The former trend includes disciplines such as ecology; the latter, disciplines such as molecular biology. These trends also led to the genesis of many new fields. The interpenetration of various disciplines has led to massive transformations and developments in the theoretical base.

Modern archaeology has similar trends of development. One direction is the division of the globe into several major regions of study; another is the interpenetration with other disciplines to generate new disciplines or new branches of learning, such as archaeozoology, archaeobotany, hydroarchaeology, and seismoarchaeology. On the other hand, the field can be divided in terms of such subjects as environmental studies, technological studies, and artifacts preservation.

3. After the October Revolution, the Soviet Union established an Institute of Material Cultural History. Later the name "Institute of Archaeological Studies" was restored. At the time, Mong-gai-te [translit.], the author of the book *Archaeology in the U.S.S.R.*, reaffirmed and restated the significance of typology as the foundation of archaeology.

In China, we established the archaeology concentration at Beijing University in 1952. At the time, in terms of curricular design, in compiling syllabi and lecture outlines, we referred to and emulated the teaching plan for the archaeology concentration at Moscow University, and also some of their syllabi in key courses. Around 1958, China underwent a major pedagogical reform. When formulating pedagogical plans at that time, we proposed in the draft concerning the objectives of training that we would "establish a Marxist system of Chinese archaeology." At the time we had different perspectives on the status of typology in archaeology, and we expect different perspectives to remain over this issue today and in the future.

The immediate issue is that we should now have a more sober and clearer perception of the direction and path along which archaeology is to develop. Also, on this premise, we should reassess the role that typology plays in the development of field archaeology as well as the topics that will arise in its development today and hereafter. This is mandated by the development of the discipline itself and is our responsibility.

4. Our goal ought to be the establishment of a Chinese archaeology that has Marxism as its guiding ideology and is marked by a Chinese character. This should be the orientation of our efforts. It is the inevitable path that China's archaeology must take.

Archaeology is a historical science. Therefore, China's archaeology ought to possess the characteristics of China's history, namely, a vast territory (9.6 million square meters), a large population (close to 1 billion), a long and uninterrupted history, a highly developed culture, both colorful and diversified, and the fact that as far back as two thousand years ago, China had already joined into a solid, unified, multinationality nation.

To achieve this goal, China's archaeological studies must shoulder within the parameters of the discipline the following tasks:

a. The regionalization, systematic differentiation, and typologization of archaeological cultures.

b. Analysis and study of social relationships within specific parameters (i.e., communities).

c. Analysis and study of the mutual relationships among different communities that existed at the same time (and in particular those that were adjacent geographically and maintained close relations with each other) within certain specific, temporal parameters (i.e., within certain stages of social historical development), and of their development.

d. To restore, in a very basic sense, the true face of our country's history.

The accomplishment of these various tasks will be a great contribution to the achievement of the grand goal of "uniting together to rejuvenate and revive China."

5. The history of science as a whole proves that the development of the theoretical foundation of all disciplines follows the logical pattern of "practice—theory—practice again" (i.e., the principle of Marxist epis-

temology) in their forward progress. Archaeology is no exception. The enterprise of archaeological studies in our country took its first steps in the 1920s, precisely at a time when modern archaeology as a discipline had formed its own academic system. The theoretical foundation of archaeology in our country in its earliest stages of development (including archaeological stratigraphy and archaeological typology) developed precisely along this track.

The basic concept (one may even call it a law or principle) of archaeological typology can be summed up in the following:

a. The species, types, shapes, and forms of typical artifacts and objects.

b. The developmental sequence of typical artifacts and objects.

c. Cogenerative or parallel relationships among the developmental sequences and diverse types of artifacts and objects.

d. Combinative relationships among diverse types of typical artifacts and objects.

Since the founding of New China, the development of archaeological studies has been very rapid. The scale of field archaeological work is quite large, and the majority of the huge amount of data [excavated and collected] was obtained only in the last ten or twenty years. What has been published is only a very small portion. The phenomenon of adversely affecting the scientific soundness of the data owing to [a weakness in] the understanding of archaeological typology (lack of clarity in terms of basic concepts) and inadequacy of experience (misjudgments) is by no means uncommon. It is very important to strengthen this inadequacy in the area of teaching of archaeology and especially in the area of field practice.

Of even greater importance is the fact that with the achievements in recent years in which we have carried out more systematic, carefully planned research work, our vision of the prospects of the future development of China's archaeology has been greatly broadened. This has also proposed new topics and new clues for the theoretical foundation known as archaeological typology. This requires that we move beyond our original level. For example:

We should no longer remain at the level of discovering the partial and localized developmental sequences of typical artifacts and objects; rather, we should move beyond that to find out about the complete process of their generation and development (including both sources and developmental trends).

We should no longer remain at the level of analyzing the relationships among diverse artifacts and objects at any individual relic site, but must move beyond that to make synthetic comparative analyses of the relationships among the typical artifacts and objects of many relic sites of the same type.

Only in this way can we possibly come up with data in the studies that explore the regional-systematic typology of archaeological cultures that are, as in the natural sciences, qualitatively and quantitatively convincing (related to temporal as well as spatial parameters).

At the same time, on the basis of achieving the kinds of research results in the study of regional-systematic typologies of archaeological cultures just described, we must, under the guidance of the Marxist doctrine of social development history, carry out penetrating and synthetic studies of the mutual relationship and mutual influence between the developmental stages of society and the various cultural types.

We hope that this generation of archaeologists will make further efforts to deal with these new topics in archaeological typology, and that they will achieve breakthroughs in the establishment of the discipline of Chinese archaeology.

ZENG QI

# 6 Characteristics and Sequence of Development of Neolithic Cultures in China

CHINA contains abundant relics of cultures of the Neolithic Age. According to incomplete statistics, over 6,000 to 7,000 Neolithic sites have been discovered in China. In the last thirty years, contemporary archaeology based on field excavation has given a new complexion to Chinese archaeology. The large-scale excavation, exposure, ordering, and study of the many typical relic sites and grave sites of the Neolithic era in many regions have greatly deepened our understanding of the cultural attributes of this period. Since the 1970s, the adoption of the Carbon[14] dating in the field of archaeology has provided a precise scientific basis for dating Neolithic objects from preliterate times. This has helped each region to establish reliable criteria for dating.[1]

**Special Characteristics of Neolithic Cultures**

How are we to periodize the preliminary stage of human cultural development? One opinion holds that in general this stage may be divided into three periods:

1. The period of mountain forest culture, characterized mainly by a hunting and gathering economy based primarily on products of nature.

"Zhongguo xinshiqi shidai wenhua de tedian he fazhan xuelie," in *Minzu kaogu yanjiu lunwen ji* (A collection of research essays on ethnoarchaeology), ed. Zhongshan University, Department of Anthropology (Guangzhou, 1984), pp. 111–19. This essay was originally published in *Kaogu yu wenwu* (Archaeology and cultural relics), 1983, 1.

[1]Xia Nai, "Tan-14 ceding niandai he zhongguo shiqian kaoguxue" (Carbon14 dating and prehistoric archaeology in China), *Kaogu* (Archaeology), 1977, 4.

This would be a period of transition from total ignorance to barbarism, and it belonged to the category of the Paleolithic period.

2. The period of hillslope culture (also known as hillfront culture). This would be the period of transition from the Paleolithic to the Neolithic age; sometimes known as the Mesolithic age. It was a stage of transition from a high-level collecting economy to agriculture.

3. The period of river valley (river basin) culture. This would be the Neolithic period. It was the time when human beings invented agriculture and animal grazing and the breeding of domesticated animals. Humankind entered the stage of creating for themselves means of living so as to continue to exist.[2] We believe this periodization method gives an in-depth expression to the close and mutually dependent relationship between human beings and nature in primitive times.

Starting with the Holocene Age, the glacial era began to recede and the earth was thawing out. Our ancestors began to move out of the forest toward the plains and the wilderness. They moved toward the broad plains along the river basins to greet the springtime of a new era. In this period of great general renewal throughout the realm of nature, humanity gradually entered the Neolithic Age. This was true also in China. In the late Pleistocene period, there were many important Paleolithic cultures within our country's boundaries, including the Zhiyu, Shandingdong, Shuidonggou, and Xiachun cultures. In terms of physical shape and formation, we can tell from human fossils of this period that human beings of this era already possessed what were clearly the attributes of primitive Mongoloids. In the area of material culture, they also had quite a few creations and inventions. The art and craft of manufacturing stone implements were greatly enhanced, and their types and shapes already moved toward fine craftsmanship. New technology of the time included the usage and popularization of polishing and grinding, hole-drilling, and color by dyeing. Bows and arrows were invented, decorations used, and burial customs designed. All these implied the imminent arrival of a new era. Following the expansion of the hunting activity of primitive human beings, small, loosely structured social groups appeared. Evidently the primordial community of human beings already had difficulty in meeting the growing needs of the production forces. As a result, a new social

[2]Shi Xingbang, "Guanyu zhongguo xinshiqi shidai wenhua tixi de wenti" (On the question of the systematic relationships of Neolithic cultures in China), *Nanjing bowuyuan jikan* (Bulletin of Nanjing Museum), 1980, 2.

organization with blood lines as the chief modal connection emerged, namely, the matriarchal tribal commune.

Thus the Paleolithic age, at long last, came to an end, and the Neolithic age arose to take its place. This new age possessed many new characteristics: People left their caves and began to build domiciles, thus forming a relatively settled primitive community. In the north, the domicile that appeared earliest could have been some sort of movable, nest-like shed. About eight thousand years ago, in the Yellow River basin, cellar-type dwellings, semicellar-type dwellings, and then roundish or squarish edifices of earth and timber were put up above ground in succession. In the Yangzi River basin, people of the Hemudu and Majiabang cultures were able, accommodating to local conditions, to create shield and railing structures and full sets of mortise and tenon constructions to improve the dwelling conditions of people in the low, damp, swampy regions. In the Neolithic Age, when people formed into a village or a settled tribal commune, they generally followed a deliberate pattern of deployment. For example, the Banbo settlement in today's Xi'an was organized in an oval shape, facing the Chan River to the west. On the other three sides the village was surrounded by large, moat-like ditches. Roundish or squarish dwellings were scattered within the village, and there was both a public "cellar" and an open-air "stove." In the southwestern portion of the village there was a large house that was approximately 160 square meters in floor area. The other houses, of medium or smaller size, had their doors facing south toward the large house. The communal grave site and kiln were located outside of the ditches that surrounded the village, to the north and east respectively.[3]

Another example is the settlement at Beishouling in Baoji. The site of the settlement is located on the terraced land on the west bank of the Jinling River. At the center of the village there was a "square" approximately 100 meters in length from north to south. To the western side of the square there was a large house approximately 90 square meters in floor area. The other houses, of medium and small size, were deployed to the north, northeast, southwest, and south of the square, with their doors all facing it. The grave site was located to the south of the residential area, at a distance of about 30 meters.[4]

[3]*Xi'an banbo* (The Banbo culture at Xi'an), ed. Institute of Archaeology, Chinese Academy of Sciences (Wenwu Chubanshe, 1963).
[4]Su Bingqi, "Jiangzhai yizhi fajuede yiyi" (The significance of the excavation of the Jiangzhai site), *Kaogu yu wenwu* (Archaeology and cultural relics), 1981, 2.

At the relic site of Jiangzhai in Linzhong, the village deployment is very much like that at Beishouling with more improvements. [The excavators] cleaned up five groups of buildings and three public grave sites. Each group of buildings had one large house and more than a dozen medium and small houses. These various clusters of buildings, each from a different direction, faced the square at the center and thus formed a united, centripetal village, surrounded by small ditches. Beyond the ditches were the grave and kiln sites.[5]

The early houses were simple in form and crude in structure. But later houses became complex in structure. In addition to simpler houses, such formations appeared as several houses lined up in rows (e.g., at the F1-F4 sites at Dahe Village in Zhengzhou), several houses linked up in "suites" (e.g., at the F1 site at Paomaling in Xiushui County and the F11 site at Huangjianshu in Xichuan County), or double housing and with a cellar inside the house (e.g., at the F98 and F174 sites at Keshengzhuang in Changan). At other sites, such as Wangchenggang in Gaocheng or Dengfeng and Pingliangtai in Huaiyang, we even find fortresses and earthwork structures.[6] There were evidently also considerable improvements in building structure. For example, floors were treated with white chalk paving, ditches and troughs for water were dug, fillings of burned clay and sand or stone were used in cracks at the base of walls to firm up the foundation, stone bases were used under the posts, and house foundations were built on a raised platform with shielding slopes.

The production of tools evidently broke through the ancient chipped stone tool tradition with the use of a new technology of carving and polishing. With the appearance of polished stone tools as a foundation, people could strive toward even greater reform of tool manufacturing methods. Tool specialization became more evident; there were tools for agriculture, for handicraft industries, for animal husbandry and herding, for hunting and fish-catching, and so forth. The types of raw materials used for manufacturing tools also became more extensive. In addition to stone implements, we also found evidence of such things as wood, bone, horn, clam shells, and pottery as tool-making material. There was also extensive usage of such technologies as polishing, sawing, drilling,

---

[5]Gong Qiming and Yan Wenming, "Cong Jiangzhai zaoqican buju tantao qi jumin de shehui zuzhi jiegou" (A study of the organization and structure of the society of residents of the early period of Jiangzhai from looking at the deployment of the village), *Kaogu yu wenwu*, 1981, 1.

[6]Yan Wenming, "Longshan wenhua he Longshan shidai" (The Longshan Culture and the Longshan Era), *Wenwu* (Cultural relics), 1981, 6.

knocking, carving, compressing, and stripping. Large-scale stone implement manufacturing "plants" such as those at Emaokou in Huairen and Xiqiaoshan in Nanhai appeared. This progress in the development of productive forces finally led to the creation of a metal-using civilization in the late Neolithic. We have found bronze artifacts, for instance, in the Majiayao, Longshan, and Qijia cultures.[7]

The development of agriculture and domesticated-animal breeding were salient benchmarks of the "Neolithic Revolution" in China. For example, dry farming and millet tilling in the Yellow River basin was a slash-and-burn type of agriculture that can be traced as far back as eight thousand years to the Cishan and Peiligang cultures. At that time, crops included millet (e.g., at Banbo and at Jiangzhai), sorghum (e.g., at Dahe village), and vegetables (as at Banbo). The Hemudu culture in the Yangzi River basin as far back as seven thousand years ago was already proficient in rice crop agriculture, and the major crops there included long-grain and round-grain rice. With the switchover from growing long-grain to round-grain rice, there was a gradual expansion of the area accessible to rice-growing production. In addition to Hemudu, there are traces of rice crops at many other sites, including Luojiajiao, Shuitianban, Caoxieshan, Songze, Qianshanyang, Honghuatao, Dadunzi, Baiyangcun, Qujialing, and also southern China's Maba. Of these sites the majority are located in southern provinces.

Animal husbandry appeared in the Cishan and Peiligang cultures in the Yellow River basin as early as eight thousand years ago. When we come to the Banbo type of the Yangshao culture, we find not only the presence of pigs and dogs among the animals domesticated, but also evidence of pigpens and fences. At a later date, and gradually, domestication of all six types of tamed animals became complete. In the Yangzi River basin, there was already the domestication and breeding of pigs, dogs, and water buffaloes in the period of the Hemudu culture. By the late Neolithic Age there was a prosperous and ascendant enterprise of breeding pigs in both the Yellow River and Yangzi River basins. According to one suggestion, the ratio between the length of the head of a wild pig and the length of its body is 7:3. The same ratio for a modern-era domesticated pig is 3:7. In the excavation of the Hemudu culture, we found small pottery models of pigs. The ratio between the fore portion

[7]History of Metallurgy Study Group, Iron and Steel Industry Institute of Beijing, "Zhongguo zaoqi tongqi de chubu yanjiu" (A preliminary study of the early bronzes of China), *Kaogu xuebao* (Archaeology bulletin), 1981, 3.

of the body and the hind portion is 1:1, which means that it is in between the wild pig and the modern domesticated pig. In terms of its overall shape, it is very different from that of a wild pig; therefore we classify this as a primitive domesticated pig.[8] When we come to the Dawenkou, Qijia, Qingliangang, and Qujialing cultures, we find, in the burial sites and graves of the richer people of the era, a common practice of having either the head or lower jaw portion of a pig, or in some cases even the whole pig, being buried along with the corpse of the deceased person. This indicates that domesticated animals already had become a "liquid asset" when reckoning private property.

People of the time also created many types of pottery and ceramic vessels, woven fabrics or knit material, and all sorts of decorative items. They also created, on top of their material culture, an art of painting that is rich with vitality and color. This particular art is epitomized in the colored, painted patterns on pottery items in the Yangshao and Majiayao cultures in the Yellow River basin and in the Dawenkou culture on the seacoast to the east. The colored pottery weaving wheel of the Qujialing culture in the Yangzi River basin is also very distinctive. As the colored pottery craft and art disappeared [from these cultures] we begin to find, taking its place, the eggshell black pottery of the Longshan culture along the eastern seacoast. The thickness of the wall [of the shell] in these items is [no more than] 0.5–1 mm. This represents the zenith of the art of pottery manufacture by China's primitive societies.

Decorative items originate from the late Paleolithic Age and seem to have been related to people's hunting activities. Most were made of such things as animal teeth, bone shafts, bone beads, and clam shells. In the Neolithic Age, we find among the primitive cultures of the Yangzi River basin earlier appearances of decorative items made of jade, stone and agate, in the shapes of hollow cylinder, beads, semiannular pendants, rings, and penannular rings. Subsequently, such decorative pieces as hollow rectangular jade, round, flat jade, and jade tablets also appeared. The latter became luxury items possessed by rich folks among the tribal people and gradually developed into ceremonial instruments of the Shang and Zhou dynasties. The public grave sites for clans and tribes in the Neolithic Age included many different forms and customs of burial,

[8]Zhong Xia, "Cong Hemudu yizhi chutu zhu gu he tao zhu shi lun wuo guo yangzhu de qiyuan" (A tentative proposition regarding the origins of pig breeding in China: Based on the pig bones and ceramic pig figurines excavated at the site of Hemudu), *Wenwu*, 1977, 8.

indicating the differences in blood relationships among people at different times. In the earlier stage, for instance, we find such things as the same burial site being used twice, the burial of a single person, the burial of people of the same sex together, and so forth. These practices revealed an equality of social status among members of the tribe. At a later stage, we find such burial practices as the burying of adults of different sexes together, the coexistence of large, medium-sized, and small graves at the same burial site, etc., indicating the differentiations of people's status and wealth in terms of the scale of the burial and the compositions of items buried along with the deceased. The private ownership of "liquid" property and the practice of burying such property together with the deceased provides increasing evidence of dramatic and intense changes in society.

The late Neolithic saw the appearance of such things as oracle bones and indications of the worship of male ancestors manifested in stone and pottery figures. These are indicators of the emergence of a patriarchal tribal organization of society.

As hunting and gathering was a key mode of production of the Paleolithic Age, the hunter was the master of this era. With the dawning of agriculture, the farmer raised the curtain of the Neolithic age. In a short period of just four to five thousand years, the farmers created a material culture that could in no way be matched by that produced by their ancestors, the hunters, in the long stretch of the Paleolithic Age. In a very short time, the people of the Neolithic went through two stages of development—matriarchal tribal society and patriarchal tribal society. With the development of the forces of production and the emergence of private ownership, primitive society inevitably disintegrated. This is a period that played an important transitional role in the history of social development.

The Yellow River basin possesses remains of an abundant and colorful material culture of a very remote ancient past, and quite naturally it is taken to be the cradle of the most ancient civilizations in China. To focus exclusively on this individual region, however, would not be in conformity with the reality discovered through archaeological excavations. The archaeological discoveries and studies done on locations in the middle and lower stretches of the Yangzi River as well as along the eastern seacoast over the last thirty years have indicated that the Yangzi, with its long history, was equally a nurturer of ancient civilizations. From today's perspective, we can say that the genesis of China's civilization came not from one source, but from many sources. It is precisely the many primitive tribes that were scattered throughout the different regions of the fatherland that, through their close contacts with one another, and through their mutual influence and blending, created a radiant, splendid civilization of the ancient past.

The Yangshao culture is a branch of the culture of the Neolithic period that had a large area of distribution in the Yellow River basin and continued over a fairly long period of time. In general, we have found that the cultures physically adjacent to the Yangshao culture (the early Dawenkou culture, for instance) already demonstrated some elements similar to Yangshao. This type of mutual influence continued in a sustained way for over nine thousand years. Then, by the time of the Longshan culture, which existed four to five thousand years ago, those elements that were common to the primitive societies in all these regions gradually began to come to the forefront and occupy a dominant position. Among the pottery or ceramic utensils for everyday use there emerged combinations of the types known as *ding* [a cooking vessel with two loop handles and three or four legs], *dou* [a tall-legged dish or tray usually used for displaying food], and *hu* [a pot with handles for liquid food]. Tripod utensils that were commonly used at the time, such as . . . *jia* [a round wine container], *li* [a cooking vessel with hollow legs], and *yan* [a double-boiler] type of cooking vessel often made up vessels and utensils that were characteristic of the various cultures of this period, and these later evolved to become the primary combination of utensils among the ceremonial vessels of the Shang and Zhou dynasties, namely, the bronze *ding*, the bronze *dou*, and the bronze *hu*.

Paleoanthropologists, based on published data concerning human bones of the Neolithic period in China, have made comparisons of the length and width of the skulls, the features of the upper face, the nose and eye sockets, and the protuberance and general angularity of the face, and have studied their distributions. In general, the residents of China in the Neolithic age were of the rounded-skull type and the high-forehead skull type. The features of the morphology of the upper face were primarily of the medium face type. In terms of the degree of facial protuberance, most of the residents belonged to the regular jaw type and the medium jaw type. In terms of the shape of eye sockets, they mostly belonged to the middle type. Noses belonged to the medium- and broad-nose types. In terms of regional distribution, the physical attributes of residents of our country in the Neolithic age can generally be differentiated into three regional groupings: those in the middle and lower stretches of the Yellow River basin had round and high skulls, with relatively narrow and long upper faces; their eye socket-placement was relatively high and the positioning of their faces was relatively vertical. They also had noses of medium width. Those in southern China had a longer and lower skull. Their upper faces tended to be lower and shorter. We find more incidences of a protruded jaw type among them; their noses are broader; their eye sockets are placed lower; they had more developed brows and also a more developed nose-bridge. Then there are the people in the Han River basin, whose skull and facial features consist of many elements that seemed to lie between the two above types.

This type of regional differentiation can be traced back to the human fossils of the late Paleolithic. For example, Liujiang Man already had a face or skull that, in terms of the upper-face indices, clearly belonged to the broad upper-face type, a general facial index that put it in the category of the protruded-jaw type, and a vertical-face index that came close to the type of the residents of South China in the Neolithic age. Also, the index of its skull length versus breadth, and its index of skull length versus height, came close to the long-skull type and low-skull type respectively. On the other hand, Shandingdong Man had a face that clearly had an upper-face index that put it in the category of a medium upper-face type, and a vertical-skull versus face index that distinguished it clearly from people of South China in the Neolithic age, and instead drew it closer to people of the middle and lower stretches of the Yellow River region.[9]

## Sequence of Development of Neolithic Cultures

In this section the cultures of the Neolithic Age are divided into six regions, according to the results of archaeological excavations and research on these various areas, in order to explore the sequence of development of the various Neolithic cultures in China.

A. The steppeland in the Northeast, Inner Mongolia, Ningxia, and Xinjiang: Neolithic cultures in these places were characterized by microlithic tools and woven-pattern pottery. In the past this has been general-

[9]Zhang Zhenbiao, "Wuo guo xinshiqi shidai jumin tixing tezheng fenbu quxiang" (Trends in the distribution of resident peoples of the Neolithic age in China according to their physical attributes), *Gu jizhui dongwu yu gu renlei* (Vertebrata Pal Asiatica), 1981, 1.

ized as the "microlithic culture." Here I would like to differentiate the various microlithic-related cultures located in the Northeast and Inner Mongolia into three types:

1. The Ang'angxi type (based in Qiqihar in Heilongjiang Province): This culture is characterized by a fishing-hunting economy.[10]

2. The Guochengzishan type (based at Chifeng and Linxi): A typical site of this culture that has been excavated is that at the mouth to the main channel of the Fu River in the Zhaowuda League region; the main economic type of this culture is agriculture.[11]

3. The Zhuanlongzang type (based at Baotou in Inner Mongolia): Here the culture includes agriculture with animal husbandry and herding as a sideline.[12]

These three types are somewhat different from the microlithic cultures to the west in Ningxia and Xinjiang, which are represented by the sites at Gaorenzhen and Asitana. In terms of periodization these three may be separated into an earlier-later sequence, but they may also overlap and crisscross in terms of the upper and lower time-reaches of each.

$C^{14}$ dating has yielded the following:

1. The lower sedimentary level of the Xinle site at Shenyang: 6145 B.P. ± 120, recalibrated by dendrochronology to 6800 B.P.

2. The Xiakailiu site at Mishan, grave site at upper sedimentary level: 5430 B.P. ± 90, recalibrated by tree-ring dating to 6080 B.P.

3. The F30 site at the mouth of the main ditch of the Fu River at Zhaowuda League: 4735 B.P. ± 1,100, recalibrated to 5300 B.P. dendrochronologically.

These three periods can include representative dates of both the early Neolithic and the mid-Neolithic. As for the lower reaches of these periods, they may extend for a very long time and reach a very late part of the late Neolithic.

The region west of the Liao River lies to the north of the Great Wall. It was the key passage to the Northeast from the region of the central

[10]*Liang Siyong kaogu lunwenji* (Collected essays in archaeology by Liang Siyong) (Kexue Chubanshe, 1959), pp. 58-59.

[11]Inner Mongolia Work Team, Institute of Archaeology, Chinese Academy of Sciences, "Nei Menggu balinzuo qi fuhe goumen yizhi fajue jianbao" (Brief report on the excavation at the site of the gate to the main channel of the Fu River in Balinzuo Banner, Inner Mongolia), *Kaogu*, 1964, 1.

[12]Inner Mongolia Work Team on Relics, "Nei Menggu zizhiqu faxian de xishiqi wenhua yizhi" (Microlithic culture site discovered in the Inner Mongolia Autonomous Region), *Kaogu xuebao*, 1957, 1.

plain. The sequence of the development of Neolithic cultures in this region is Hongshan culture → Xiaoheyan culture → Xiajiadian (lower levels) culture.

All these cultures included developed agriculture, and they also had close relationships with the primitive cultures of the Yellow River region. However, these agricultural cultures all contained a certain quantity of microlithic material.

Recently, Tong Zhuchen published an essay discussing the various northern and northeastern cultures that contained microlithic tools.[13] He differentiated these cultures into nine types, belonging to three economic modes: primarily agricultural, primarily fishing-hunting, and primarily pastoral. Tong pointed out that the term "microlithic" in fact connotes a certain type of tool that coexisted with chipped stone tools and with polished stone tools, and which was possessed in common by many nationalities over a very long period of time, from the late Paleolithic to the Iron Age. Its economic forms were also very broad and diverse.

B. The middle and upper reaches of the Yellow River region: Neolithic cultures in this region include the Cishan-Peiligang, Yangshao, Majiayao, Qijia, Miaodigou (secondary stage), and Longshan cultures, among others. In other spots we have also discovered the Qujialing culture (such as at Gushui River of Yu County) and the Dawenkou culture (such as at Dahe Village at Zhengzhou); however, these are not the primary elements of the cultures of this region and may only be elements of mutual influence and interchange with other cultures.

The Cishan-Peiligang culture was discovered on the great plain of northern China. Dated 8000 B.P., it had relatively simple pottery heated at low temperatures, but the culture's stone tool types were advanced, reflecting both agriculture and animal husbandry. From the complexion of this culture, and from its relative position in the chronology, it ought to be considered a precursor of the Yangshao culture.[14] Somewhat similar and close to it we find the "Laoguantai culture," which is within the borders of Shaanxi Province, and the culture at the lower sedimentary

---

[13]Tong Zhuchen, "Shilun Zhongguo beifang he dongbei diqu hanyou xishiqi de zhu wenhua wenti" (A tentative discussion of the question of the various cultures containing microlithic stone tools in northern and northeastern China), *Kaogu xuebao*, 1979, 4.

[14]The discovery of the Cishan-Peiligang Culture was a major breakthrough in the archaeological studies of the Neolithic age in China in the 1970s. The characteristics of this cultural type are in many instances similar to those of the Yangshao culture, and yet its dates are earlier. We may call it an early Yangshao culture.

level of Dadiwan in eastern Gansu Province.

The Yangshao culture was mainly distributed in the territories of Shanxi, Shaanxi, and Henan provinces, but reaching into the provinces of Gansu, Qinghai, Ningxia, Inner Mongolia, and Hubei. It consists of a relatively larger number of types and variations. Relatively many $C^{14}$ dates have been done for this culture yielding recalibrated dates ranging from 7100 to 5000 B.P., which means the Yangshao lasted over two thousand years, with the major types being the Banbo, Miaodigou, and Qinwangzhai. If we take Tongguan as a point of delineation, we can see this culture divided into two with parallel lines of development, one northeastern and one northwestern. However, there are also some intersections and crossovers between the various types.

The sequence of development of the Yangshao-type cultures in the northeast is as follows:

Shuangmiaogou (lower levels of Xiawanggang) culture → Xiawanggang (middle levels), Hougang type → Miaodigou + Dasikongcun types → Wangwan (period II) → Dahe Village (levels 3 and 4) → Qinwangzhai type.

The sequence of development of the Yangshao-type cultures in the northwest, on the other hand, goes this way:

Beishouling (lower levels) → Banbo type (early) → Miaodigou type → Xiwang Village type (late Banbo).[15]

From the above description, we can see that the Miaodigou type represents the peak of Yangshao culture, and that it had a very broad sphere of distribution and influence, reaching as far as the eastern sector of Gansu Province.

Another view holds that while we can distinguish four types in the region of the loess plateau, we can separate cultures of the Yangshao type on the southeastern fringe of the loess highland into two types, namely, the Miaodigou and Dahe Village (periods 3 and 4) types. The cultures on the North China plain bordering the slope of the Taihang Mountain range can be differentiated as the Hougang and Dasikong types. In all areas, however, there are still a number of missing links in each of the aforementioned schemes of differentiation.[16]

A third view believes that the Yangshao cultures are primarily distrib-

[15]Yan Wenming, "Lun Banbo leixing he Miaodigou leixing" (On the Banbo type and the Miaodigou type), *Kaogu yu wenwu*, 1980, 1.

[16]An Zhimin, "Zhongguo de xinshiqi shidai" (China's Neolithic age), *Kaogu*, 1981, 3.

uted in the region of the central Shaanxi plain, western Henan, and southern Shanxi, and that the so-called Hougang type, Dasikong type, and Qinwangzhai type should not be considered as parts of the Yangshao culture system.[17]

The Longshan culture is in the region of China's central plain. It consists of an early stage represented by the period II culture at Miaodigou and a late stage represented by the Longshan culture. On the basis of different characteristics in different regions, the Longshan culture can also be divided into the Keshengzhuang type, the Hougang type, the Sanliqiao type, the Taosi type, and so forth. According to $C^{14}$ dating, the chronological data for the Longshan culture includes a range from 4700–3815 B.P., with a continuity span of about one thousand years. Thus Yangshao culture was superseded by the Longshan culture sometime around 4,900 years ago.

Neolithic Age cultures that were discovered somewhat earlier than others in the Gansu and Qinghai region (the latter including Ningxia) were the Banbo and Miaodigou types of the Yangshao culture. These were primarily distributed along the basin of the Wei River and in the area known as Longdong. About 5500 B.P., the culture in this region evolved from the above-mentioned types to the Shilingxia type (at Wushan). Its cultural content included attributes from the Miaodigou type and the Majiayao type, and it was suppressed beneath the stratum that represented the Majiayao type. Thus from that it evolved to form the Majiayao culture.[18]

To put it graphically, therefore, the sequence of evolution and development of this culture is as follows:

Banbo type →
↓          ↘ Shilingxia type → Majiayao culture
Miaodigou type

The Majiayao culture can, for the time being, be tentatively divided into the Majiayao, Banshan, and Machang types. $C^{14}$ data date it in a period from 5,100 years ago to 4,500–4,300 years ago. The Machang type

[17]Zhang Zhiheng, "Shilun Cishan-Peiligang wenhua yicun de xingzhi" (A tentative discussion of the nature of the cultural relics of Cishan-Peiligang), *Kaogu yu wenwu*, 1981, 1.

[18]Xie Ruiju, "Lun Shilingxia leixing de wenhua xingzhi" (On the cultural character of the Shilingxia type), *Wenwu*, 1981, 4.

continued to exist for a longer period in Qinghai Province. In some places the Machang type was basically coterminous with the Qijia culture.

The latest of the Neolithic cultures in the upper stretches of the Yellow River basin is the Qijia culture. It contained elements of the Majiayao culture but also received influences from the Longshan culture of the Wei River basin to the East. According to $C^{14}$ dating, the Qijia culture existed in a period from approximately 4200 to 3800 B.P. or even a bit later. Its lower reaches already enter the range of the Erlitou culture (possibly a culture of the Xia dynasty).

Because the Yangshao culture displayed a close relationship with the Majiayao culture, some people hold that the Majiayao culture should be absorbed into the system of the Yangshao culture. Such an opinion, however, would disturb the sense of coordination between the eastern and western parts of the development of the Yangshao culture. Moreover, we do not think that there is a stage-like character to the ending of any culture. We find it hard to envision a situation in which a culture is practically ended in its central region and replaced by another culture while at the same time the original culture is preserved in its western region. Furthermore, we find that the ceramic utensils of the Majiayao culture—its *ping* (bottles), *hu* (cooking pots), and *weng* (double-eared jars)—and the style of its painted pottery are different from those of the Yangshao culture.

C. The lower stretches of the Yellow River and Yangzi River basins and the eastern coastal region: The primitive cultures in this region include the Hemudu, Majiabang, Liangzhu, Dawenkou, and Qingliangang cultures as well as the Longshan culture of Shandong Province, among others. With the Yangzi River as the line of demarcation, we now tentatively and for the time being separate these into two series.

In the region south of the Yangzi River, we have first the Hemudu culture, whose upper range may go back as far as 7000 B.P., and whose continuity span was approximately a thousand years. Following in its wake were the Majiabang culture, the Songze culture, the Beiyingyangying culture, and finally the Liangzhu culture. The lower range of these cultures was approximately 4300 B.P. The Hemudu and Majiabang cultures were two branches that at one time coexisted.[19] The Hemudu

[19] Archaeological Team for Luojiajiao, "Tongxiang xian Luojiajiao yizhi fajue baogao" (Report on the excavation at Luojiajiao, Tongxiang County), *Zhejiang sheng wenwu kaogu suo xuekan* (Bulletin of the Institute of Cultural Relics and Archaeology of Zhejiang Province), 1981.

culture already possessed advanced agriculture. As to what its forerunner might have been, we have very good clues in the pottery shards discovered in recent years in the site of Shenxiandong (Immortals' Cave) at Sushui County in southern Jiangsu.[20]

In the region north of the Yangzi River, there is the Qingliangang culture represented by the lower strata finds at the site of Dadun in Pi County which can be dated as early as 6300 B.P. (There are also people who advocate that the strata of Dadunzi belongs to the early phase of the Dawenkou culture.) In recent years the Beixin site was discovered in Teng County of southern Shandong Province. Its cultural contents resembled those of the Cishan-Peiligang culture, and the four pieces of data that have been subjected to $C^{14}$ dating reveal relatively early times. Among them, the ZK-632 specimen is 6725± 200 (without dendrochronological adjustment just yet). This makes it no later than the Hemudu culture south of the Yangzi.

The next culture to develop, after the Qingliangang culture, was the Dawenkou culture. It lasted for nearly two thousand years. The date of its early cultural phase may be as far back as 6400 B.P. (The ZK-468 specimen found at Dawenkou, Tai'an County, is dated 5555 B.P.± 95). The later-phase culture is represented by the sites at Sanlihe in Jiao County and at Dafanzhuang in Linxin County. The stratigraphic evidence for the transition from Dawenkou culture to typical Longshan culture is represented by the middle stratum of the site at Donghaigu in Rizhao County.[21]

According to the analysis of numerical data at Sanlihe, the lower chronological range of the typical Longshan culture may put it at a time of coexistence with the Erlitou culture in the central plain; as for its upper range, it is about 4500 B.P.

D. The middle stretches of the Yangzi River basin: Here the primitive cultures include the Qujialing, Daxi, Honghuatao, and Longshan cultures, among others. In the plain between the Yangzi and Han rivers and in the southern part of Henan Province, the sedimentary strata that represent cultures even earlier than the Qujialing culture belong to the Yangshao culture. The sequence of development here is as follows:

Yangshao culture → Qujialing culture → Longshan culture.

In the region of Sichuan Gorge and in western Hubei Province, the

[20]Wenwu Editorial Board, *Wenwu kaogu gongzuo sanshinian* (Thirty years of archaeological and cultural relic studies) (Wenwu Chubanshe, 1979), p. 198.

[21]Museum of Shandong Province, "1975 donghaigu yizhi de fajue" (The 1975 excavation at the Donghaigu site), *Kaogu*, 1977, 6.

excavations of Honghuatao (at Yidu) and of Guanmiaoshan (at Zhijiang) revealed the Honghuatao (period I) culture. The sequence of development here is as follows:

Honghuatao (stage I) culture (early Daxi) → Daxi culture → Qujialing culture → Longshan culture.

We can see from this that at an earlier time, the primitive cultures in the plain between the Yangzi and Han rivers and those in the region of the Sichuan Gorge were somewhat different, but from the time of the Qujialing culture onward, they had become basically unified. By approximately four thousand years ago, the entire middle stretch of the Yangzi River was blended into the Longshan culture.

E. The South China region: The cultures in this region that can be named include the Xianrendong (Immortals' Cave) culture (at Wannian), the Tanshishan culture (at Minhou), the Dapankang culture (at Taibei), the Shixian culture (at Qujiang), the Xiqiaoshan culture (at Nanhai), and the Shanbei culture (at Xiushui). For the time being, they are tentatively classified into three types, namely, the cave cultures, knoll cultures, and terrace (or hillslope) cultures. Although each of these three types of remains has its own internal sequence of development, in an overall sense, the sequence of cave knoll terrace basically reflects a chronological order in itself; this sequence is in general accord with the sequence of economic development represented by hunting → fishing/hunting → agriculture.

The upper range of the Neolithic Age in the South China region is represented by the clusters of caves at Xianrendong and Qingtang, dated to approximately 8000 B.P.[22] Also, the microlithic material discovered not long ago at Xiqiaoshan in Nanhai [Guandong Province] may be of an even earlier age.[23] The lower range, on the other hand, is represented by the cultures discovered at Shixia, Jinlansi (in Zengcheng), and Zhuweicheng (in Qingjiang). These are dated at about 4300–4000 B.P. This is consistent with the lower range of the Longshan culture in the Yellow River basin and that of the Liangzhu culture in the Yangzi River basin. As the Neolithic Age came to an end in this region, a phenomenon

[22] Association of Cultural Relics Management of Jiangxi Province, "Jiangxi wannian dayuan xianrendong dongxue yizhi shijue" (A test excavation of the cave site at Xianrendong of Dayuan in Wannian County, Jiangxi Province), *Kaogu xuebao*, 1963, 1. Also Museum of Guangdong Province, "Guangdong Wengyuan xian qingtang xinshiqi shidai yizhi" (A Neolithic site at Qingtang, Wengyuan County, Guangdong Province), *Kaogu*, 1961, 11.

[23] Zeng Qi, "Xiqiaoshan dong lu de xishiqi" (The microlithic stone tools on the eastern slope of Xiqiaoshan), *Kaogu yu wenwu*, 1981, 4.

known as the "*Bai Yue wenhua*" (culture of the hundred Yues) arose wherein "the hundred Yue peoples mingled and lived together in a common territory, but each had its own lineage and family name." In archaeological discoveries, the cultural attributes found for this phase of development include the use of geometric forms and patterns for impression on pottery, double-shoulder stone tools and stone tools with sections, and the cultivation of paddy rice.

F. The Southwest region: Not many typical sites have been excavated in this region. [Of those that have been excavated], the Daxi culture at Dongchuan belongs to a relatively early age. But it is a culture that forms a system with the Neolithic cultures in Hunan and Hubei provinces in the middle stretches of the Yangzi River, and by and large it is not widely distributed in this region. According to what we now know, the earliest Neolithic culture in this region is that represented by the Ka-ruo site at Changdu in Tibet. $C^{14}$ dates this culture to 4230 B.P. ± 80 years (recalibrated tree-ring dating to 4690 B.P. ± 153).[24] Resembling this culture are the stone tool remains discovered in the general area of Linzhi and Motuo. The Baiyang Village site in Binchuan in western Yunnan Province is $C^{14}$ dated at 3770 B.P. ± 85 (dendrochronologically recalibrated to 4115 B.P. ± 105).[25] At several spots such as at Manghuai in Yun County in the middle stretches of Lancangjian River in Yunnan Province, a primitive culture has been discovered that has as one of its chief characteristics the making of shouldered stone axes from stone pebbles in the river by the clipped stone method. The number of pottery shards excavated at these sites is extremely small, and the age of this culture may be slightly earlier than that of the Baiyang Village site.[26] The Dadunzi site of Yuanmou is $C^{14}$ dated at 3210 B.P. ± 90 (recalibrated to B.P. 3420 ± 115).[27] Cultural relics that resemble it include the excavated site of the Lizhou Middle School in Xichang.[28] Then, in the region of Tianchi in

[24]Association of Relics Management of Tibet, "Xizang changdu karuo yizhi shijue jianbao" (A brief report of the test excavation at the site of Karuo in Changdu, Tibet), *Wenwu*, 1979, 9.
[25]Museum of Yunnan Province, "Yunnan binchuan baiyang cun yizhi" (The site of Baiyang Village in Binchuan, Yunnan Province), *Kaogu xuebao*, 1981, 3.
[26]Cultural Relics Work Team, Museum of Yunnan Province, "Yunnan Yun xian wanghuai xinshiqi shidai yizhi tiaocha" (A survey of Neolithic sites in Wanghuai, Yun County, Yunnan Province), *Kaogu*, 1977, 3.
[27]Museum of Yunnan Province, "The Yuanmou Neolithic Site of Dadunzi," *Kaogu xuebao*.
[28]Lizhou Joint Excavation Team, "Sichuan Xichang lizhou xinshiqi shidai yizhi" (Neolithic site at Lizhou, Xichang, Sichuan), *Kaogu xuebao*, 1980, 4.

Yunnan Province, a number of sites of the knoll-culture type are widely distributed. These carry the distinctive characteristic of containing dish-shape utensils of red pottery. They produce stamped ornamentation pottery on shouldered stone axes, and pottery with sand pebbles in it; their age is generally later than that of Dadunzi.[29] The site at Haimenkou in Jianchuan is $C^{14}$ dated at 3115 B.P. ± 90 (it has not been subjected to recalibration). It is characterized by the cultivation of paddy rice, by the presence of fence structures in architecture, and by the appearance of copper utensils. This last indicates that it represents a time that has already entered the phase in which stone and copper were used together[30] and therefore may be taken to be the lower range of the Neolithic cultures of this region. From the above we may get a rough outline of the Neolithic Age from about 5,000 to 3,400 years B.P. in the southwestern region of China. However, we may assume that since the Neolithic cultures and their remains are distributed over such an expansive region, distinct regional or local differences and different cultural characters are bound to exist, and that at the same time they are most likely to contain many elements of influence that came from primitive cultures in the heartland of the Northeast and the coastal region of the Southeast; they thus reflect the historical lineage of the region and its characteristic of being a place where many different ethnic groups had gathered and settled. Therefore, the developmental sequence of the primitive cultures of the Southwest cannot be a monistic one.[31] We have to say that the sequence of the development of the Neolithic cultures in this region is as yet not completely clear. We must wait for more sites to be excavated, compared, and studied before we can compile a credible sequence.

[29]Cultural Relics Work Team of Yunnan Province, "Yunnan tianchi zhouwei xinshiqi shidai yizhi diaocha jianbao" (Brief report on the survey of Neolithic sites in the environs of Tianchi, Yunnan Province), *Kaogu*, 1961, 1. Also see Huang Zhan and Zhao Xueqian, "Yunnan tianchi dong an xinshiqi shidai yizhi diaocha" (Survey of Neolithic sites.on the eastern shores of Tianchi, Yunnan Province), *Kaogu*, 1959, 9.

[30]Planning Office, Museum of Yunnan Province, "Jianchuan haimenkou gu wenhua yizhi qingli jianbao" (Brief report on the putting in order of the ancient cultural site of Haimenkou in Jianchuan), *Kaogu tongxun* (Correspondence on archaeology), 1958, 6.

[31]Regarding the Neolithic cultures in the territory of Yunnan Province, the current opinions and viewpoints are inconsistent with one another. Wang Ningsheng, for instance, divides them into four types (see *Yunnan kaogu* [Archaeology in Yunnan], 1981, pp. 11-27), but Li Kunsheng et al. divide them into eight types (see *Wenwu jikan* [Cultural relics magazine], 1980, 2:133-42).

LIANG ZHAOTAO AND ZHANG SHOUQI

# 7 On "Ethnoarchaeology"

SINCE 1979, a new scholarly term, "ethnoarchaeology," has come formally into ethnological and archaeological usage in the United States and Britain. For example:
—A collection of essays on archaeology published by Columbia University Press in New York in 1979 used this noun as its title.[1]
—In 1980, University of Chicago Press published an anthology that contained essays focused on fossils and primitive ecologies. Its title was *Fossils in the Making: Vertebrate Taphonomy and Paleoecology*. In this book there was an article that focused on the discussion of the role played by this new field of science known as "ethnoarchaeology."[2]
—In 1980 also, the *Cambridge Encyclopedia of Archaeology*[3] published by Cambridge University Press and *A Dictionary of Terms and Techniques in Archaeology*[4] published by Phaidon Press both introduced this new term (a new field of study, really) as a special entry.
 In recent years, some of our Chinese translators have translated the English term "ethnoarchaeology" as *zhongzu kaoguxue* (racial archaeology). We feel that the translation is somewhat lacking in precision.

"Lun minzu kaoguxue," in *Minzu kaogu yanjiu lunwenji* (Collected essays in ethnological studies) (Guangzhou: Zhongshan University Press, 1984), pp. 1–10.

[1] Carol Kramer, "Implications of Ethnography for Archaeology," in *Ethnoarchaeology*, ed. C. Kramer (New York: Columbia University Press, 1979).
[2] D. Gifford, "Ethnoarchaeological Contributions to the Taphonomy of Human Sites," in *Fossils in the Making: Vertebrate Taphonomy and Paleoecology*, ed. A. Behrensmeyer and A. Hill (Chicago: University of Chicago Press, 1980), pp. 94–107.
[3] Andrew Sherratt, ed., *Cambridge Encyclopaedia of Archaeology* (Cambridge: Cambridge University Press, 1980), pp. 36–37.
[4] Sara Champion, *A Dictionary of Terms and Techniques in Archaeology* (Oxford: Phaidon Press, 1980), pp. 42–43.

In studying the composition of this term, we find that it originates from a combination of *minzuxue* (ethnology) or *minzuzhi* (ethnography) with the term *kaoguxue* (archaeology).

Since the 1950s, in order to investigate the specific and concrete contents of the Neolithic cultures along the southeastern coast of China so as to trace the prehistoric conditions of the ancient *baiyue* [peoples], we have combined archaeology, ethnology, and historical diplomacy as a route for verification, authentication, and study.[5] Later we called this method *minzu kaogu* [nationality archaeology].

Since the English term "ethnoarchaeology" connotes the blending of ethnology and archaeology to become a new science, it has a conformity and unanimity with the contents and connotations of the term *minzu kaogu* that has been in use in our country for these many years. Therefore we feel that instead of translating this term as *zhongzu kaoguxue* [racial archaeology], it would be more accurate and precise to translate it as *minzu kaoguxue* [ethnoarchaeology].

As for why this field of study has been generated and what influence it may have on the study of ethnology, history, and archaeology as well as its prospects in the future, we would like to offer some analysis so as to elicit critical opinions and corrections from our colleagues in academic circles.

## Factors in the Formation of Ethnoarchaeology

To understand this question we must go back to the time of the Second World War. During that period, numerous renowned cultural sites and historical edifices [around the world] were devastated. The work of repairing and restoring cultural relics, artifacts, and historical buildings after the war was formidable. In the onerous and complex process of carrying out this task of repairing and restoring, in order that accuracy and detail may be achieved, many experts were involved in the study of the original shape of these cultural and historical relics. Even earlier, and over the course of the last century, the archaeologists of many countries had already been involved in the study of the restoration of the original shape of a number of historical objects. For example, they had created

[5]See "Wuoguo dongnan yanhai xin shiqi shidai wenhua de fenbu he niandai tantao" (An exploration of the problems of the distribution and dating of the Neolithic cultures along the southeastern coast of China), *Kaogu* (Archaeology), 1959, 9:491–93.

some preliminary restorations of such things as the conditions of ancient human beings with regard to their food, techniques of production, communal residences, burial customs, and seasonal migrations. After the World War, with the impact of the large-scale projects in repairing and restoring, the "restoration" studies that were already carried out in the field of archaeology were bound to be promoted and propelled forward. This also stimulated archaeologists to advance new conjectures and new ideas. To do restoration work, we must rely on data in several areas, namely, (1) fossils and archaeological data. Undoubtedly data in this area can only provide us with clues and can resolve only some of the problems. (2) We must also seek out the conditions regarding the continuities and changes in the social organization of human beings in the remote ancient period and their activities and behavior. This means that we must rely on data from elsewhere, that is, data concerning those unusual human communities in certain areas of the contemporary world where they are still leading a life of gathering and hunting. Their various modes of adapting to their own natural environment, their societal organization and social behavior, and, in general, their modus vivendi somewhat resemble those of early human beings. They also continue to possess vestiges of ancient customs and are what we call "living fossils." To restore the shape of remote, prehistoric societies, we can take all these data and compare and contrast them with ancient documentary evidence. This forms the contemporary background and social origin for the genesis of "ethnoarchaeology."

Second, as science marches forward, under certain conditions each field of science must, inevitably, absorb from other sciences and branches of learning certain theorems and techniques that are conducive to the deepening of the study of the science itself. Among each science and among many different sciences there is bound to be mutual supplementation and penetration.

We may take archaeology as an example. In the last thirty years or so, archaeology has absorbed from "physical chemistry" a new methodology for determining the date of things. From "physical anthropology" it has absorbed the technology of authenticating the bones found buried in ancient graves; from zoology, botany, and meteorology it has absorbed the technology of analyzing the conditions of the natural environment in ancient times and the technology to distinguish specific conditions pertaining to ancient flora and fauna; from geography it has introduced the techniques of "locational analysis"; from geology and pedology the methods relating to stratigraphy and sediment analysis.

Recently the combination of archaeology with certain other sciences has also formed some new disciplines.

The blending of archaeology and seismology has given rise to the formation of the new "seismo-archaeology." In the late 1970s, seismologists Chen Enmin and others in Guangdong used precisely this method, supplemented by "folklore" studies, in discovering the actual devastation wreaked by the massive earthquake that took place at Qiongzhou in the 33d year of the reign of Wanli in the Ming dynasty (1605 A.D.)—an earthquake that would have registered close to 8 on the Richter scale and was so forceful that it led to parts of the seacoast crumbling into the sea and caused numerous villages to collapse and be overrun by the ocean.[6]

The combining of archaeology with agronomy also brought about the formation of "agro-archaeology." Professor Zhang Zhongge, a specialist in the science of animal husbandry at Beijing Agricultural University, used this method, and also some ethnological data as secondary evidential data, to clarify the picture regarding the origins and evolution of the breeding of high-class pigs in our country in ancient times, as well as the transmission of such techniques to Europe. He also used these methods to study the methods and techniques adopted among common Chinese in breeding and raising pigs.[7]

Since, as we have seen, in both the study of "seismo-archaeology" and the study of "agro-archaeology" certain types of data from folklore and ethnology were involved, it stands to reason to make the argument that, simply from the perspective of scholarly functionality, there is bound to be some integration between "archaeology" and "ethnology," owing to their own intrinsic needs as a science. The archaeologist, to reconstruct the concrete contents of certain prehistoric sites and to explain how certain stoe tools were manufactured and used, would need

[6]For details see Chen Enmin and Huang Yongyin, "Yi liu ling wu nian hainan dao qiongzhou da dizhen ji qi fazhen gouzao chubu tantao" (A preliminary investigation of the great earthquake of Qiongzhou on Hainan Island in 1605 and its structural factors), *Dizhen dizhi* (Seismology and geology) 1, 4 (December 1979).

[7]See Zhang Zhongge, "Wuoguo yangzhuye lishi" (A history of pig breeding in China), in *Dongwu xuebao* (Bulletin of zoology) 22, 1 (March 1976); Zhang Zhongge, "Chutu wenwu suojian wuoguo jiazhu pinzhong xingcheng he fazhan" (The formation and evolution of the species of domesticated pigs in China as seen from excavated cultural relics), *Wenwu* (Cultural relics), 1979, 1; Zhang Zhongge, "Wuoguo zhu zhong de xingcheng ji qi fazhan" (The formation and evolution of pig species in China), *Beijing nongye daxue xuebao* (Bulletin of the Beijing Agricultural University), 1980, 3.

to borrow from ethnology. Similarly, for an ethnologist to clarify some aspect of a particular nationality's history, especially when dealing with the question of origins, as well as to ascertain how the primitive cultures of various nationalities have influenced each other, he would need archaeology.

In 1961 a team of nautical archaeologists made up of Turkish and American scholars led by the internationally renowned nautical archaeologist Professor George F. Bass carried out an undersea excavation in the waters to the north of the island of Rhodes in the Aegean Sea. They dug up pieces of wooden planks from Roman and Byzantine ships that had sunk in the fourth to seventh centuries as well as large batches of ancient glass and pottery items. These archaeologists distinguished, out of the large quantity of artifacts that came from the seabed, certain pottery items whose shape and model appear to indicate they were made long ago in emulation of ancient Chinese ceramic porcelain ware. Moreover, they also discovered an ancient sword whose hilt bore decorative carving patterns that clearly indicated motifs strongly influenced by comparable decorative patterns of China.[8] That these nautical archaeologists were able to make such an analysis and distinction was largely and inseparably owing to the knowledge of ethnology that they possessed.

In the last thirty to forty years, a number of scholars at the Bishop Museum of Hawaii, in order to trace the history of Polynesia, carried out excavations in certain spots on the Hawaiian Islands, Marquesas Islands, and Society Islands. They carried out comparative studies of the fishhooks excavated from the various archipelagoes, and they also compared these with the primitive fishing technologies still prevalent among certain Polynesian people today, and by doing so, they were able to clarify the choice of material and techniques employed by ancient Polynesians in manufacturing their fishing hooks.[9] This kind of research is a study in Pacific basin archaeology and at the same time a study of Pacific basin ethnology.

Such examples exist in China as well. The restoration of the Banpo site called for making reference to ethnographic data from Yunnan. In turn, the remaining primitive societies revealed in the Banpo site ap-

[8]For details see the brief introduction to this expedition in "Treasure from the Aegean," *National Geographic* (Washington, D.C.) (June 1978): 729, 772, 790. Also, in the same issue, George F. Bass, "Glass Treasure from the Aegean," pp. 768–793, gives a detailed description of this nautical archaeological expedition.
[9]See Yosihiko H. Sinoto, "Artifacts from Excavated Sites in the Hawaiian Marquesas and Society Islands: A Comparative Study," in *Polynesian Culture History*, ed. G. A. Highland (Honolulu: Bishop Museum Press, 1967), pp. 341–61.

peared to be similar or contiguous to some of the phenomena retained by a number of nationality societies that are "fraternal" [to the Han people of Yunnan]. This evidence also serves, then, as proof that these currently existing social phenomena are vestiges of primitive societies.

Therefore, it is evident that in terms of the intrinsic and individual needs of both sciences, there is bound to be mutual combination and mutual penetration between ethnology and archaeology.

Furthermore, we can also see [the significance of such a viewpoint] from the perspective of the intrinsic structure of anthropology. Ethnology, archaeology, linguistics, and physical anthropology are the four basic components that make up the science of anthropology. In the realm of anthropology, these four parts all take "human beings" as their major target of study. They study not only the conditions that pertain to all aspects of the existence of the human race in the past, but also the conditions that pertain to current human beings. Within the parameters of anthropology as a science, archaeology and ethnology both pay attention to questions relating to the cultural origins, development, changes of, and mutual influences among the various communities of the human species. In the research and study process, these two fields inevitably are integrated with each other, and would also integrate with the other two components together to form a comprehensive entity.

Professor Jason W. Smith, an archaeologist at the University of California at Los Angeles, posed the problem in a very succinct and precise way in a monograph he wrote in 1976. He said: "As of now, we feel that archaeology and anthropology are like the warp and weave on a single piece of scientific fabric. They both take 'Man' to be the object of their study; and we find it very difficult to separate the two."[10] Indeed, this is how things actually stand.

From the above analysis we can see that there are social, historical, and scientific causes for the gradual formation, over the last twenty or thirty years, of a new field of study among the social sciences, known as "ethnoarchaeology." Indeed, this is inevitable.

**The Function and Role of Ethnoarchaeology**

In recent years, a number of scholars have raised ideas about the academic usefulness of ethnoarchaeology.

[10]Jason Smith, *Foundation of Archaeology* (Beverly Hills, Calif.: Glencoe Press, 1976), p. 31.

The British archaeologist Andrew Sherratt stated in a book that he edited, published in 1980, that "most recently, some archaeologists have come to feel that they must themselves take hold of ethnography and use it to explain certain peculiar problems in archaeology. This methodology is commonly known as ethnoarchaeology."[11]

(Note: The phrasing here is, in fact, overly abstract. There are many peculiar problems in archaeology. When we encounter certain 'peculiar problems' such as the question of the origins of certain specific cultures or of the formation of certain specific social customs, ethnoarchaeology by itself will not be able to explain these on the spot. Indeed, many such problems can be resolved only when we bring together the methods of many fields of science and only if we dig deeply into them and make penetrating, in-depth inquiries and analyses.)

Also, Professor of Archaeology Carol Kramer of Lehman College of the City University of New York offered: "The term 'ethnoarchaeology' has most often connoted problem-oriented ethnographic research conducted by anthropologists trained as field archaeologists. It is designed to meet the special needs of archaeologists, who can rarely question informants about the remains with which they work."[12]

We feel that although these suggestions have indeed provided a certain explanation for the function of ethnoarchaeology, we should take the question a step further in order to clarify it. At this point we think we must cite the statements of some researchers who have long-term practical experience in this area.

First, let us look at the conditions in the late 1960s surrounding the expedition that an American archaeologist, Richard Gould of the University of Hawaii, made to Western Australia. At the time, in the company of his wife, he ventured into the Gibson Desert with the theories and techniques of archaeology at his disposal and carried out a fifteen-month systematic ethnological survey of the aboriginal communities in the region that were still using stone tools and leading a life of gathering food and hunting. He learned the languages of these aboriginal communities and often accompanied them on treks of four to five miles in gathering food. At night he slept in the camps of these small communities. December and January were the months during which the Australian climate was at the peak of extreme heat. After the sun rose in the morning the weather could be unbearably hot. People tended to wait until the late

---

[11] Sherratt, *Cambridge Encyclopedia*, p. 37.
[12] Carol Kramer, "Introduction," in *Ethnoarchaeology*, ed. Kramer, p. 4.

afternoon, at six or seven o'clock, before they would venture forth to carry out their food-seeking activities. Gould did the same and persevered in his efforts. He lived among these aboriginal communities, to understand the compositions of the hunting groups among these communities and their methods and to observe the techniques of gathering that they employed. He studied the composition of their night-camps, the organization of their society, their systematic social behavior, their child-rearing methods, their religious practices and ceremonies, and so forth. At the same time, he also studied in detail the stone tools that these aboriginal communities used and the techniques they employed to manufacture them. He found that what these communities used was a slice-shaped stone wedge, which is a crudely made tool with a steep edge. This type of tool is very similar to the scraper that has been excavated at prehistoric sites. He found that they also used a type of stone axe that had a plane resembling the stone axe of the Mesolithic Age of some ten thousand years ago. These aboriginal residents [of Western Australia] also used animal teeth as tools. In general, their production technology resembled that prevalent some thirty thousand years ago.[13]

Afterward, when Gould spoke of the understandings that he gathered from this period of field work, he concluded that the investigation "suggests new possibilities and analogies to us, and helps us to get unstuck [from] a limited range of ideas."[14] Gould obtained a massive amount of "live" data that constituted a reliable foundation in his work of explaining certain prehistoric cultural sites and restoring the original shape and outlook of prehistoric life.[15]

Quite clearly, then, ethnoarchaeology can indeed propel both ethnology and archaeology to make their own developmental advances.

Second, in southern Venezuela and northern Brazil, there is an Indian ethnic community known as the Yanomamo. This ethnic group was using stone tools right up to about forty or fifty years ago. They used stone axes and spades to dig holes as well as to fell and cut up huge trees. They generally led a life of primitive, nomadic horticulture. This kind of slash-and-burn primitive agriculture was originally one of the characteristics of production in the Neolithic Age and at one time existed widely throughout the world. However, as for how, in the Neolithic Age, people

[13]See Frank E. Poirier, *In Search of Ourselves: An Introduction to Physical Anthropology*, 3d ed. (Minneapolis: Burgess, 1981), pp. 113-14.
[14]Ibid., p. 114.
[15]Ibid., p. 113.

actually used a stone axe to fell a huge tree, or what the actual process was, not only would we be unable to see it happening today, but even explorers and travelers of the eighteenth and nineteenth centuries or the early part of this century, if they indeed had incidentally come upon such a scene, failed to pay it adequate attention and certainly failed to carry out a careful observation. Therefore we are unable to find any explanation of such an activity in the documented evidence. Nevertheless, if the scholar of the history of primitive societies or the archaeologist is to find out the complete picture of the food production of the people of the Neolithic age in the world as a whole, and if they have to draw certain conclusions about this on the basis of the excavated evidence of stone axes, then they must obtain concrete data regarding how those people felled trees with stone axes and cleared the ground.

It was precisely with such a purpose in mind that, on March 31, 1975, the American ethnoarchaeologist Robert L. Carneiro of the American Museum of Natural History, ventured deep into the region of the upper stretches of the Orinoco River in southern Venezuela, at a place called Hasubowateri, and found a Yanomamo village where the villagers still knew how to use a primitive stone axe to fell trees. There he lived for a time with a young native by the name of Dobrabewa. While this young man carried out a sustained experiment of cutting down a big tree with a traditional stone axe that was firmly hafted with thongs, Carneiro carried out an on-site observation and recorded the process in detail. He collected a batch of extremely valuable data. Afterward, he recalled with insight: "Such information would help us not only to reconstruct the culture history of a particular group, but also to elucidate the general relationships that have obtained between environment, technology, subsistence, labor, and society. And that, as becomes clearer every day, is the common objective toward which ethnologists and archaeologists are rapidly converging."[16]

In speaking of this insight, Robert Carneiro has in fact spoken of the basic function and role of ethnoarchaeology.

Third, since 1967, a group of scientists from Harvard University have carried out an extended investigation and study in the Kalahari Desert of the Botswana region of Africa. The object of this research is the Bushman people who live in the region and still, even today, lead a life of food

---

[16] See Robert L. Carneiro, "Tree Felling Out Among the Yanomamo Indians of South Venezuela," in *Ethnoarchaeology*, ed. Kramer, pp. 21–58. The quotation is from p. 54.

gathering and hunting. At the time, this group of Harvard scientists focused on the observation and study of such topics as the health care of the Bushman people, their nutritional conditions, their family composition, their child-bearing practices, their group structure, their interpersonal relationships, their mores, ceremonies, and customs, their production technologies, and how they adapt to the local natural environment. Some among these scientists who are involved in archaeological studies have also inquired into the sites where the Bushman people have resided. They have dug up their residential sites and taken the artifacts they excavated to the Bushman people, asking on the spot their opinions and explanations as to the names and usages of these artifacts. These archaeologists also carried out excavations of the ancient "refuse dumping sites" that had been left behind from long ago at places where the Bushman people had lived, so as to find out what prehistoric artifacts and relics might have been left behind and to see what might be learned from the artifacts that had been buried and the sedimentary accumulation that has piled up.[17]

These archaeologists also studied the question of how the Bushman people selected their residential sites and reconnoitered the distribution of their residential relic sites throughout this lengthy strip of desert. They studied the factors that prompted the Bushman people to migrate from one site to another. They distinguished, for example, the shape and type of different camps that the people had as they moved around in search of food. There are, for instance, camps where the Bushman people stayed for "several weeks" at a time, and others where they stayed for "several months." These various shapes and types were compared to arrive at a clearer picture.[18]

Undoubtedly, the material obtained by the Harvard scientists will help our historians of primitive societies to explain the migratory patterns of prehistoric human beings.

Fourth, the research work of ethnoarchaeology is applicable not only to explaining some historical facts related to prehistoric human beings but also to the explanation of a number of problems related to the slave and feudalistic society, problems on which doubts remain.

A couple of years ago, a debate arose within China's historical circles over whether or not there was actually the phenomenon of "drilling wood to obtain fire" in ancient China. The problem was resolved eventually

[17] See Poirier, *In Search of Ourselves*, p. 116.
[18] Ibid., pp. 116–17.

by bringing together and comparing ethnological, archaeological, and documentary data. It was thus proved that the technology of drilling wood to obtain fire indeed existed in primitive society in China, and that indeed the technology was applied and retained by people for a long time well into the feudalistic society.[19] This is an example of how ethnoarchaeology may be employed to explain problems in this area.

Over the last twenty years, we have discovered a number of grave sites of the Warring States period in southern China. The local nationality characteristics epitomized in the unearthed artifacts (in fact, they would be the cultural attributes of the ancient Yue cultural group) have yet to be studied. As we continue to discover more and more ancient grave sites in the region of nationality groups, and as more and more artifacts are excavated, the need for us to be guided in their study by [the principle and methodology] of ethnoarchaeology will become increasingly evident.

We believe that ethnoarchaeology is a new science that has opened up a new path of research for ethnology, archaeology, and history, and for the study of the history of primitive societies. For the study of primitive cultures, it is certainly an indispensable new science.

## On the Issue of Research Methodology

From 1960 to 1979, according to what we must acknowledge as an incomplete count, more than a hundred scholarly essays have been published in the United States and Britain on "ethnoarchaeology" and its topics.

Taking these essays into account, we can, in general, subsume the many research methods that they have either suggested or proven by experimentation under four major categories: (1) carrying out direct observation of corresponding ancient things that have remained as survivals; (2) making comparisons of related or similar survivals of ancient objects [from different ethnic groups], or comparing these to related ancient artifacts, and then carrying out analogous comparisons and deductions regarding the contents of related ancient objects; (3) in-depth analysis; and (4) making interim conclusions and reports. However, such a "methodology" has been the subject of debate in Western academic circles.

[19]For details, see Zhang Shouqi, "Zhongguo gudai quhuo fangfa kaozheng" (A study in the authentication of methods for obtaining fire in ancient China), *Shehui kexue zhanxian* (Social sciences battlefront), 1981, 1.

The sharpest opposing opinion was held by the scholar Freeman of the United States. In an essay written in 1968 entitled "A Theoretical Framework for Interpreting Archaeological Materials," he proposed: "To carry out direct analogous and comparative deductions regarding the conditions of ancient human beings on the basis of remnants of communities that exist today and are still leading a life of food gathering and hunting is prone to lead the study of things in the remote past into a detour or a blind alley. This is because when we study these types of conditions, what we are getting at are really the cultural behavior or people under a system that is adaptive to and reflects the excavated artifacts, which serve as the foundation of the study, and such a basis is vastly different from [the data that we gather from studying] such communities that remain in remnant fashion today."[20]

In fact, Freeman simply believes that the past and the present are two different things altogether.

Second, Martin Wobst also raised objections in an essay written in 1978. He offered the opinion that the primitive clans that remain in remnant form in the world today are confined to small areas. The restrictions that they experience are much greater than those experienced by the ancient communities of the Pleistocene period in selecting their habitats and spheres of activity. Therefore, he believes, if we are to carry out a comparison and above all a restoration of the ancient and remote past on the basis of some primitive things that remain in the contemporary era, we are running a great risk of distorting the archaeological record.[21]

[We do have to note that] with regard to those primitive communities still leading a life of food gathering and hunting today, their places of residence are not all or always confined to small areas. For example, among the communities in western Australia cited earlier, and among the Bushman people in Africa, the population density is extremely low and they have very expansive regions in which to maneuver and move about.

With regard to these opposing opinions, responses have already been made in Western scholarly circles: First, the fossil records, archaeolog-

[20]L. Freeman, "A Theoretical Framework for Interpreting Archaeological Materials," in *Man the Hunter*, ed. R. Lee and I. DeVore (Chicago: Aldine, 1968), pp. 262–67.

[21]H. Martin Wobst, "The Archaeo-Ethnology of Hunter-Gatherers, or the Tyranny of the Ethnographic Record in Archaeology," *American Antiquity* 43 (1977): 303–309.

ical data, and the traces of activities and behavior of ancient human beings that are retained even today are things that we should feel fortunate about, and which can serve as an outline to help us restore the history of the past. Second, with regard to those groups that are still leading primitive lives, the question lies with our ability to discover their ancient and remote origins, as well as things that currently exist but are extremely similar to things in their ancient and remote past. Only when we compare these things can we find the appropriate answers to our questions. Third, the remnants of these food gathering and hunting groups can help us—by seeing how their own traditional cultures adapted to all sorts of natural environments, by seeing their way of life and existence—to clarify the contents and temper of human social behavior in the historical past.[22]

As for the authors' personal views on this question, we believe that ethnoarchaeology is not a matter of simply and extemporaneously attaching some little bits of ethnological material to archaeological data so as to make some forced comparison or incidental combination. Nor is it adding some archaeological data to ethnological material to carry out analogous deductions arbitrarily. Insofar as ethnoarchaeology is truly as its name suggests, it is, in the continuous process of the forward development and progress of science, to bring together the methods and data of ethnology and the methods and data of archaeology, as well as the data of historical documentation, to compare and criticize and verify one another, to supplement one another, and to be synthesized with one another, so as to bring about a more penetrating and more careful explanation of certain historical subjects. Let us cite one incident as an example to prove this point.

In 1972 Joseph Birdsell, an anthropologist at the University of California at Los Angeles, published a book entitled *Human Evolution*.[23] In this book he formally proposed what he called the "magic number" concepts of the number 25 and the number 500. The number 25 referred to the fact that as he studied the population growth rate among primitive communities of Australia's aboriginal residents, he noticed that the number of people in each of these communities fell between 20 and 50. He chose the number 25 to stand for a representative number of people in the primitive communities that are still leading a life of food gathering and hunting. This number is proven among the Bushman people in the Kalahari Desert in southern Africa and among the Birhar

[22]See Poirier, *In Search of Ourselves*, pp. 108–10.
[23]Joseph Birdsell, *Human Evolution* (Chicago: Rand McNally, 1972).

people in northern India. There is a great resemblance, he found, among these groups in terms of the number of people in each community. He also found a similarity and conformity [to this number] from the conditions that were represented by the prehistorical residential sites [in these regions]. This number, 25, is most certainly not an absolute figure, but it does indeed seem to represent an equilibrium figure [for the population] of primitive groups. Furthermore, there is also a similar or approximate situation with regard to the numbers that make up communities of chimpanzees.[24] As for the number 500, this refers to the average number of people in a tribal grouping that still leads a life of food gathering and hunting and speaks the same dialect. This is an average number that Birdsell suggested after he had done a very careful demographic survey, and it is based on his understanding that, among the currently existing tribal groups that still lead a hunting and gathering life, their population numbers fall between 200 and 800. These figures reflect actual situations among human groupings and are thus true not only of the Australian aborginals, the Bushmen of Africa, and the Birhar of northern India, but also of the average numbers of people in primitive tribal groups that speak a common dialect, including the Shoshone people of the Great Basin area of the United States in the states of California, Nevada, and Utah.[25]

This is the result of Joseph Birdsell's efforts in employing an "ethnoarchaeological" method to investigate the conditions related to the population of primitive communities. We do not see how this is a distortion of archaeological material. On the contrary, we think this is an effort to bring about a reasonable explanation of something that we had not previously comprehended, namely, the population numbers of food gathering and hunting in communities in primitive society. This, we believe, will deepen our understanding about the primitive societies.

[24]According to the understanding of Jane Goodall, the famous anthropologist renowned for her studies on chimpanzees, each chimpanzee community is made up of about forty members. This is derived from her observations of the settlement in the Gombe River area of Tanzania in Africa. (See Jane Goodall, *The Chimpanzees Are Calling*, trans. Liu Houyi and Zhang Feng [Science Press, 1981], p. 322.)

Also, the Japanese scholar Kano Takashi observed in 1973 in the Congo basin of Africa that among the pygmy chimpanzee communities, the tendency is for each group to have fifteen to thirty members. See "The Dual Structure of Pygmy Chimpanzee Groups," in Yuanhou shehui (The Society of Apes and Monkeys), ed. Zheng Kaiqi et al. (Knowledge Press, 1982), p. 21.

[25]See Poirier, *In Search of Ourselves*, p. 118.

## The Prospects of Ethnoarchaeology

At this point we would like to take a look at this question from the vantage point of the actual conditions in our country.

1. The need to study the history of primitive societies in our country. In the past, in some general histories of China, in dealing with the history of primitive society, authors have commonly used archaeological material as the principal basis for their narrative as well as analysis, while branching out to encompass, supplementarily, documentary material and ethnological data. This methodology already involves the employment of ethnoarchaeology in this area.

Many problems in the history of primitive society in China remain to be explored. For example, with regard to questions such as the society's structure and evolution, conditions of production, mutual relations between the cultural behavior and the material base of the people, and the origins of all sorts of scientific knowledge and cultures, we are still extremely limited in our understanding. If we are to explore problems such as these we must rely on archaeology. Yet we must also depend on ethnology and the study of history. In other words, we must rely on ethnoarchaeology. The late Professor Lin Huixiang integrated ethnological material with the study of archaeological relics in his successful effort to restore to its original shape the method of assembling and using a piece of stone sectional wedge that was excavated along our country's southeastern coast.[26] For another example, we cannot dispense with ethnological data if we are to explore the actual conditions pertaining to the fenced human residences in the Hemudu relic site in Zhejiang Province.

2. Regarding the need to study the histories of the many ethnic groups in our country: At present the work of ethnoarchaeological studies has not yet been developed in many vast tracts of territory in China inhabited by minority nationalities. In some minority regions certain artifacts and relics have already been excavated but await further investigation and treatment. Therefore, there is much room for the exercising of ethnoarchaeology in these aspects.

In the past, Professor Feng Hanqi has taken the artifacts that belong to the period of the Western Han dynasty that have been excavated at Shizhaishan in Jinning County, Yunnan, and by integrating the methods of ethnology and archaeology he has sorted out the questions of the

[26]See Lin Huixiang, "One of the Traits of Southeast China's Neolithic Culture," *Kaogu xuebao* (Journal of archaeology), 1958, 3.

national identities reflected in these artifacts.[27] Then there is also the double-hulled boat whose existence we deduced from the decorative patterns on the bronze drum excavated at Luobo Bay in Gui County, Guangxi. Without reference to ethnological data, we simply could not have clearly understood its significance.[28]

Another thing that needs to be explained here is that, at the moment, a number of ethnology research institutions have already successfully written or compiled "brief ethnic histories" of the various nationalities with which they are affiliated. However, if we are to expand and develop these brief nationality histories, or historical outlines, into complete and comprehensive historical accounts, we will have to use massive amounts of excavated relics and artifact data as we carry out research and study that integrates such data with the ethnological data above ground. The narrative work of nationalities' histories is based on historical documentary material as well as ethnological material (including existing data on the folklore of currently extant societies) and on the data of excavated relics. Therefore, this new science will evidently play a significant role in the work in this area.

3. Regarding the needs in the area of archaeological studies: Every cultural relic excavated, whether it belongs to slave society or to feudal society, is an object that epitomizes a fragment of the social culture and mores and customs of the time. If we are to trace the contents of these fragments, we will need data in ethnology as well as in folklore studies. At the same time, if we are to carry out a synthetic, coordinated study, we will have to explore social customs and functions. This means, again, a reliance on the theories of ethnology and folklore studies.

Clearly, then, ethnoarchaeology is indispensable to archaeology as well as to ethnology and to the study of history.

**An Interim Summary**

Twenty to thirty years have gone by since the earliest sprouting of ethnoarchaeology, and today it has completed its initial phase of forma-

---

[27]See Feng Hanqi, "A Tentative Exploration of the Question of Nationality Identity of Excavated Artifacts at Shizhaishan in Jinning County, Yunnan Province," *Kaogu*, 1961, 9; and "A Study of the Bronze Artifacts Unearthed at Shizhaishan in Jinning County of Yunnan Province: A Tentative Explanation of Several Major Graphic Depictions of Human Activities," *Kaogu*, 1963, 6.

[28]See "A Preliminary Exploration of the Tribal Origins of the Xi-ou People," in *Xueshu yanjiu* (Academic studies) 1 (1978): 129–35, originally published in *Shehui kexue zhanxian*, 1983, 4.

tion. In the West, before the term "ethnoarchaeology" was formally ratified and accepted by archaeological and ethnological circles, various scholars had given this research methodology "in which ethnology and archaeology are blended" various names; some have called it "action archaeology," some "living archaeology," some "archaeoethnography," and still others "ethnographic archaeology." Eventually, the designation "ethnoarchaeology" was accepted by archaeologists and ethnologists alike, and since then it has been put to common and formal usage.

Undoubtedly, this field of science is still in its earlier stages of formation, and many problems, whether in terms of its ontology or methodology, remain to be explored. What we are doing here is to throw out some crude ideas in the hope of eliciting others' valuable and refined thoughts, and to propose some questions for discussion in the hope that that will strengthen the growth of this new twig on the tree of science. We hope that our efforts will succeed in bringing out the criticisms and corrections of our esteemed colleagues and comrades.

# Part IV

# Paleoanthropology and Neoanthropology

WU RUKANG

# 8 Paleoanthropology and Neoanthropology

PALEOANTHROPOLOGY is also known as human paleontology; it is the science that studies the origins and development of the human race.

The human being is a species of primates. When we study the origins of human beings we will inevitably be involved in the study of primates; this includes knowledge of existing primate species as well as of ancient primate species and fossils of primate species. During the long process of human development, stone implements were the primary type of tool used by human beings. Therefore the study of paleoanthropology is also inevitably the study of stone tools, particularly tools of the Paleolithic age.

The primary data for the study of the evolution of the human race are human and ape fossils, all of which are excavated from geological strata. Therefore we must also have a general knowledge of geology and stratigraphy. In particular, we need to have knowledge of geology and stratigraphy relating to relatively late geological ages, such as the Cenozoic era. This is because that era is the geological age during which humanity evolved.

For us to have a broader understanding of ancient human beings we must comprehend the environment in which they existed, including the geological conditions and the configuration of the Earth's surface at the time, the relative movements of the continents, the major climate zones, quantities of rainfall, changes in surface temperature, as well as changes in the [locations and shapes of] rivers, mountain ranges, glacial movements, deserts, grasslands, and forests, and changes in flora and fauna of all sorts.

Since fossils are the foundation on which we can study the processes

"Gurenleixue yu jinrenleixue," *Kexue bao* (Science journal), September 27, 1986, p. 2.

of human evolution, we must, as we approach the study of the formation of human fossils, have a rich knowledge of morphology and human anatomy. Furthermore, form is closely related to function; the two are mutually dependent and mutually determining. Therefore, to understand the meaning of specific morphological structures, we must pay attention to the issue of function. This means that we must have a knowledge of physiology. For example, by measuring a human skull we can tell the size of the human brain and also find out some of its functions. From studying fossilized limb and torso bones we can deduce the mode of motion. From studying hand bones, we can understand something about the human being's ability to grasp and hold objects. And by studying related bones we can also deduce such things as speech and other cultural habits.

In studying the morphological attributes of fossils, we must, in accordance with the principles of system studies and categorization, determine the categorical position of these fossils and their systems relationships.

When we excavate fossils we must make specific observations and records of the position, distribution, and interrelationship of these fossils. This is the science of deposits, which is becoming a popular subject of study. Another newly emergent science is behavioral science, which studies the behavior of groups or communities of animals in their natural environment. The results of this study can serve as reference data for the study of the behavior of the earliest human beings.

To understand the age of ancient human beings in terms of chronological distance from today, and to understand the process and speed of human evolution, we must be able to determine dates. This calls for the science of chronology, the science of dating, or determining ages.

Human beings evolved from ancient apes. Therefore we must, in this science, also understand the basic principles of the theory of evolution. Human beings are special animals. They share the commonality of evolution with other animals, and at the same time there are particularities to their specific process of evolution: Humans have culture, and this makes for an evolutionary process different from that of other animals.

Therefore, [because of all the above,] we can say that modern paleoanthropology is a synthetic science that makes use of the research results of many different disciplines.

In contrast with paleoanthropology we have neoanthropology. However, whether in China or in other countries, the term neoanthropology has not been established as a formal title for a particular field of study.

In recent years there have been great developments in the study of the physical transformation and development of the human body in modern times. The results of these studies, however, are scattered among the many different sciences related to the human body. I believe that we now have sufficient reason and the necessary conditions to establish this new science of neoanthropology as a field of study.

The object of neoanthropology is to describe and explain the processes of transformation and development of the physical attributes of modern human groups and the laws that govern these transformations. Its principal contents of study should include the following: the connection and distinctions between human beings and other animals; humanity's closest relatives, the apes; the structure of the human body and the laws governing the changes in this structure (this ought to include the layers of human body structure, the deviations and correlations of human body structure, human body structure and diseases, age-related changes in the human body and differences in terms of sex, menopause, age-related health deterioration, longevity and life expectancy, the biological clock, the physiological responses of the human body to environmental and climatic changes, and problems related to the quantitative and qualitative changes in the human body through a life span); the meaning and categorization and attributes of human races as well the causes for their formation and a criticism of racism; and the specific physical attributes of Chinese people, etc. Some of this, such as when we study the near relatives of human beings, is similar to paleoanthropology. However, we should note that in this case, for instance, the study of neoanthropology will focus mainly on the explanation of present primate species, whereas paleoanthropology focuses on the fossils of ancient primates. For another example, in the study of race, neoanthropology will focus on the attributes, categorization, and formation of races, whereas paleoanthropology focuses on the origins of races. In these branches, there will be differences in emphasis between neoanthropology and paleoanthropology, but they supplement each other.

HUANG XINMEI

# 9 The Impact of Physical Anthropology on Construction of the "Two Civilizations"

PHYSICAL anthropology is the science that studies the physical attributes of human groups and the laws that govern the formation and development of these attributes. By groups of human beings we mean all sorts of commonality-bound groupings of human beings, including all races and nationality groups. Cultural and physical anthropology make up the two major aspects of the field of anthropology. The study of anthropology has by now, in some scientifically and technically advanced countries of the world, a history of almost a hundred years. In our country, too, it began over forty years ago. However, for all sorts of reasons, this science remains today a weak link in the chain of scientific undertakings in our country, and within it the study of physical anthropology is the weakest. And yet we must acknowledge that anthropology, physical anthropology included, can have a profound impact on our country's socialist construction. It is bound to become, in the future, a flourishing science in China in the contemporary age, and it will surely play its rightful role—a role that cannot be ignored—in the construction of the material and spiritual civilizations of socialism.

The following essay takes a look at the importance of physical anthropology and its impact. It begins with a reflection on the question of why it is necessary to ban marriage between close relatives.

The prohibition of marriage between close blood-relatives is an important legal restriction in our country. Article 6 of the "Marriage Law of the People's Republic of China" ratified by the Third Session of the Fifth National People's Congress on September 15, 1980, stipulates that

"Tizhi renleixue dui jianshe 'liangge wenming' de zuoyong: Cong jinzhi jinqin jiehun tanqi." *Zhongshan daxue xuebao* (Bulletin of Zhongshan University) 2 (1984): 87–89.

"Marriage is prohibited in situations wherein any one of the following conditions applies: (1) Direct blood relationship or collateral blood relationship within three generations...." This important stipulation has an impact on whether or not our country's general policy on population development, which is spelled out as "reducing the quantity of the population while enhancing the quality of the population," and our policy of planned parenthood, in which we promote the idea that each married couple should have only one child, will be smoothly implemented. It indeed affects the issue of the prosperity and flourishing of the Chinese people as a whole. The basis for making such a stipulation comes directly from the research results in the field of physical anthropology and related sciences.

According to the proof from archaeological investigations, the Peking Ape-man [*Homo erectus pekinensis*] in the caves at Zhoukoudian incestuously married close relatives. As a consequence, the species had a very short lifespan. Among the forty Peking Ape-men excavated, 39.5 percent were found to have died under the age of fourteen, 7 percent under the age of thirty, and 7.9 percent between the ages of forty and fifty. Only 2.6 percent died between the ages of fifty and sixty; and 43 percent of the specimens of Peking Ape-man were of indeterminate ages.[1] Naturally, when Peking Ape-man lived, there was a very low level of productivity and the living conditions were extremely inhospitable, which certainly affected their life expectancy. However, incestuous marriage with close relatives was also a factor causing the early deaths of Peking Ape-men.

In January–October 1983, the Yunnan Nationalities Investigative Team of the Institute of Nationalities of the Chinese Academy of Sciences and the Nationalities Research Office of the Yunnan Province Institute of History conducted a survey of the marital conditions before and after Liberation within the Naxi nationality in the Yongning area of Yunnan Province. This survey proved that in the past among the Naxi nationality, the custom known as "Ah Zhu" marriages caused repetitive marriages among blood relatives to be relatively common. This caused severe damage to the people's health and childbirth conditions. Take, for example, the prototypical study of Baqi Village, which found that many women there became infertile, and that a very high infant mortality rate and venereal diseases were prevalent. Up to the end of 1962, among

---

[1] Jia Lanbo, *Zhongguo yuanren* (Ape-men of China) (Shanghai: Longmen Lianhe Shuju, 1951), p. 130.

women over thirty-five years of age, six simply could not bear children or had infants who died immediately after birth. As a consequence, the population growth rate was extremely low, and some households were even disbanded. In the last fifty years, five families in that village died out, making up about 30 percent of the total of seventeen households which were counted at the period of democratic reform in that village. This example also demonstrates powerfully the severe adverse affects that intermarriage among close blood relatives has on the health and procreativity within the population.

Intermarriage among close blood relatives can also cause many hereditary genetic diseases among subsequent generations. They may include congenital mental retardation, severe congenital malformation, congenital deafness and dumbness, overall albinism, discoloration of the retina, etc. According to statistical data, among the twelve production brigades of Xiongerzai Commune of Pinggu County in Beijing, out of a total of 6,312 people, 90 were afflicted with congenital retardation, i.e., a rate of 1.43 percent. Thirty-two of them were from Daduanwa Brigade, representing a rate as high as 7.06 percent. Another bit of data indicates that "there may be as many as 1.6 million cases of congenital mental retardation throughout the country. Such people are incapable of taking care of their own lives, much less creating wealth. They can only become a heavy burden on the shoulders of their families and society."[2]

Clearly, the prohibition of intermarriage among close relatives has a vital bearing on the nation's endeavor to build the "two civilizations." In the first place, this prohibition will help enhance the quality of our population; it will prevent the emergence of "population refuse" and is conducive to the promotion of planned parenthood, thus making population growth in our country basically compatible with the production of material resources, and greatly reducing the pressure on the four modernizations program. We will then be able to transform more rapidly the nation's outlook of poverty and backwardness, and gradually improve the people's livelihood.

In the second place, to ban the marriage of close blood relatives is a clean break with many reactionary theories about blood lines that have plagued our country for thousands of years and have saddled us with many feudalistic traditional concepts, such as "close gets closer" [i.e.,

[2]Chen Muhua, "For the Future Happiness of the Chinese Nation, Let Us Talk about the Population Question," outline of speech given at the Central Party School, December 29, 1981, p. 17.

letting those families that are close become even closer], and "families of equal standing" [i.e., a couple must be matched in social and economic status when considering marriage]. As of now, in certain regions of the country and among certain minority nationalities, owing to their lack of knowledge of eugenics, these traditional concepts still carry on. Therefore, to insist on prohibiting the marriage of close blood relatives is one element of the construction of a socialist spiritual civilization.

The necessity of prohibiting the marriage of close blood relatives is a scientific conclusion resulting from the integrated development of several modern sciences, including genetics, eugenics, and physical anthropology. In the field of genetics, it has been proven that every type of living thing is able to transmit its attributes to the next generation because of the working of hereditary genes (also known as codes). The [biological] structure that carries these genes is known as a chromosome. There are twenty-three pairs of chromosomes in the human cell. Of the chromosomes in the cells of an embryo, half come from the father's body and the other half from the mother's. Certain diseases or illnesses among human beings are related to this genetic transmission primarily because the chromosomes in the cells of either the father's body or the mother's may carry certain illness-causing genes. In general, the closer the blood relationship between a husband and a wife, the greater the likelihood that they would be carriers of similar illness-causing genes. If both husband and wife are carriers of a certain illness-causing gene, their children will likely become a recipient of this type of illness as a dominant genetic carrier. The reverse is also true. The further apart in terms of blood relationship a husband and wife are, the smaller the possibility would be that they are carriers of the same illness-causing gene. Even though the husband or wife is a carrier of a certain illness-causing gene, their children would become only a recessive recipient of the illness. The further apart the blood relationship, the greater the possibility that the genetic inheritance of the illness will be recessive, and the greater the likelihood that children will be healthy. This is a very meaningful conclusion from the science of genetics on the impact of blood relationship between spouses on the health of their progeny. However, the scientific nature of such a conclusion can elicit sufficient attention among people only when it is proven through practice and through the investigation of human communities to reveal the extent of the impact of marriage among people with blood relationships on the health of their children. This becomes the responsibility of the science of physical anthropology. According to statistical surveys conducted by the World Health Organization, the mortality rate among children of marriages between close relatives is generally three times as high as that among children of marriages between people who are not close relatives, and the rate of dominant recipiency of genetic illnesses is as much as 150 times higher! Therefore, through the integrated study and proof of physical anthropology and genetics, there should be no doubt about the scientific accuracy of the conclusion that marriage between close blood relatives should be prohibited.

Similar cases are too numerous to be cited. For instance, the examination of the compatibility of the blood type of the Rh gene in the husband's body and the wife's body is a new subject of study in eugenics that deserves to be given attention in our country today. Genetics proves that the Rh gene [also known as the Rh factor] in human blood-types can come in many forms and types. At present we have discovered that the human body has received five types of anti-Rh sera, thus forming an Rh blood-type system. In the Rh blood-type system of human beings there are six antigens, respectively labeled as C, c, D, d, E, and e. Since there are five types of anti-Rh sera that these antigens elicit, the sera are respectively known as anti-C, anti-c, anti-D, anti-E, and anti-e. We have not yet discovered the anti-d serum, and therefore the d-type antigen is merely a theoretical supposition. In terms of practical application, when red blood cells contain the D-type antigen, it is called an Rh-positive type; when red blood cells contain other types of antigens, such as C, c, E, e, it is known as an Rh-negative type. If the Rh-genetic codings in the blood of husband and wife are similar, the children's health will not be greatly affected. However, if the Rh-genes in the mother's body are negative and the Rh-genes in the father's body and the embryo's body are positive, then the Rh-positive genes in the embryo's body will be transmitted into the Rh-negative blood-type body of the mother; this will cause the mother's body to instantaneously produce the antibodies to resist the Rh-gene. When these antibodies flow back into the bloodstream of the embryo, it will cause haemolytic anemia in the embryo or the newborn baby. This means that the embryo or the infant would die instantly, unless its life could be prolonged by constant blood transfusions. According to medical statistics, about 99 percent of the people of the Han nationality and most other nationalities have Rh-positive blood, and only 1 percent have Rh-negative blood. However, among a number of nationalities, the Rh-negative type is relatively prevalent. For example, in the Miao nationality, the percentage of Rh-negative blood-type is 12.3 percent; in the Buyi nationality, 8.7 percent; in the Tatar nationality, 15.8 percent; and in the Uzbek nationality, 8.7 percent.[3] If this kind of physical anthropological population statistics were more widely known, it would certainly draw the attention of the birth control authorities, who would clearly stipulate that couples must undergo Rh-gene blood-type testing before marriage. Doing this would help guarantee better genetic and childbirth conditions for the next generation.

Physical anthropology can play an extensive role in building up all aspects of the "two civilizations." Where there are human beings there are human communities, and there will be room to utilize the study of physical anthropology. Although at present there are not many workers in the field of physical anthropology, they have, in coordination with the efforts of workers in related fields, begun to do a great amount of work beneficial to the four modernizations. For example, the investigations and analyses that have been conducted from the viewpoint of physical anthropology have helped promote standardization in the clothing, footwear, and headgear manufacturing industries, so that our products can better fit the physiques of people in different regions of the country, resulting in better fitting and more aesthetically appealing styles. It has helped improve designs in the transportation and communications industries (including automobiles, airplanes, tractors, and tanks), making them more fitted to the physiques of Chinese people, allowing for greater facility in driving as well as safety and comfort for the passengers, and ease and convenience in boarding and alighting. It has also helped in making classroom furniture (desks, chairs) in secondary and primary schools more suitable for the standard physique of students, thus facilitating the growth and maturity of our children. It has helped in the design of a whole series of modernized machines and instruments, making them more suited to the physique of Chinese people, and thus facilitating operations and enhancing labor efficiency as well as providing assurances of safety, etc. The above-mentioned achievements have begun to elicit the attention of the relevant ministries and departments.

Although our strength at present in the area of anthropological studies is still relatively weak, we have no doubt that the construction of the material and spiritual civilizations of socialism calls for a broadening and more rapid development of the study of anthropology, including physical

[3]*Physiology* (experimental textbook for institutions of higher education), pp. 92–93.

anthropology. As long as we are able to take a firm hold of the special characteristics of this field, be good at our studies, and take the initiative in cooperating with related subjects and sciences, this newly emergent field of anthropology is bound to make great strides forward in step with the advance of the four modernizations.

ZHANG ZHENBIAO

# 10 Modernization Requires Anthropometry

BECAUSE mathematics, physics, and chemistry have already been broadly applied in the practice of production, people generally have a better understanding of their content and applicability. On the other hand, many people are still very unfamiliar with the field of anthropometry. What does this discipline study? Of what use is it? In many cases, people know nothing at all about it.

Actually, anthropometry is a branch of anthropology. In terms of subject matter, it consists of the measurement of the human skeleton and the body. Its primary responsibility is to carry out a numerical analysis of the physical attributes of the human body on the basis of numerical data gathered through measurements, and then to describe the laws that govern the evolution of human physical characteristics. For example, skeletal measurement can provide us with the dimensions of human bones in each stage of human systemic growth and individual growth and thus help us understand transformations and developments in terms of bone structures at different stages of human evolution and in different races or nationalities, and thereby understand the mutual relations as well as changes in human bone structures in the processes of growth and aging. The measurement of a living body, as the term itself suggests, is simply the measuring of various parts of the body, including the head and face, torso, and limbs. Afterward, we can apply the method of mathematical statistics to the resulting dimensions of the various parts measured and carry out a quantitative analysis of the body's physical attributes.

From the above description, we can see that if we were to think that

"Xiandaihua xuyao renticeliangxue." *Huashi* (Fossils) 3 (1981): 1–2.

anthropology was just a field of science that studies the theoretical problems relating to the origins and development of the human race, that would not be a complete picture. In fact, anthropology (including anthropometry) is extremely closely related to the construction of the national economy, and its specialized knowledge and techniques have broad practical value in the modernization endeavor.

## Standardization of Protective Equipment for the Head and Face

With the development of modern industry, there is an increasingly urgent demand for labor protecting measures. Especially in the mining, chemical engineering, and national defense industries, recent developments have made the need for all sorts of head and face protection a matter of dire urgency, because this affects the safety and life of humans. Since the First World War, the United States, Britain, France, Japan, and the Soviet Union, in order to resolve the problem of how to standardize the design of gas masks, have organized their anthropologists in a project to conduct anthropometric measurement to protect their people from toxic gases. Since Liberation, related departments in our country have also conducted sporadic surveys and measurement projects, but the problem of how to standardize the protective equipment for the head and face remains unsolved. In terms of production design, the common tendency has been to copy the specifications of other countries. As a result, many products have not been able to meet the standards of practical use, and this has caused tremendous waste. Through anthropometric studies, we have proven that people of different races, regions, or nationalities have differing facial and skull measurements; therefore, in drawing up the product specifications for head protection equipment, each country must follow its own design instead of copying the specification of others.

In accord with the construction of modernization in our country, we have to develop a standardized series of specifications in the design and production of different products. To resolve this problem, we have in recent years, in cooperation with relevant departments, carried out an anthropometric survey of the adults of all provinces and have collected a massive amount of numerical data. By analyzing these data, we have come to understand the laws that govern changes and variations in the dimensions and locations of the various parts of the head and face of the contemporary people of China. In general, we have found, the length of the head of a person in Northeast China is relatively short, the width is relatively large, and the overall height of the head is medium. People in the Southwest, that is, the provinces of Yunnan, Guizhou, and Sichuan, generally have longer and lower heads, with a medium width. The people in South China—Guangdong, Guangxi, and Fujian provinces—generally have a higher, wider head of medium length. The residents of the Beijing region in general tend to have a shorter, wider head of medium or higher height. People of different regions also have different facial dimensions. The faces of people in the Northeast are wider in both the upper and the lower parts, and on the long side. The residents of Fujian, Guangdong, and Guangxi in South China generally have faces that are, in terms of their upper and lower parts, both narrower and shorter in comparison with faces of northerners. In very general terms, the changes in dimension of the facial features of China's residents are such that, in a basic sense, these measurements become gradually narrower and shorter as we move southward.

The measurement and statistical recording of the dimensions of thirty-two positions on the heads and faces of contemporary Chinese people have provided scientific data for the specifications and standardization of the design and manufacture of all sorts of protective headgear for adults. This will help enhance the quality and design of related products. For example, the departments concerned may refer to the dimensions of various positions on human heads and faces and design appropriate specifications accordingly, to produce gas masks suitable for the use of adults to insure their safety. They can also design and manufacture dust-repellent surgical mouthpieces according to measurements of the human mouth and nose. Similarly, standard specifications for eyeglass frames can be designed according to measurements of the length between the outer points of the two eyes, between the inner points of the two eyes, and the height of the nose bridge.

If we have a standard skull shape and various standard measurements of the human head and face, we can apply these standards to the inspection of related products and use the measurements as a basis for quality control.

## Standardization of Garment, Shoe, and Headgear Industries

People in northern China have a penchant for sending away as far as Guangzhou to purchase a pair of nylon pants that fits the body and is both relatively cheap and pleasing in style. This may indeed be the intention, but often things do not work out as originally hoped for. Instead, the pants that are purchased from Guangzhou turn out not to fit. This involves a knowledge of anthropometry.

Anthropometric surveys inform us that residents of different regions of our country are different not only in facial dimensions and complexions, but also in physical form. For example, in comparison with northerners, southern people are a bit shorter, and somewhat more conspicuous in the curvature of the chest and waist. In particular, the women of Guangzhou are slender, have relatively small waists, and have relatively smaller diameters around their derrieres and thighs. In contrast, northerners have less curvature variation between their chests and their waists, and in general terms their torsos are stouter and stronger. Their derrieres are somewhat broader, and their thighs are thicker. Therefore, when northerners, especially women, purchase a pair of trousers from Guangzhou, in spite of the aesthetic appeal and style, it will always feel too tight; in some cases they simply cannot not wear it at all. This, of course, affects the marketing of garments from Guangzhou. If, on the other hand, the designers in the garment industry could obtain valid anthropometric data and were able to come to grips with the principles governing the proportionate differences between the residents of the North and South in terms of overall body height, torso height, length of limbs, and so forth, and if they could also understand the laws governing the variations in the standardization series with regard to such things as chest, waist, thigh, and derriere circumference, etc., they would be able to design a series of standardized specifications for garments that would fit the needs of both northerners and southerners respectively. In that case, the garments produced at one factory may apply to markets far away throughout the country, they will satisfy people's needs and help increase the garment industry's usefulness.

For the same reason, if we can establish a standardized series [of indices] for the physiometric measurements of Chinese people, the designers in the various related areas will be able to design the specifications for hats [and other headgear] according to such [indices] as the head's circumference, its arrow-like arc, its crown-like arc, the height of the ears relative to the head, etc. They can also design the style, shape, and sizes of shoes according to such [indices] as the length and width of the foot and the height of [the arc] of the foot.

## Design in the Transportation Industry

The quality of an automobile is primarily measured in terms of the quality of its mechanical equipment. And yet, when it comes to the question of how the automobile's functions and abilities may be applied, the answers have a lot to do with the driver of the automobile. In that case these questions will also involve the placement of the driver's seat, the position of the steering wheel and its dimensions, the position and design of the gas pedal and brake pedal, etc. Naturally, if we are talking about a bus, then the design of the passengers' seats will also be involved. We have seen, for instance, such a case as a relatively short driver driving an automobile imported from Europe. The driver's foot cannot reach the gas pedal and he has to stretch his leg, forcing him to move forward. And when it comes to braking, he is almost off the seat and has to apply his whole body's strength to the brake pedal. All this makes the driver exhausted. This is because in a European-made automobile, the various controls in the driving chamber are designed according to the standardized physiometric series of Europeans, such as the standard measurements of the height of their seats, length of lower limbs, length of upper limbs, and arm strength. Therefore they are suitable for use by Europeans and not by Chinese, who have different physical forms and proportion of limbs.

Furthermore, the design of tractors, tanks, and airplanes must also give consideration to this problem. This means that we must have a better understanding of the dimensional proportions of every part of the human body and create a standardized physiometric series to provide scientific data for designing transportation and communication vehicles suitable to the conditions in our country.

In addition, we have also discovered that the desks and chairs of some middle schools do not meet the specified standards, and the desks and chairs in primary schools in general are even further from suitable standards—either the chairs are too low or the desks are too high. The students are very uncomfortable in such furniture, and this not only affects their efforts at listening in class, paying attention, and taking notes, but also is detrimental to their growth and physical development. This situation is caused by a lack of understanding of the physique of middle and primary school students, and of the proportions of the dimensions of their limbs. To solve this problem, we have to begin with basic anthropometric work, investigate and survey the physical properties of middle and primary school students, and find out their growth patterns so that we can formulate a standardized physiometric series. Consequently we can standardize classroom desks and chairs in our efforts to facilitate the development of educational undertakings.

**Applications in Forensic Medicine**

When forensic medical workers proceed to crack criminal cases, they rely on knowledge of anthropometry. For example, when they encounter what is called a "headless case," forensic medical experts have to rely on knowledge provided by anthropology to determine the gender and to estimate the age of the deceased. Furthermore, they use the numerical data from the measurements of limbs to estimate the overall height of the victim. Naturally, if the forensic medical expert understands the proportional relationships between the measurements of various parts and positions of the human body—such as the relationship between the length and width of the foot and overall body height—he can estimate body height and stoutness of the torso from the length and breadth of traces of footsteps. All these data are very useful in cracking cases.

If, through anthropometry, we can establish a "standard" head shape using the measurements of the various parts and positions of the head and face, then forensic medical experts can use the standardized measurements of such things as the width of the face, length of the nose, width of the mouth, distance between the eyes, and other data such as the thickness of tissue in various parts of the head and face that they have obtained to restore a skull to the facial features and complexion it had when the deceased was alive, and through that they may be able to determine the identity of the victim.

Anthropology has a history of only about fifty years in China. Because the majority of our research has been confined during these years to the study of fossil humans and apes, many people do not fully understand the applications of anthropology. However, if we can develop anthropometry on a nationwide scale and come to understand the physical types and shapes of people of different regions and nationalities and identify the laws that govern the variations in these shapes and types, we will not only provide critical data for the study of the theoretical questions concerning the origins of the people(s) of China, but also perform a great service for the socialist economic construction of our country. In sum, the study of anthropometry has an extensive future within the context of our modernization endeavor.

ZHANG SENSHUI

# 11 Paleolithic Research in China, 1980–1984

*Commemorating the Fifty-fifth Anniversary of the Discovery of the First Homo Erectus (Sinanthropus Pekinensis) Skull*

ON DECEMBER 2, 1929, Mr. Pei Wenzhong excavated the first complete skull of *Sinanthropus pekinenesis* in the "Lower Cave" of Locality No. 1 at Zhoukoudian, thereby writing a new chapter in the history of the research project at Zhoukoudian and also a new chapter in the history of paleoanthropological studies.

In the history of the study of the Zhoukoudian site, 1929 was a particularly meaningful year. That year saw the rising of the curtain on the study of the culture of *Sinanthropus pekinensis*, and also the beginning of the study of China's Paleolithic cultures by Chinese. In directing the excavation work at Zhoukoudian, Mr. Pei Wenzhong paid special attention to the gathering of cultural artifacts and was able to come up with excellent results. "In the Lower Cave, where the first piece of skull of *Sinanthropus pekinensis* was discovered, we also found a quartz flake that had clearly been struck" (Pei Wenzhong 1931). At the same time, he also collected burned bones that were excavated from the same geological stratum from which *Sinanthropus pekinensis* was dug. As D. Black later pointed out, "Since 1929, it has been possible for us to find, at any time, scattered fragments of animal bone that had clearly been burned, or in some cases, partially carbonized, among the excavated

"Wu nian lai Zhongguo jiushiqi wenhua de yanjiu: Jinian Beijing yuanren diyi tougaigu faxian wushiwu zhounian." *Renleixue xuebao* (Acta Anthropologica Sinica) 3, 4 (November 1984): 304–11.

material in the chief accumulated pile at Zhoukoudian. Because of suspicions that these were evidence of the use of fire, these specimens were carefully stored and preserved in a smaller room'' (Black 1931).

These discoveries and further studies later fully established that *Sinanthropus pekinensis* was an ancient hominid that already knew how to manufacture tools and use fire. This helped to resolve a debate that had been raging for many years at the time, namely, the debate over whether Java man was human or ape. Anthropologists then came to recognize that morphologically speaking, Java Ape-man (*Pithecanthropus*), which is akin to Peking Ape-man (*Sinanthropus pekinensis*), was a primitive human. This established without a doubt the existence of the *Homo erectus* stage in the process of human evolution.

Through macrocomparative studies and repeated chemical analyses, it was proven that the burned bones and ashes discovered in Locality No. 1 at Zhoukoudian were doubtlessly the remains of the use of fire by Peking Man. Therefore the history of human use of fire was back-dated from the Middle Paleolithic to the Early Paleolithic. This represented a pushing back of several hundreds of thousands of years. The excavation and study of stone tools allowed us to trace the time of ancient human beings in our country's territory as far back as 400,000 to 500,000 years ago.

In 1979, a conference in commemoration of the fiftieth anniversary of the discovery of the first skull of *Sinanthropus pekinensis* was convened in Beijing. Participants reviewed comprehensively the findings of the research done in our country on human fossils, the Paleolithic cultures, and related fields. They shared their experiences, summed up the past, and opened up avenues for the future. Since that conference, much new material has been discovered, and our researchers have published quite a few new research findings and some new interpretations. There has been, in this relatively short time, a rather brisk forward pace in the development of the study of Paleolithic cultures, and this has been very heartening. It would seem beneficial for us to take a brief look backward and analyze this development, because this would be useful for our work from here on in. We hope also to use this as a commemoration of the fifty-fifth anniversary of the discovery of the first skull of Peking Man.

**Brief Summary of the Research Findings**

From early 1980 to the summer of 1984, new material on more than forty sites has been published.[1] Most of the material on these site reports was discovered after 1980, not before. Some were materials that had been discovered in the late 1970s and worked on continuously into the 1980s. Only a small portion was made up of new research findings that came from research work newly done in the 1980s on the basis of discoveries made in the 1970s.

These new sites of Paleolithic culture being studied belong to many different stages of the Paleolithic age. Among them, five are, or possibly are, sites of the Early Paleolithic. They were discovered in the provinces of Hebei, Shanxi, and Shaanxi. There are also sites that are, or possibly are, from the Middle Paleolithic, and they are found in the territories of Shanxi and Shaanxi. In at least thirteen provinces and autonomous regions, namely, Heilongjiang, Jilin, Liaoning, Shanxi, Shaanxi, Gansu, Henan, Hubei, Yunnan, Guizhou, Sichuan, Jiangsu, and the Guangxi Zhuang Autonomous Region, we have found relics of the Late Paleolithic.

The new discoveries have greatly expanded what we understand to be the area of distribution of Paleolithic culture in our country. In comparison with [the area we knew of] five years ago, [this new territory] represents an expansion, in terms of latitudes, one degree northward. In the new configuration, the territory extends as far north as Mohe County in Heilongjiang province. In the southern part [of the territory] there is also a slight expansion [in the east-west dimensions]; we discovered a Paleolithic site in Hekou County of Yunnan. As a result [of collating] this new material and past findings, it appears that we can now perceive the general trends of the development of Paleolithic culture in our country, in terms of the temporal and spatial dimensions, in the following way: Early Paleolithic culture was distributed in the territory between 101°55′E and 124°8′E longitude and between 25°41′N and 41°15′N latitude. Then, in the mid-Paleolithic, the Paleolithic culture expanded, but we cannot be clear on the degree of diffusion eastward, southward, and northward—it appears that [in these three directions] the area of distribution generally remained the same as in the early period, but there seems to have been a greater development to the west. It is possible that cultural diffusion in this middle period may have reached as far west as

---

[1]The actual sites discovered are much more numerous. It is reported, for example, in Baise Prefecture, Guangxi, seventy-one sites have been excavated. In an area of close to 20 square kilometers at Longgang in Hanzhong, Shaanxi, stone tools have been found in many places, but they are all counted as findings of one site.

87°21'W; that is, to the area of the Sure Locality in Dingri County of the Tibetan Autonomous Region. Then, in the Late Paleolithic, the culture diffused even farther to the west and north and came to be distributed over a vast territory encompassed by the 80°01'E and 126°21'E longitudes and 20°40'N and 53°20'N latitudes.

In these last five years, a rich inventory of artifacts and Paleolithic culture remains from all stages has been excavated. The count of stone implements discovered is in the tens of thousands, and there are also hundreds of bone implements and several dozen pieces of horn tools and decorative fragments. In quite a few sites we have discovered traces of fire, and we found large quantities of burned bones and layers of ash deposits in varying degrees of thickness. All these have allowed us to gain a greater understanding of Paleolithic culture in our country. As for stone tools, although we have found no clear evidence of sudden breakthroughs in flake-making technology or in the type of tools used, or in the repair and maintenance technology of these stone implements, we have nevertheless found evidence of clear progress in making and using bone and horn scrapers and polished stone tools. This has greatly enriched our knowledge in these areas.

In the forty-some years from the 1930s to the 1970s, very few polished or scrape bone and antler tools of the Paleolithic age have been [excavated, reported, and] published. In total, only five bone implements[2] and three deer antler pieces were reported to have traces of artificial processing, but none of them was a tool used in production. All in all, we had then a sense of the shortage of bone and antler implements. This situation has greatly changed since 1980. In 1982, Cao Zetian published a research report on the bone and antler implements excavated at Maomaodong. That site is in the territory of Xingyi County of Guizhou. It was excavated in the mid-1970s. The specimens described [in the report] included four pieces of bone implements[3] and eight pieces of antler tools. Since early 1980, repeated excavations have been conducted at Chuandong and Hongtudong (Red Earth Cave) of Puding in Guizhou, and at Xianrendong (Immortals' Cave) in Haicheng County of Liaoning, and these yielded very rich discoveries of bone and antler tools exceeding

---

[2]This does not include a bone tool drilled with a hole discovered in the cultural stratum at the C Site of Jinniu Mountain in Yingkou, Liaoning. This is because it is difficult to determine the bone tool's category. This also does not include the bone tools of the Changbin culture found in Taiwan as they belong to a later age.

[3]The bone awl with a tilted point listed in the original classification is not included here.

five hundred pieces. This is a finding of tremendous significance in the study of Paleolithic culture in our country in the last five years.

As for the typology of bone tools, we have been able to increase the number from just two categories, namely, bone awls and bone needles, to six categories, adding bone knives, bone shovels, pronged bone implements, and bone clubs. Within the category of bone awls, the blunt-pointed bone awls discovered at Maomaodong are a bone tool never recorded before.

Owing to the discovery of large quantities of bone tools and the finding of quite a lot semifinished products, we have attained a certain understanding of the production process [of bone implements]. We believe that the manufacturing of bone tools goes through the following general steps: First, a long piece of bone of a mammal would be selected and cracked into pieces. From the various pieces a fragment suitable for use would be selected, and this would become the rough form [of the tool]. The next step would be to hammer this rough form into a gross shape of the type of tool desired. Additional gouging, scraping, and paring down would then be done on this grossly shaped tool, and the scars left on the fragment of bone during the hammering stage would be smoothed out. This then becomes the preliminary form of the eventual tool. The last step would be grinding and polishing—first a coarse grinding [of the surface] and then a finer polishing, resulting in the final shape of the tool. In this way, bone instruments of various types that are regular in form and shape and are either polished or somewhat polished would eventually be produced.

As for antler implements, there are mainly two types of such tools: antler shovels and fishing fork-spears.[4] The former type is divided into two subtypes, namely, shovels made of the trunk of the antler and shovels made from [flat] pieces of the antler. The steps in making antler implements are relatively simple. First, there is the selection of a rough form, and second, the production of the implement by scraping and paring down. In concrete terms, a section of antler must be chopped off, either from the main trunk (of the antler) or a piece of tine. If the antler implement [to be produced] was to be of a [flat] piece of antler, then this section had to be chopped into [flat] pieces. Then the cross-section [of antler] where it was chopped off would have to be smoothed out. [When this was done], the first step, i.e., the selection of the rough form, would be completed. The second step would be to scrape out a blade edge

[4] According to the news release by Fu Renyi in *Liaoning Daily*, February 25, 1984, p. 2.

longitudinally, on one end of the section of antler, using a scraping or paring tool. This blade edge is essentially a slanted, sloping edge. The angle of the blade is about 45 degrees. This would then be the full process of preparing an antler shovel. In the main, this is processing on one side [of the object]; only a small number [of specimens] were made with the blade edge on both sides.

Since the beginning of the 1980s, a relatively large amount of knowledge has been gathered about the Paleolithic culture in our country, and this has made it possible, after many years of uncertainty, to resolve questions about the dates of the stone implements at a number of sites. Nevertheless, due to the discovery of new material and further research, a number of new questions have been raised, and these will be briefly discussed below, period by period.

**The Early Paleolithic**

[ . . . ]

**The Middle Paleolithic**

[The essay here sums up much of the recent work reported in English and in greater detail in *Paleoanthropology and Paleolithic Archaeology in the People's Republic of China*, edited by Wu Rukang and John W. Olsen (Orlando: Academic Press, 1985).]

**Late Paleolithic**

We can see from the newly discovered material and the new studies made of material discovered in the past that there is a considerable difference between the Late Paleolithic cultures in northern China and those in southern China. Let me discuss them in terms of the different regions.

*Northern China*

In the North, the cultural tradition of the Early and Middle Paleolithic, which was predominantly represented by small stone tools, was continued and developed. There are discoveries of this continuing culture in an area reaching eastward to Jilin and westward to Gansu. Among these discoveries are representative sites such as at Yumenkou in Hancheng of Shaanxi, and at Xianrendong in Haicheng of Liaoning. Then there is the Xueguan site in Puxian County of Shanxi, which is representative of another cultural type altogether.

Among the relics at the caves of Yumenkou over a thousand stone tools have been excavated, along with traces of the use of fire and fossils of deer and rhinoceros (Liu Shiwo et al. 1984). The stone tools here are primarily made of quartz and flint and are basically small in size. Except for the choppers and cores among them, there are extremely few pieces that exceed 40 millimeters in length. Flaking is done by the percussion method, and flakes and cores are mostly of irregular shapes. A small number are relatively regular in shape; for example, the flakes that are triangular or trapezoidal and the cores that are shaped like a tray. The tools found here are primarily made from flakes and are relatively simple in categorization. There are three types altogether, namely, scrapers, points, and choppers. The primary type is scrapers and single-edge instruments. Those tools are all made by the percussion method, and for the most part they bear finishing work done on the obverse side. Retouching is in general relatively coarse and crude. The stone tool industry that we have found at the Yumenkou site basically retained the characteristics of the cultural tradition that prevailed in northern China, which is represented predominantly by small stone tools. It is a major member of this cultural tradition. Its discovery has served to link together, in a very intimate fashion, the components of this type of culture on both sides of the Yellow River.

The Xianrendong site was discovered in the spring of 1981. It was excavated once in October of the same year and then again in 1983, yielding abundant cultural artifacts and remains. In addition to almost ten thousand stone tools (mostly small ones) and rich traces of the use of fire, there are also many decorative pieces made of animal teeth and stone in which holes have been drilled, bone needles and awls made by grinding of deer antler and bone pieces, and fishing spears with reverse hooks on both sides (see Fu Renyi 1983, 1984). Bone needles and decorative pieces with holes in them that are made of wolf or badger teeth (in these cases the holes are found in the center of the root of the tooth, and are evidently made by drilling with sharpened, pointed tools on both sides of the tooth) have been found earlier in the Shandingdong site at Zhoukoudian. But the discovery of fishing spears here is the first time such a discovery was made among the cultural relics of the late-Paleolithic cultures in our country. This provided direct evidence for the claim that human beings of this period had engaged in the activity of catching fish. These relics indicate that the age in question cannot be "the early period of the Upper Pleistocene era" (see Fu Renyi 1983). Undoubtedly, it would have to belong to the Late Paleolithic, or the later period of the Upper Pleistocene. It is clear that this culture is closely related to the Shandingdong culture. It supplements [our understanding about the culture of this period] by providing a very large quantity of stone implements, which are not found in considerable quantity at the Shandingdong site. It therefore allows us to have a better, more comprehensive understanding of the cultural type that contains a large amount of microlithic tools and also, at the same time, a considerable amount of decorative pieces and bone and antler tools.

The Xueguan site at Puxian County [southern Shanxi] was discovered in 1964. Two excavations have been made here, one in 1979 and another in 1980. These yielded 4,777 stone tools, which are $C^{14}$ dated to 13,550 ± 150 B.P. These tools can be divided into two categories, one of which is microlithic tools, consisting of large quantities of stone leaves, some long flakes, and cone-shaped and wedge-shaped cores, as well as small stone tools made from these. The other category is of relatively large stone tools, mainly made of flakes that appear to have been manufactured skillfully by the "finger-padding" method. The forms and shapes [of those tools] are quite regular. The most representative tools among these are convex blade scrapers and sharpeners. The finishing work on these is very fine, as evidenced in the sharpness of the blade and the balance in the line of the blade.

Combinations of tools including both microlithic tools and finely finished scrapers and sharpeners were discovered as early as the late 1950s at Qingshuihe County and the Zhunge'er Banner in Inner Mongolia, at Bianguan County in Shanxi, and in 1963 at Lingwu County in Ningxia. These earlier sites were all located at the base terraces on the banks of the Yellow River. Furthermore, all of these sites were excavated on the surface of the earth. At the time of their discovery, they were deduced to be artifacts of the Late Paleolithic on the basis of the typology of the shapes of the stone tools and of the finished technology that they represented (see Zhang Senshui 1959, 1960). The findings at the Xueguan site provide reliable comparative stratigraphic and dating evidence for the claim that this culture type was broadly distributed throughout the banks of the Yellow River (reaching Ningwu County to the west and Puxian County to the east).

## Southern China

Last year, an interim summary was made regarding [the study of] Late

Paleolithic cultures in the southern part of our country. In general, the Paleolithic cultures of this region at this period represented, on the one hand, the continuation of an earlier legacy, and, on the other hand, a peculiarity of their own type of development (see Zhang Senshui 1983). When the study of the Tongliang culture was made, it was proposed that we "ought to pay attention to the problems of the unevenness, tortuousness, and complexity of the development of Paleolithic cultures in our country." Also, it was suggested that "the viewpoint of linear development, and the doctrine of cultural development in which [culture is seen to have] originated from one central point and then radiated outward on all sides, has become less and less explicable as the study of Paleolithic archaeology in our country has developed" (see Li Xuanmin et al. 1981).

The discovery of stone tools at Caohai, Weining, Guizhou, in 1982 was not mentioned in the interim report. The stone tools here were all manufactured by the percussion method; finishing work was often done by reduplicative facet processing and steep facet processing, resulting in an irregular polygonal shape in many cases. There are more cases of multiple edges than of single edges, and edges are often blunt, with the angle frequently larger than 80 degrees. From this we can see that the cultural complexion of this site very much resembles that of Guanyindong culture. We may consider the stone tools of Caohai to belong to the same cultural tradition as the Guanyindong culture. It might be an inheritor of the early phase of Guanyindong culture, or it might be a variant of the late phase. From the discovery of the stone tools of Caohai, we may surmise that a cultural type exists in northwestern Guizhou that is represented by these stone tools, or, in other words, a late version of the Guanyindong culture.

## Major Findings in Related Disciplines

Here I am referring to the chronological and climate studies in ancient times with regard to ancient hominid and Paleolithic cultural sites. Although these studies do not themselves belong within the boundaries of the study of Paleolithic culture, they are deeply related to the latter and have significance for the study of sequential relationships among various Paleolithic cultures, and of the relationship among human beings, their culture, and the sphere of nature. For these reasons let me pick out the most significant findings [in these fields of study] and briefly describe them, so that we may have a more complete understanding.

Since 1980, in addition to $C^{14}$ dating, we have successively published data on the determination of the age of ancient hominid and Paleolithic sites using such methods as archaeomagnetic dating, thermoluminescence, uranium isotopes, and amino acid analysis. The greatest amount of work was done on the site of *Sinanthropus pekinensis*. As for the findings in this area, such issues as the discrepancies [among findings regarding the] data of Yuanmou Ape-man [a *Homo erectus* form] determined by the archaeomagnetic dating method have been discussed in great length by Professor Wu Rukang. Here we will omit this and mention instead, as a supplement, the findings of other research projects. For example, regarding the age of Hexian Ape-man, it has been determined by thermoluminescense that "the date of Hexian Man's existence at that particular site ought not be more than 200,000 years ago" (Li Huhou et al. 1983). The date of the Xujiayao culture, determined by the uranium isotope method, is placed at about 100,000 years ago (Chen Tiemei et al. 1982). The date of Salawusu is determined to be 37,000-50,000 years B.P. (Yuan Sixun et al. 1983). Also, An Zhimin has, on the basis of $C^{14}$ dating of a number of sites, made some changes in the estimates of the age of a number of individual sites. For example, he suggested that the site of Shandingdong should not be placed at $16915 \pm 420$ years B.C., but should be at $8520 \pm 360$ years B.C. instead. He also made similar adjustments to, or in some cases raised questions and doubts about, the age, or the nature of the culture, of nine other sites.

Studies on climate conditions in ancient times have been published only in regard to the *Sinanthropus pekinensis* site and the Dingcun site plus a few neighboring cultural sites. A relatively commonly held opinion is that the climate during the period in which Peking Man lived at Zhoukoudian was a generally temperate one, but that there were also, over time, several changes between dryer and damper periods and between colder and warmer periods. As for the explanation of the climatic conditions related to the different geological strata, however, there have been many opinions, and it is impossible to tell which one is right and which is wrong. As far as the studies of the Dingcun site and others [around it] are concerned, the general opinion maintains that during the Upper Pleistocene period the region around Dingcun went through two cycles of change between cold and warmth. "The human beings of Dingcun lived in a climatic environment that is located in the southern part of the warm and humid temperate zone and the northern part of the subtropical zone." The top part of its fifth stratum and its sixth stratum, on the other hand, "reflect a similarity with the grassland type of climate, that is, dry and generally cool." Near Ding Village, on the other side of the Fen River, there is site 7701 ($C^{14}$ dated at 26,400 ± 800 B.C.). The stratum at this site that contains microlithic tools belongs to a "climatic environment that is warm and moist," whereas the various strata above reflect climatic conditions that have become "dry and cool" (Chen Wanyong 1983).

At this time, as we commemorate the fifty-fifth anniversary of the discovery of the first skull of *Sinanthropus pekinensis* and the beginning of the research on its culture, we are mindful, with deep gratitude, of the tremendous efforts and sacrifices of those scholars who have preceded us as pioneers in the work on the Zhoukoudian site and given so much of themselves to the development of the study of paleoanthropology in China. These are professors Li Jie, Yang Zhongjian, and Pei Wenzhong. If we could learn from their determined professionalism and their spirit of being bold in inquiry and diligent in work, and if we could mobilize all the active and enthusiastic elements among us to strengthen our basic training, take solid steps, and work hard, we believe we would see major strides in the progress of archaeological study of Paleolithic cultures in our country.

## References Cited

An Zhimin (1983). "Zhongguo wanqi jiushiqi de C-14 duandai he wenti" ($C^{14}$ periodization of the Late Paleolithic finds in China and its problems), *Renleixue xuebao* (Acta Anthropologica Sinica) 2:342–51.

Li Xuanmin and Zhang Senshui (1981). "Tongliang jiushiqi wenhua zhi yanjiu" (The study of Paleolithic culture at Tongliang), *Gu jizhuidongwu yu gu renlei* (Vertebrata Pal Asiatica) 19:359–71.

Li Huhou and Mei Yi (1983). "Hexian ren de shangxian nianling" (The upper boundaries of the age of Hexian Man), *Kexue tongbao* (General bulletin of the sciences) 11:703.

Chen Wanyong (1983). "Shanxi 'Dingcun ren' shenghuo shiqi de gu qihou" (Climatic conditions of ancient times during which "Ding Village Man" in Shanxi lived), *Renleixue xuebao* 2:184–95.

Zhang Senshui (1959). "Neimeng zhongnanbu he shanxi xibeibu xinfaxian de jiushiqi" (Newly discovered Paleolithic finds in Central-South Inner Mongolia and Northwest Shanxi), *Gu jizhuidongwu yu gu renlei* 1:31–40.

Zhang Senshui (1960). "Neimeng zhongnanbu jiushiqi de xincailiao" (New material on the Paleolithic finds in Central-South Inner Mongolia), *Gu jizhuidongwu yu gu renlei* 2:129–40.

Zhang Senshui (1983). "Woguo nanfang jiushiqi shidai wangqi wenhua de ruogan wenti" (Some questions concerning the Late Paleolithic cultures in southern

China), *Renleixue xuebao* 2:118-30.

Yuan Sixun, Chen Tiemei, and Gao Shijun (1983). "Yong youzi xi fa ceding Hetu ren he Salawusu wenhua de niandai" (Using the uranium isotope method to determine the age of Hetu Man and the Salawusu culture), *Renleixue xuebao* 2:90-94.

Cao Zetian (1982). "Maomaodong shiqi de yanjiu" (A study of the stone tools of Maomao Cave), *Gu jizhuidongwu yu gu renlei* 20:155-64.

Cao Zetian (1982). "Maomaodong de guqi he jiaoqi" (The bone tools and antler implements of Maomao Cave), *Renleixue xuebao* 1:36-41.

Fu Renyi (1983). "Anshan haicheng xianrendong jiushiqi shidai yizhi shiqu" (An experimental excavation of the Paleolithic sites at Xianren Cave in Hiacheng, Anshan), *Renleixue xuebao* 2:103.

Black, D. (1931). "Evidence of the Use of Fire by Sinanthropus," *Bulletin of the Geological Society of China* 11:107-108.

Pei, Wen-chung (1931). "Notice of the Discovery of Quartz and Other Stone Artifacts of the Choukoutian Cave Deposit," *Bulletin of the Geological Society of China* 11:109-46.

# Part V

# Developing Ethnology

LIN YAOHUA

# 12 New China's Ethnology: Research and Prospects

THE SCOPE of ethnology, as a specialized field of study that takes as its object nationalities or human communities, is both broad and deep. The breadth lies in the fact that from ancient times and up to the present, as long as human groups or communities have existed, there has been something for ethnologists to study. Similarly, throughout the entire world, wherever there are peoples, there will be subject matter for ethnologists to study. The depth lies in the fact that with regard to every nationality, regardless of how powerful it may be, everything about it needs to be studied—its origins, developments, attributes and characteristics, language, economy, culture, and even the customs and habits of everyday life. In today's world there are more than two thousand nationalities, and in our country alone there are more than fifty. The origins of nationalities can be traced all the way back to the earliest times when the human race and human society first appeared. From this we can easily perceive that the task confronting our ethnologists is a heavy and difficult one. We must be able to acknowledge the achievements already attained, sum up the fruits of our research, plan new research, and nurture new talent in the field so as to continue to open up a broader avenue for study.

I

Since the founding of New China, the study of ethnology has attained great achievements. Even though it has traversed a circuitous path, and although during the period when the "Gang of Four" rode roughshod its achievements were negated wholesale and the field was thoroughly

"Xin Zhongguo de minzuxue yanjiu yu zhanwang." *Minzu yanjiu* (Nationality studies) 2 (1981): 48–55.

strangled, nonetheless, the results that China's ethnologists have produced under the guidance of the party are not to be denied. The results of thirty years of effort eloquently prove that the field of ethnology in our country is a scientific and Marxist-oriented field that serves the interests of the party's work in dealing with minority nationalities.

The path on which New China's ethnology has progressed is closely connected to the practice of revolution and construction undertaken by people of all nationalities in China under the party's leadership. As far back as the Yan'an period, for instance, we already had such things as historical and social study of the Hui nationality and the Mongol nationality, which exemplified how we could be guided by the party to employ a Marxist standpoint, viewpoint, and methodology to analyze and study the problem of minority nationalities. For example, the book *Hui-hui minzu wenti* (Questions on the Hui nationality) involved the inquiry into the origins of the Hui nationality, its name, distribution, socioeconomic development and contemporary conditions, etc. What the book employed was precisely the ethnological method of investigation and analysis. Even though at the time the terminology of "ethnological studies" was not yet used, in reality what was done then was the work of ethnology. This book had a profound and long-lasting significance by its determination that the Hui-hui people were indeed a nationality, and by guiding the Hui people in pursuing a path of revolutionary struggle. This is a good example of how the work of ethnological studies can serve the interests of the party in dealing with nationalities.

After Liberation we had, for the sake of the unity of the great family of the motherland and the solidarity of the various nationalities, an urgent need to carry out the party's nationality policies and do work among the national minorities. At that time, our great historical task consisted of identifying the various nationalities and acknowledging their status as such, guaranteeing the equality of all nationalities in the areas of rights and privileges, implementing the autonomous self-government in the minority regions, helping the minority people to carry out social reform, to develop their economy and culture, and to gradually abolish the inequality that existed among the different nationalities, which had been handed down through the ages, and to help the more backward nationalities move ahead to join the ranks of the more advanced so that they could develop together and make the transition to socialism in step with one another. This task could not have been accomplished without the huge amount of scientific research carried out by scholars and workers in related disciplines under the guidance of the party. The labor of ethnologists is to be counted among these efforts.

In the first few years after Liberation, ethnological workers undertook a great deal of investigative work, particularly in the area of identifying nationalities. Prior to Liberation, the Guomindang reactionaries had executed a policy of oppression and discrimination against nationalities. They had deliberately negated the existence of minority nationalities and deepened the sense of hatred and alienation among the minorities. After Liberation, the people of all nationalities attained, under the leadership of the party, national equality. The system of national oppression and suppression was abolished. Many minority nationalities who had been so oppressed in the past that they had not dared to use the name of their nationality now had the courage to proclaim publicly their national identities and express the wish to become an honorable member of the great family of nationalities. Following the publicity about the nationalities policy and its implementation, gradually there emerged a wave of new names of nationalities and tribes that had not often been heard in the past. In the general election of 1954, it was said that the number of self-claimed nationality identities amounted to several hundred. Were each of these several hundred names or designations truly representative of an individual nationality in our country? To resolve this problem the party proposed that we embark upon the task of identifying the nationalities. This question not only affects the policy of equality and solidarity among the nationalities, but it has a very close relationship also with a whole series of questions, such as carrying out the autonomous self-government of minority regions, exercising self-governing rights among the national minorities, developing the politics, economics, and cultures of the nationalities, and so forth.

To launch the scientific work of identifying and distinguishing nationality groups we had to integrate the principle of Marxist-Leninist nationality theory that dealt with the formation of human communities or nationalities with the concrete conditions prevailing among each group that laid claim to the identity of a nationality, and study these situations analytically. At that time, in addition to affirming the minority nationalities that have historically been recognized as such, we also carried out investigations, surveys, and studies with regard to the very large new batch of groups that laid claim to the name and identity of a nationality having cropped up in the various minority regions throughout the country. This task of identifying and distinguishing nationalities was accomplished by ethnology workers in cooperation with workers in other fields of science, especially linguistics. Language being one of the most important attributes of a nationality, without linguistic knowledge the identifying work could not possibly have been done. For example, at the time, there were some three million people of the Yi nationality widely distributed in the four provinces of Yunnan, Sichuan, Guizhou, and Guangxi. Among them there were over one hundred ethnic groups with different claims to tribal or nationality identities and titles (including those both self-proclaimed and touted by others). Through the comparative analysis of the language of each of these groups, by tracing the historical migrations and transformations of each of them across the vast territory covered by the four provinces, by tracing these groups' crossmingling and cohabitation with other nationalities and the disequilibriums thus generated in their socioeconomic development, and by comparative studies regarding their cultural life, customs, practices, and psychological conditions, we concluded that all of these groups with different claims on nationality titles were members of a common nationality, the Yi. In the end, the broad masses of the Yi nationality also concurred that they should be presented as a united minority nationality.

As a result of nationality identification, in 1956 the State Council proclaimed that there were a total of fifty-one minority nationalities in China. Since then, there has been added to the list the Pumi nationality of Yunnan, the Menba and Luoba nationalities of Tibet, and, most recently, the Jinuo nationality of Yunnan. Thus at present we acknowledge that there are fifty-five minority nationalities in China as a whole, or fifty-six nationalities including the Han. It is our country's unique, creative achievement to undertake to determine the number of nationalities through such scientific research work. How many nationalities are there in the world as a whole? No one knows for sure. The Soviet Union is a multinationality country, but as for how many nationalities there are in the Soviet Union, Soviet scholars seem each to have a different figure. The same is true of India. In 1956 I was invited to attend the All-Soviet Ethnography Conference of the Soviet Union, which was attended by quite a few international delegates. In my conference report, "The Tasks Raised for Ethnology by the Current Nationalities Work in China," I cited our experience in identifying and distinguishing nationalities. This report, and the work that we had done, received much praise at the conference.

In the spring of 1979, while attending an international conference in

Mexico, I found Latin American and Mexican scholars to be very interested in our work. They especially inquired about ethnological studies in our country, and they were extremely intrigued by questions related to nationality identification, such as the methods, criteria, and standards used. Indeed, the ethnological circles of New China have made significant achievements in the identification of nationalities, work that has not been done in any other country of the world. If we can successfully sum up our experiences and raise our theoretical level, we will undoubtedly elicit the broad attention of ethnological circles throughout the world.

The principal research method of ethnological studies is field investigation. In addition, documentary historical materials are also used to study nationality communities around the world that were, or are, at different stages of social development. The focus generally is on observing and studying in the field the various social and economic conditions of a nationality, to analyze these conditions and draw conclusions therefrom. Since Liberation, our ethnology and other social science workers have performed unprecedented large-scale social surveys. Their arduous and penetrating efforts have been witnessed by us all, nobody can deny them. The portion that relates to the study of ethnology, the material that has been accumulated, and the results that have been attained all are a most valuable treasure that China's ethnology workers are able to offer to the motherland and its people.

From 1950 to 1956, when ethnology workers participated in the work of the visiting delegations or work teams sent by the party center to the various regions inhabited by minority nationalities, and as they took part in the research and survey organizations of the various minority nationality areas in the name of research groups, they always started by getting to the bottom of the actual conditions prevailing in those nationality areas and striving to attain at least a preliminary understanding of such things as the stage of development of the society and the economy, class situation, and relations among the various nationalities, so as to provide [the relevant authorities] with the necessary data and basis for ethnic guidelines and the formulation of concrete nationalities policies. For example, in Yunnan Province, ethnologists and cadres involved in nationalities work attained excellent results in social investigation and survey and provided valuable material for formulating the policy of social reform among the minority nationalities. Yunnan is a province consisting of many nationalities. In addition to the Han nationality, there are twenty-two minority nationalities in that province. Owing to a variety of historical reasons, however, and chiefly to the long-term oppression and exploitation by the reactionaries both inside and outside the province, there has been a severe imbalance in the patterns of socioeconomic development among the various nationalities. Prior to the democratic reform, many minority nationalities still retained a primitive commune system, or even a slavery or serf system. Therefore, it was essential that first a social survey be conducted among the various minority nationalities. As a result of the great effort put into the investigative work, it was possible to ascertain the ethnic distinctions between the various minority nationalities and the [patterns of] distribution of their populations, and to get to the bottom of the socioeconomic structure and class relations within each group. This provided a systematic, scientific basis for carrying out the [policy of] regional nationality autonomy and implementation of democratic reform among the minority people.

From 1955 to 1957, democratic reform was carried out in the regions inhabited by minority nationalities in Yunnan. In those areas where the slavery and serf system still existed, reform was carried out by adopting a policy of "peaceful negotiations." On the premise of abolishing the system of ownership by feudal masters and slaveowners, the policy of redemption was adopted vis-à-vis the upper echelons of the nationalities; this was a principle of eliminating [their ownership status] as a class while uniting with, educating, and reforming [them] as people. At the same time, with regard to those few areas that were making the transition from a primitive commune [state] to a class society, the policy of "direct transition" was adopted. As there was no concentration of land ownership in those areas, there was no need to make the redistribution of land an active stage [in the reform process]; rather, it was possible, on the basis of gradually abolishing the special privileges between nationalities and within each nationality, to launch a movement of mutual aid and cooperativization and thus directly make the transition to socialism. As a result, a tremendous victory was attained in the democratic revolution of the minority nationalities regions of Yunnan. From 1950–1955, when the research work was underway, to 1957, when the democratic reform was accomplished, nationalities research consistently marched at the forefront of the nationalities work in Yunnan. By investigation and research, we discovered the laws governing the development of work among nationalities, and by setting guidelines and policies in accordance with the actual situations and testing and improving these policies and guidelines through practice, in the end we were able to make headway in nationalities work.

In 1956, after the (Draft) National Twelve-year Plan for Scientific Research was formulated, and under the direct leadership of the Nationalities Commission of the National People's Congress, minority nationalities social history investigation groups were formed, to launch a project of social history investigation and research of unprecedented dimensions. In 1958, the investigation groups expanded their coverage from eight provinces and regions to sixteen, and at their height involved some one thousand staff. The study of the social history of the minority nationalities was a comprehensive research undertaking. People engaged in the work included researchers in many different fields, and the result of the project was the crystallization of the joint efforts of researchers from many disciplines.

Each social history research group launched into its work with enthusiasm. From 1959 on, they wrote drafts for three sets of collective publications, namely, outline histories of the minority nationalities, outline geographical-historical gazettes, and descriptions of the general conditions of autonomous zones. According to the statistical records of the Institute of Nationalities Studies of the Chinese Academy of Social Sciences, over 190 publications emerged from the many investigative materials that were put together, totaling approximately 14 million words. In addition, more than 150 items have been put together but are not yet at the printers, covering about 15 million words. This does not include the raw data that served as the subject matter of the investigations, not to mention the many documents that were compiled and published locally by the sixteen investigation and survey groups. These drafts of books and compilations of survey material provided a sound basis for the party's work among the nationalities, and for its formulation of plans and guidelines on how to carry out social reform and reconstruction in minority regions.

These investigative groups also produced more than a dozen scientific documentary films on minority people who still preserved primitive social forms—the slavery system or the serf system. These documentaries photographed valuable and rare material on actual forms and phenomena, and they serve to supplement the oral material on social and historical investigations. They provide material for and enrich the study of the history of the social development of various nationalities and ethnic groups in our country, as well as the history of the social development of humanity.

During the social history investigations, the question of the nature of minority nationality societies emerged as one of the most significant lessons in ethnological studies. Through living material we were able to perceive the actual process through which human society evolved and developed. Prior to Liberation, for many historical reasons, the various minority nationalities in our country existed in a state of inequality in terms of socioeconomic development. The fifty or so minority nationalities, which made up approximately 6 percent of the country's population, possessed many different modes of social economy. In general, about thirty of these minority nationalities, which together made up about 30 million people, retained a feudalistic landlord economy. Of these, a few nationalities produced in varying degrees capitalistic elements. These were mostly the people who had closer contact with the Han nationality, and many were commingled with the Han. They were therefore deeply affected by Han influences. Still, in terms of development they were different from the Han nationality, and in terms of form they retained systems and attributes that were inconsistent with those of the Han. There were also many other minority nationalities that, prior to Liberation or before the democratic reform, retained even more backward forms of society and economy. Of these, about 4 million people retained what can be called an early feudal system, that is, a feudalistic serf system; and about 1 million people retained the slavery system, and about 700,000 people retained a primitive communal system. Someone once said that the social conditions of the various minority nationalities of China, before and after Liberation, epitomized a living history of the social evolution of the human race. In light of the ten years (1956–1966) of investigation, we may say that this is by no means an exaggeration. Our country's ethnological workers came to grasp first-hand material through field investigation and came to understand and acknowledge the various conditions of the society, economy, and cultures of the minority nationalities. This not only promoted the development and progress of the various nationalities, but also greatly enriched the treasury of our ethnological studies and allowed the ranks of our ethnological researchers to grow to maturity and strength in the crucible of actual practice.

Our country has always paid attention to the study of ethnology and its development, and at the same time to the nurturing and cultivation of ethnological research personnel. As early as in 1950, Premier Zhou personally instructed immediate action in implementing the plan to construct the Central Institute of Nationalities. Later, nine more nationalities institutes were set up in provinces and autonomous regions. Within the Central Institute of Nationalities' history department, an ethnology specialty was established. In it a curriculum on ethnology was taught; courses included, for instance, "Foundations of Ethnology," "History of Primitive Societies," "Chinese Ethnography," "World Ethnography," and courses in related disciplines such as anthropology and archaeology. To further cultivate research personnel, the institute also offered two terms of an ethnological studies research seminar. Other places, such as Fudan University, Zhongshan University, Xiamen University, and Yunnan University, as well as many local nationalities institutes, also established courses or even specialties in ethnology. The graduates and graduate students in ethnology of these institutes are distributed throughout all minority areas in China to pursue research and teaching work. They have become the backbone force of ethnological studies in our country and down the years have produced many good results contributing to the party's cause of nationalities work.

In the early 1960s, ethnology workers of this country took part in compilation and editing the entries related to the nationalities issue in the *Cihai* [a Chinese encyclopedic dictionary]. In particular, two categories, Chinese nationalities and nationalities around the world, were principally the responsibility of the participating ethnologists. In compiling and editing those glossaries and entries in *Cihai* and in scrutinizing and examining the drafts of those three sets of collected books on the issue of nationalities, many difficult items, terms, and questions were raised. At the time, under the sponsorship of the Guidance Committee for the Study of Nationalities History, a series of forums, seminars, and discussions of major scholastic significance were held. They included, for example, seminars on the meaning and content of the terms "ethnology," "nation," "tribe," etc.; on the origins and formation of certain minority nationalities; on the relationships among nationalities in history; and on the question of how to assess certain minority historical figures. Some of the problems were resolved through these discussions; others remained the subject of continued debate. In any case, these discussion times did enliven the academic atmosphere within the realm of ethnology and truly carried out the party's principle of "let a hundred flowers bloom, let a hundred schools of thought contend."

In addition to the above, ethnologists in China have also done much work in other areas; but let us not attempt to describe it all here.

From Liberation to right before the Cultural Revolution, research work in the field of ethnology, led by the party and sustained by its concern, had moved forward uninterruptedly and achieved gladdening results. However, just as we were forging ahead with confidence, Lin Biao and the "Gang of Four" and their ilk brought a great calamity upon the country. As in other spheres, nationalities work and ethnological studies also suffered severe damage. Lin Biao and the Gang of Four opposed the party's policy toward nationalities, negated the nationalities work, undermined their solidarity, spread discord among them, and stifled nationalities research work. For more than a decade the study of nationalities was suspended, and the entire organization became paralyzed. Much valuable material was lost, and in many places the research teams were disbanded. All this caused irreparable loss. In particular, they fabricated many absurd theories about the nationalities issue, thus creating both ideological and theoretical confusion. This brought about severely adverse effects on ethnic research. Lin Biao and the "Gang of Four" slandered the Marxist-Leninist study of ethnology, which had, since Liberation, been carried out under the correct leadership of the party, and labeled it bourgeois ethnology. They negated it in a wholesale fashion and thoroughly strangled it. As a result, the field of ethnology was entirely eliminated from our country. Many ethnologists and researchers suffered destructive attacks, and some even were persecuted to death. Those who survived did not dare even to mention the word "ethnology."

After the "Gang of Four" was crushed, the party and the government proposed that the socialist undertakings of science, education, and culture, including ethnology, once again flourish. It was unequivocally proposed to launch the study of ethnology, a move that not only restored ethnology to its former reputation, but also encouraged ethnology workers to strive for new achievements. The broad ranks of our ethnology workers truly feel as if we were given a new lease on life. Since then the research work in ethnology has begun to be restored and spruced up, and there is now an aura of a new dawn, filled with the energies of youth. As an old veteran of the study of ethnology myself, I deeply feel a sense of bright hope for ethnological research; I feel that there is much worth in what is being done, and there is much to be done. I would like very much to work together with the younger folks to make something of the situation.

## II

For us to see more clearly the future prospects for the development of ethnology, we must discuss and come to understand other issues as well. The first is the question of the relationship between the theory of the nationalities issue and ethnology. I feel that the theory of the nationalities issue belongs to the sphere of philosophy; it is a component of historical materialism, whereas ethnology belongs to the category of concrete social sciences and is a discipline that specializes in the study of nationalities. We propose to carry out the study and research of ethnology under the guidance of a Marxist-Leninist theory of nationality; there is no contradiction between the two. An essay written by the commentator for the journal *Zhexue yanjiu* (Studies in philosophy), no. 5, 1979, entitled "Historical Materialism and Sociology," offers, I believe, some enlightenment with the questions that it raises. It says, "With regard to natural phenomena, neither Marx nor Engels ever said that such philosophical explanations of natural phenomena could or should take the place of natural sciences. . . . The same is naturally true of the social sciences." From this I realized that the same can be said of historical materialism, which cannot take the place of the various specific social sciences. Historical materialism provides us with a basic viewpoint, a fundamental method, and a theory for the study of the massive and long-range aspects of social life and social development, but historical materialism itself has not replaced and does not attempt to replace the various disciplines related to the different aspects of social phenomena. The article goes on to say, "Marx and Engels, the creators and founders of historical materialism, used their own extensive research efforts to demonstrate clearly that even they never attempted to use historical materialism to take the place of sociology or the specialized studies in other fields of the social sciences. . . . For another example, Marx and Engels never attempted to use historical materialism to replace social history. Marx and Engels both employed the historical materialist methodology that they founded to study social history, and to this study they devoted a tremendous amount of work. Engels' *Origin of the Family, Private Property, and the State* was a famous scientific work that dealt with the history of primitive human society. We can say that the viewpoint and methodology of historical materialism provided a clear sense of direction for the study of social history and provided it with a scientific tool; and yet this does not mean that it is tantamount to the science of social history itself; nor does it mean that once we learn historical materialism, all the problems in social history will be readily resolved." The "history of primitive society" mentioned here is precisely a component of the study of ethnology. This essay clearly explained the relationship and also the distinction between historical materialism (including the theory on the nationalities issue) and social science (including ethnology). [It tells us] that we must not confuse the two issues. In fact we have always thought in the same way and acted along these lines; it is only that Lin Biao and the Gang of Four muddled up the theoretical issue, thus making it necessary for us to clarify this important matter of right and wrong.

Second, with regard to the questions of what the objectives of ethnology are and what its scope or parameters ought to be, there are differences of opinion and understanding. This is a natural phenomenon, especially with regard to a newborn discipline. The age of ethnological studies abroad is relatively greater, and yet even they are involved with incessant debates over the definition and objectives of the discipline. Still, the controversy has not prevented them from developing ethnological studies. On the contrary, it seems that [with these debates] the objectives and parameters of their field of study have become ever broader, and more topics calling for immediate studies have cropped up. In general, we can say that as an independent discipline, ethnology takes as its objectives of study nationalities or human communities (including clans, tribes, tribal alliances, and the nationalities produced in class society). No other discipline is like ethnology in the sense that it specializes in nationality as an object of study. From this perspective we can say that ethnology is a discipline that possesses its own special character. Naturally there are many other fields of study that may study questions related to nationalities from this or that angle, but none of them would be like ethnology in taking nationality as a subject to be studied as an integral entity. Ethnology is closely related to many social sciences as well as some natural sciences. They include, for example, sociology, history, archaeology, anthropology, and geography. These, however, are only crisscrossing relationships; none of these sciences can replace or include one another.

In summing up what we have discussed, we can say that ethnology is a discipline of unique objectives and with a special investigative methodology. It is a social science indispensable in our effort to carry out socialist construction and develop the national culture. As of now there are still some debates as to whether or not we need such a discipline as ethnology in our country. I don't think this is a bad thing. Discussion and debate can help promote the development of science. Throughout history, the development of all new fields of study came with circuitous and difficult struggles. Even though the methodology of the study of ethnology, and the records related to this field, may have existed for a very long time, as an academic field of study its establishment is only a matter of the last hundred years or so. In particular, because imperialists and colonialist elements had attempted to exploit it as a tool for colonial rule, some people even today have difficulty comprehending the real meaning of ethnology; this is no surprise. What is important is that the broad ranks of our ethnological workers must not be overcome by the difficulties and the debates; instead, we must be bold in exploration, must dare to carry out our research. Practice is the criterion for the examination of truth; the facts will prove that ethnological studies are extremely essential.

At the moment, the four modernizations demand that the minority nationalities rapidly develop their economy and culture, and that ethnological study develop with greater speed. Although our ethnological research has already attained considerable achievements, there are still quite a few shortcomings. Particularly under the current circumstances when things are moving forward by leaps and bounds, our ethnological studies are lagging far behind the needs. The urgent task that ethnology workers face is to figure out how we can establish and develop a Marxist-Leninist ethnology and make it more effective in serving the interests of the four modernizations. A great deal of work needs to be undertaken if we are to accomplish this task, and I believe that the following items are currently the most pressing.

1. We should take Marxist-Leninist nationalities theory and the party's policy as the guide for our ethnological study and research. Since our efforts in this field are for the progress of the human race and the development of our country, and, at this moment in particular, for the economic and cultural development of our minority nationalities, our study and research must not depart from the guidance of Marxist-Leninist theory. Otherwise, our ethnology will not be different from bourgeois ethnology, or from the Soviet Union's ethnology. We must put our diligent efforts toward studying the Marxist-Leninist theory regarding the nationalities issue and learn well the party's nationalities policy. In turn we will, in our work, supplement the Marxist-Leninist theory in this regard, and also provide basic data to facilitate the party's formulation of its nationalities policy.

2. We must continue to carry out research and investigation regarding

nationality identification. We have discussed the significance of identifying and distinguishing nationalities within our country and how it has elicited the attention of international ethnological circles. Today, the vast majority of this project has been accomplished. In addition to the minority people in Taiwan that remain to be investigated and identified in the future, there are also still some ethnic groups of relatively small numbers that are demanding to be recognized as individual nationalities. There are, for instance, the Deng and the Xiaerba people in Tibet, the Kuchong, Be, Kongge, Shanda, Xiandao, Ake, Kalao, Bajia, and Chaman people (the latter call themselves the "Kemu" people) in Yunnan, the Dabu people of Pingwu County in Sichuan (who are currently called the "Zang" people of Baima), the Paimei and Nari people in the Lugu Lake region of Sichuan and Yunnan, as well the Lingao people on Hainan Island in Guangdong—a dozen or so groups altogether—which need to be investigated, identified, and distinguished. In fact investigation and research is already underway in some of these cases. Most recently we learned that there are about twenty groups with claims to nationality titles among the Gedou (who call themselves the "Gemo") and the Chuanqing in Guizhou who have requested that nationality identification be conducted for them. According to our information, the local research organizations there are already planning research and investigation that would immediately begin the identification process. In addition, there are some minority nationalities that have already been identified but need to be reevaluated. These include, for instance, the Jiayong "Zang" people in Sichuan and the "Miao" people on Hainan Island. In response to the opinions of the people of those "tribes" and groups, we need to carry out investigation and research among them again. In doing so we must base ourselves on the research data available, but we must, at the same time, respect the will of the nationality or the group itself. We must take care of both the interests of the development of that nationality and the solidarity among all other nationalities. We must carefully consider all factors involved and handle the issues with caution and prudence.

3. We need to take a good hold of the studies of the nature of societies of the minority nationalities and bring them to completion, especially those projects that were already planned, namely, the compiling of works on the three types of social formations—primitive society, slave society, and serf society. On the basis of existing investigative results and materials, and, in conjunction with the work of the various local nationalities research organizations, we must carry forth synthesized, analytical

studies in accordance with Marxist theory and strive to explain systematically and completely the genuine nature of the various types of societies among our minority nationalities. This research project will not only enrich our new knowledge of the history of human social development but also be conducive to the study of the formation and development of the Han nationality, and will at the same time play a major role in the study of the history of China as a united multinational country.

4. We must develop the study of the Han nationality. The Han nationality is our country's main nationality, for it comprises about 94 percent of the total population and is well covered in the historical record. However, when we come to treating the Han people as a nationality, there are still such questions as its origins, national formation, and development which remain open to discussion and research. In the 1950s, our academic circles carried out a discussion of the origins of the Han nationality, but it was suspended. Furthermore, from the perspective of the objective and task of the study of ethnology, there are many research projects revolving around the Han nationality that have yet to be formally launched. For instance, the transformations in the lifestyle and culture of the people living in the Han regions (especially the profound transformations that have taken place since Liberation), their family histories, the study of their folk customs and folklore, and indeed even the study of the history and current conditions of the several tens of millions of overseas Chinese, should all be put on the agenda. The culture of each nationality makes a valuable contribution to the motherland, and these contributions are all closely linked to the creations of the laboring masses. It should be admitted that the study of the Han nationality is a major task for ethnological circles in China today. According to the information we have at hand, the bourgeois ethnological studies in Europe and America have long transcended the confinement of being studies of minority nationalities, and in the Academy of Sciences of the Soviet Union, the largest group of people in the Institute of Ethnic Studies is the group that studies the Russian nationality; the scope of its research is also the broadest. These are by no means accidental phenomena; rather, their special significance ought to draw adequate attention.

5. A very important task is for us to strengthen our study and research on the world's nationalities and to expand our international scholarly exchange. Following our increasingly enhanced international status and the increasing frequency of exchange and contact between our country and other countries, this issue is becoming more and more significant.

The nationalities questions occupy an especially important place in the political lives of many countries. We can even say that with regard to certain countries, we cannot understand their problems in many areas unless we first comprehend their problems regarding nationalities. Therefore, our comprehension of the conditions of the many nationalities around the world is indispensable for our handling of international affairs and developing friendly relations with them. Our study and understanding of the world's nationality groups is one of the subjects of our ethnological studies. It helps us to know the processes of ethnic development and supplements our study of nationalities in our own country in areas where we are weak or inadequate. International scholarly circles pay a great deal of attention to the study of the world's ethnic groups and nationalities. There is much scholarly exchange in this area, and there are many international conferences. It is a great loss that in the past we have, as a rule, failed to take part. We cannot do scientific research while plugging up our eyes and ears. We ought to employ the method of inviting people to come to us and going outside ourselves to broaden our horizons. Since our Society for the Study of World Nationalities was founded in June 1980, we have begun to undertake work in this area. There are many nationalities around the world, and the problems to be studied are both many and complex. We need to establish priorities and gradually open up this field of study in accordance with the human resources and material conditions available.

6. Regarding research on socialist nationalities, in our country we have habitually called all human communities in the various stages of historical development "nationalities" (*minzu*). This was necessary under the specific historical conditions prevailing in our country. However, in the discussions we find in the writings of classical Marxist-Leninist authors, we discover that the various historical types of human communities, following the development of human society, have different classifications and titles. In the book *Marxism and the Problem of Linguistics*, Stalin once said: "The continuous development of language is from clan languages to tribal languages, from tribal languages to the languages of *buzu* [*narodnost*], and from the languages of *buzu* to nationality languages." From this passage we can clearly get the idea that the sequential process of the historical types of human communities is a process in which there are to be distinctions among clans, tribes, *buzu*, and nationalities. Today in our country there is as yet no consensus on this issue, whether at a theoretical level or at the level of understanding

semantic concepts, and this has severely affected the understanding of Marxist-Leninist theory on the nationalities issue. The urgent task for the present in this area of study is to study the questions of the formation and development of socialist nationalities. The study of how, in the wake of the victory of the bourgeois revolution and under a socialist system, [nationalities have been] gradually transformed, out of the ruins of bourgeois nationalities, into socialist nationalities, ought to be brought onto the agenda.

7. The study of the history of primitive societies has a dual significance—on the theoretical front as well as on the practical front. The study of the history of primitive societies, as a component of the study of ethnology, was gradually established in the bitter and intense struggle against the false science of the bourgeoisie. Although bourgeois ethnology indeed considered primitive societies as a major subject to be studied and researched, it generally looked upon the various nationalities in the primitive period as "prehistoric barbarians" and treated the history of primitive societies as "the history of prehistory." In accordance with the scientific analysis of Marxism-Leninism and Mao Zedong Thought, we affirm that primitive society was indeed the beginning of human history, and therefore a part of human history. Our ethnology workers must work in conjunction with archaeologists, anthropologists, and scholars in other related fields to integrate broadly the materials on the various nationalities in all places around the world, in order to be able to draw a more complete picture of the development of primitive society, and to explain that human society developed according to certain laws of development. Therefore, the study of the history of primitive societies is a basic theoretical foundation. It is closely linked to the analysis of many problems such as the question of the origins of the various nationalities, the periodization of social development, and ascertaining the social character of the various nationalities. For this reason, the study of the history of primitive societies has a major theoretical significance. In our country, in the early years after Liberation, we discovered through surveys and research that some nationalities still retained in large measure the vestiges of a primitive social system. In accordance with this set of conditions, our party formulated a policy of direct transition, helping them to transcend and skip over several stages of social development and enter socialism directly. This has created splendid results. Therefore, the study of the history of primitive societies also has its practical significance.

8. In our country the study of race is also a gaping hole. Not only is there a close relationship between the racial question and the question of nationalities, but many racial questions are also subject matter for ethnology. In many of our publications we frequently confuse the two terms race and nationality, which are in fact different concepts. On the one hand, the question of race is a question of the external physical conditions and forms of human beings and belongs to the realm of physical anthropology. On the other hand, although there are distinctions between "race" and "nationality," there are also close connections between the two, and many issues of race also belong to the realm of social science. Every two years, UNESCO convenes a conference for which one of the subjects of discussion is race. Our delegation to the organization, because we have not investigated the subject, has so far not spoken a word at these meetings. We must not allow this situation to continue. In particular, we must be aware that even today the imperialists are waving all sorts of theoretical banners behind which they promote racism to serve the interests of their colonial policies and policies of hegemony. We must take them to task on every point and carry out our unflagging criticism of and struggle against all sorts of absurd racist arguments, no matter what form they may come in.

9. We must continue to put in order the material that has been gathered on nationalities studies since the founding of the republic. We must sort out and publish the manuscripts and documentary material resulting from the survey research on the social histories of the minority nationalities that have been in the process of being compiled since 1956. In the last two years, the collection known as *Minzu wenti wu zhong congshu* (Collected works on five areas of nationalities questions) has been gradually compiled, edited, and published. This is a task that confronts all the disciplines related to nationalities. Our ethnology workers can contribute their efforts to many items and sections of this overall task. In addition, the more than one dozen scientific documentary films on minority nationalities that have already been made ought to be edited as soon as possible, with a view to being publicly released and shown at an early date. The Institute of Nationalities of the Chinese Academy of Social Sciences plans to make more scientific documentaries; this is an essential project. The task of summing up and putting in order work that had been begun in the past but was not completed is not merely a job of continuing the work of the past; it will also have a promotional effect on the investigative and research work of the future. From now on, we ought

to go even deeper into the subject and, on the basis of what was done in the past, carry out more investigations and research and, in a planned and methodical way, write new collected books on ethnological issues as well as monographs on ethnology, so that the fruits of our research may be accumulated in a timely fashion and play their part even more effectively.

10. Establishing an ethnological museum is an integral component of our nationalities work as a whole. It is also a major task in the area of ethnological research. An ethnological museum is different from other types of museums. Its functions, in addition to displaying, studying, preserving, and storing artifacts and specimens, will include such important roles as publicizing to the broad masses of people the party's and the state's nationalities policy, introducing the results of our work in nationalities studies, and promoting solidarity among the various nationalities. It will not only be an ordinary cultural and educational organization, but will also serve as an organization of scientific research in carrying out ethnological studies. Ours is a country of many nationalities united together; the country as a whole is composed of fifty-six national components. In particular, since Liberation and under the brilliant guidance of the party's nationalities policy, we have achieved tremendous results in every area of endeavor. In all the world, we stand alone as an example; this is a tremendous victory for our people of all nationalities, something of which we ought to be proud. And yet today we still do not have a formal public museum of ethnology. This ought not be the case. If we can immediately take steps to plan and build a museum of ethnology, the project is bound to be enthusiastically welcomed by the people of all nationalities in the country.

11. Conduct studies in nationality statistics and the geographical record of the nationalities. On the basis of extensive nationalities surveys, the task of establishing a field of ethnic statistical studies and of drawing maps of nationalities' distribution has become an indispensable link in the chain of ethnological studies today. In the dozen or so years prior to the Cultural Revolution, we had collected and stockpiled a considerable amount of material and statistical data in such areas as industry, agriculture, culture, education, public health, and demographics of the minority nationalities. Owing to the interference and sabotage of Lin Biao and the Gang of Four, however, this was never subjected to the systematic treatment and study of specialized organizations or experts. Some of these valuable materials accumulated over a long period have been lost, and others have deteriorated into a pile of waste paper, never put to use.

This is extremely regrettable. As of now, we have not even drawn up a standardized map of nationality distribution, which is intolerable. We must immediately take action to collect related statistical and mathematical data on the nationalities in our country, and even on the nationalities of the world at large, and classify them in an orderly fashion, put them in good shape, and launch the study of nationality statistics and nationality cartography. This is a project of great necessity, because it is not only an important foundation for the launching of ethnological studies, but also will serve as important material in the interests of the four modernizations endeavor.

12. Study the ethnology of the West and the ethnology of the Soviet Union. We cannot study anything without understanding its origin and how it developed. At this moment, if we are to establish and develop the position of a Marxist-Leninist ethnology in our country, it would not be enough for us to train our vision on the situation at home. We must study the genesis, development, and current conditions of ethnology in the West; we must study all sorts of schools and trends of thought and the roles they have played in history, and we must study the nature of those reactionary schools of thought that have lent themselves to the service of the colonial rule of imperialism. At the same time we must also study the ethnology of the Soviet Union, the influence that the ethnology of the West and of the Soviet Union has had on our own ethnology, and the developmental trends in the study of ethnology in the international sphere. This will not only help us to deepen our understanding of ethnology, but will also be helpful to us in distinguishing ethnology that serves the interests of colonial rule and that which serves the interests of the proletariat. It will facilitate the firm establishment and development of our own Marxist-Leninist ethnology.

13. Put a big effort behind the nurturing and cultivating of the next generation of ethnologists to take our places. Even though this is the question that I placed last in this discussion, we feel that it is in fact one of the most important issues of all. We cannot hope to accomplish those tasks of ethnology that we mentioned in the foregoing paragraphs unless we are able to strengthen the construction of the ranks of ethnologists and make a big effort to nurture and educate qualified ethnology personnel. Just as in many other departments and fields, many of our veteran ethnology workers are very advanced in age. Some are even physically weak and in desperate need for other people to take their places. The work of training and nurturing a successor generation includes work in

two aspects. One is to help the middle-aged ethnology workers fully develop their talents and wisdom and to allow them to pick up a heavier load than they have done in the past. The work of ethnological research at the present moment is primarily dependent on them.

The second task is to nurture and train young people; in their hands lie the future prospects for the study of ethnology. At this moment the Central Institute of Nationalities is engaged in the nurturing and training of two groups of graduate students in the study of the history of primitive societies and in the study of ethnology. Some other colleges and schools have also recruited and enrolled graduate students in ethnology; but this is still not enough. Henceforth we must plan to build up departments of ethnology in all the universities, colleges, and technical colleges. We make an effort to nurture even more people in the field of ethnology to serve as the succeeding generation. If we want ethnological studies in our country to continue to move forward without interruption, it is indispensable for a large group of people with talent in scientific research to be cultivated. As the saying goes, "While it takes ten years to nurture a tree, it takes a hundred years to educate a person." This is a major issue to which our ethnology workers ought to give some thought.

HUANG SHUPING

# 13 Developing Ethnology in Our Country Is What the Construction of Socialism Needs

SINCE the exposure and criticism of the ultra-Left line of Lin Biao and the "Gang of Four," our country has stepped into a new historic era of marching toward socialist modernization. This has opened up broad vistas for the study of ethnology.

From the time of Liberation onward, the development of ethnology in our country has undergone a circuitous journey. Its experience is very closely linked to the overall path that our country has taken over the last thirty years. Practical experience over the last three decades has allowed us to look clearly at many problems and realize what they are.

Is there such a thing as Marxist ethnology? The answer is, most assuredly, yes, just as there is such a thing as Marxist history, or Marxist economics, or Marxist legal studies. Ethnology arose to become an independent field of study in the capitalist societies of the nineteenth century. The bourgeoisie and the imperialists once exploited the field of study to serve the interests of capitalist colonialism and proposed some reactionary theories. However, we cannot simply think of all ethnology as necessarily bourgeois. Many fields of study were generated in the period of capitalism, and in capitalist society, the various fields of the natural sciences and social sciences were all servants of the interests of the bourgeoisie, because all these fields of study and scholarship were in the hands of the bourgeoisie which was the ruling class. Naturally, with the field of ethnology, there are questions as to which class owns it, who exploits and utilizes it, on what standpoint it is founded, what viewpoints

"Fazhan wuoguo de minzuxue shi shehuizhuyi jianshe de xuyao." In *Minzuxue yanjiu* (Ethnological research), no. 1 (Beijing: Nationalities Press, 1981), pp. 84–92.

and methodologies are used in its study, the interests of which class it serves, etc. We believe that in a socialist country under the dictatorship of the proletariat, the various fields of study in the social sciences that are inherited from the old society of either feudalism or capitalism can, after undergoing reform, be changed to serve the interests of the proletariat and of socialism. The field of ethnology is no exception. Practice has proven that in socialist New China ethnology is in the hands of the proletariat. When research is carried out according to the premises, viewpoints, and methods of Marxism, it is entirely possible to serve the interests of the proletariat and socialism.

As for the question of whether or not the legacy of a bourgeois ethnology has been inherited in a critical way, again the answer is affirmative. The history of ethnology as an independent field of study is already more than one hundred years old. The field of ethnology in the West has accumulated a rich store of material, and it has carried out investigative research on many nationalities around the world. This material is valuable for launching of the study of ethnology and other related disciplines as well. Ethnology in Russia also has a considerable amount of useful material. The ethnologists of the Soviet Union have carried out extensive investigations, surveys, and studies of the various nationalities in their country, and their writings on nationalities both in the Soviet Union and outside of it are still useful and worthy materials for reference.

The ethnological legacy in our own country is even more abundant and rich. There are fragmentary records of ancient history dating far back to the period of legends. The chapters in the biographies section of Sima Qian's *Shi ji* (Records of history), such as the chapters "Xiong nu" and "Xinan yi," and also Fan Zhuo's *Man shu* (History of the barbarians) are all special historical monographs containing ethnological materials. Prior to Liberation, the ethnologists of an older generation in China did a great amount of work on the study of Chinese nationalities, in spite of the limitations at the time that prevented their work from fully developing. They nonetheless published quite a few original works and translations, introduced Western ethnology, and went to the border regions inhabited by minority nationalities to carry out ethnological surveys and write up reports; they studied the history of Chinese nationalities and applied ethnology to the explanation of ancient history. We must affirm and acknowledge the contribution they made, and critically utilize the material they have accumulated.

Among bourgeois scientists there have also been progressive materialists. The U.S. ethnologist Morgan was one, and the contributions that he made reached beyond the realm of ethnology. For example, his achievements in the study of the history of primitive societies enriched and proved [the validity of] the materialist historical viewpoint founded by Marx and Engels. Engels' famous work *Origin of the Family, Private Property, and the State* was written by using, in considerable quantity, the results of Morgan's research. In many of their works, Marx and Engels, basing their views on large quantities of ethnological material, discussed the laws of the development of human society as well as many major problems in social history. The classical writers of Marxist works not only accorded high praise to Morgan's outstanding achievements, but also awarded other bourgeois ethnologists fair and affirmative assessment of what is correct and reasonable in their theories in spite of their errors, and their achievements and contributions were duly noted. We must learn this critical spirit of historical materialism; we should, with regard to the ethnological studies of the West, of the Soviet Union, and of our own country in the period before Liberation, carry out penetrating and earnest study and, following the principle of discarding the dross but absorbing the essential, critically assimilate what is beneficial and useful to us.

Can we say that since we have Marxist nationality theory we no longer need ethnology? Not at all. The former cannot take the place of the latter. The theory in Marxism that deals with the nationality issue serves as the theoretical foundation for the resolution of the nationalities problem, but it cannot take the place of the concrete study of the attributes of nationalities and the laws governing the development of nationalities. This latter task has to be shouldered by a specific field of study, which is precisely the responsibility of ethnology. Similarly, historical materialism cannot take the place of ethnology. Marxist historical materialism provides a guiding principle for the study of ethnology, but we must not think that ethnology is simply using the viewpoints and methodologies of historical materialism to study nationalities. Ethnology, as a discipline, has its own concrete objects of study, its responsibility and methods; no other disciplines can substitute for it.

As we look back on the journey that ethnology has traveled in the last thirty years, we can see that we are as yet a bit short on understanding the actual conditions of this discipline and lack a scientific study of the field. On a number of issues—for instance, the actual subject matter and contents of ethnology in the West; the research results, materials, or methods that deserve our attention; the reactionary theories that should be criticized; how it serves the interests of the imperialists and the capitalists—we do not have much understanding, and in particular, with regard to the conditions of its development over the last few decades we know even less. At the same time, our lack of clarity concerning the object of study of ethnology and its task is also a reason for our confused perspectives.

With regard to the object, parameters, task, and methods of ethnology, these were the topics discussed in the 1950s and 1960s. In recent years, some comrades have also written on these issues. In these various rounds of discussions, many good opinions have been published. Ethnological circles abroad have likewise devoted much discussion to these questions over a long time, and they, too, have come up with many different views and opinions. Each country has its own set of conditions, and in different periods there will be different contents and tasks of study. Therefore we must develop our own ethnology in accordance with the conditions in our own country.

On the question of what this discipline should be called, I think it is appropriate to use the title *minzuxue* [the study of nationalities, i.e., ethnology, as it is usually translated]. In terms of scholastic nomenclature this would be equivalent to the terms "ethnology" or "anthropology" (referring to social anthropology or cultural anthropology) used in the West.

A nationality is an objectively existing social phenomenon. Ethnology is the science that studies nationalities, including all human communities at various stages of social development. It studies the laws of their genesis, development, and extinction. Ethnology, however, is not all-encompassing. Its focus is primarily on studying the nationalities' social system, characteristics of their material and spiritual culture, and way of life, and the processes by which they were formed, took shape, and developed. In terms of research method, it primarily relies on on-the-spot investigation, while also relying on using historical documents and archaeological material. Ethnology may study nationalities of any period, from the remote past to the immediate present, and of any place in the world, but it should focus on contemporary society and culture. However, to get to the bottom of the processes by which the characteristics and attributes of a nationality are formed and the causes for this formation, ethnology must also trace the steps of history. There are numerous nationalities around the world, and they each have a different outlook. The total outlook of a nationality is composed of many characteristics and attributes. In terms of an individual attribute, it may be shared by a number of nationalities, and yet, in terms of the total outlook of that particular nationality, it is unique, and it is what distinguishes this nationality from the others; it is the attributes that this nationality alone possesses. Ethnology studies the characteristics of nationalities and the laws governing their development and transformation. This is an object of study not repeated in any other discipline, and no other field of study can fully take its place.

Ethnology in the West tends to emphasize only the study of the existing societies, cultures, and ways of life of current nationalities, and to ignore their historical development. Ethnology in the Soviet Union, on the other hand, pays the latter some attention. Japanese ethnologists, however, do not merely study the social and cultural structure of nationalities, they emphasize the tracing of their historical evolution and development. This is what we ought to learn from and emulate.

Ethnology has a close relationship with many other disciplines. On the one hand, this is because the scope of study of ethnology is relatively broad. On the other hand, an even more important reason is that the distinctions between fields and disciplines of study are relative; while there is indeed a division of labor between related academic fields, we cannot impose a clear line of demarcation between them. When we study a particular social phenomenon or a particular topic, for instance, this may well be a responsibility commonly shared by several fields and disciplines, and we cannot think that because of this we only need to have one of these disciplines and that's that, or that other disciplines do not need to exist. Following the progress of society and the development of scientific culture, the division of labor between academic fields and disciplines has become more and more detailed, and each of the related disciplines has come to claim its own sphere of specialization. And yet at the same time there are also areas in which the disciplines are closely related, intersecting and penetrating one another. This is an inevitable result of the development of science. Some tasks can be handled by ethnology on its own, and other responsibilities call for cooperation with other disciplines. In return, ethnology can provide other disciplines with the material and research results they need.

Ethnology has the closest relationship with the discipline of history; yet history cannot take the place of ethnology. When ethnology studies the characteristics of a nationality, it traces the conditions under which these characteristics were formed and the historical process of their development; this is where it intersects with the discipline of history. The study of history may be devoted especially to a particular nationality; at the same time, ethnology needs to look at the formation of the characteristics of a nationality from the perspective of historical development. They therefore have certain things in common, but they are not one and the same thing. Each of the two has its own disciplinary object and responsibility, and they can supplement each other without being antithetical or exclusive. For example, in studying problems related to the familial-clan commune and the rural commune in the ancient history of China, we may find that in addition to relying on written historical documents, the studies done by ethnologists on the remnants of these communal forms in minority nationalities' societies can also serve as important data for the resolution of these problems and can indeed serve greatly to supplement the inadequacies of historical records.

Archaeology is another fraternal discipline that has a deep and close relationship with ethnology. The two in fact have similar research methods; both pay attention to on-the-spot investigation. Archaeology excavates and explores the mysteries of past human society that are buried underground, and it provides factual data and firm dates. On the other hand, ethnological data may provide living evidence and examples for the history of human society and culture. In recent years in the field of archaeology, much attention has been paid to using ethnological findings to help restore artifacts to their original shape; in determining the use and manufacture of the artifacts, tools, and vessels that are excavated; and in explaining such customs as burial practices and domicile arrangements—all to better understand the social system of the time.

The study of the history of primitive societies is by no means the responsibility of ethnology alone. To restore to original shape the picture of the history of the human race or the history of the primitive society of a particular region or a particular nationality, we must employ the research results of different disciplines, including ethnology, archaeology, anthropology, history, and linguistics in a synthetic way. Because there are no written records for primitive societies, and therefore there are no written historical data, to a great extent the study of primitive societies has to rely on ethnological material. In most countries, the convention is to consider the history of primitive society a major subject matter of ethnological studies. Since Liberation, the ethnological workers of our country have consistently given great attention to the study of the history of primitive society, deeming it to be significant in both theoretical and practical terms.

Practice proves that coordination among closely related fields of study can only propel forward the development of science, rather than giving rise to the question of who is devouring whom.

For many years ethnological research had suffered the interference of a "Leftist" line and sustained great damage. Nonetheless, some of the work was able to continue, even though it was not called "ethnology." At the present moment, the people of all the nationalities in our country are carrying out under the leadership of the party's Central Committee the construction of socialist modernization. This new situation of prosperity and development has created unprecedentedly favorable conditions for ethnological work. Ours is a multinational country; at present we count within our borders fifty-six nationalities. Each nationality has a long history and a rich, colorful culture. This is a rare situation in the world at large. Each region inhabited by a nationality is a broad and expansive universe for the study of ethnology, and as we explore and excavate this precious treasure trove we are bound to make important contributions to the world's cultural treasure chest. The period of socialism is one in which nationalities will prosper and develop. During this period, the distinction among nationalities and national characteristics of the various ethnic groups will continue to exist. Thus the question of how we may carry out the construction of the four modernizations in the regions inhabited by minority nationalities while adapting to the special characteristics of each nationality is one of great importance. Therefore, the historical circumstances and the contemporary situation both demand that we strive mightily to develop ethnological research. Indeed, to develop ethnology in our country is a necessity for the construction of socialism.

The four modernizations are focused on economic construction. In this dawning period, the various regions of our country inhabited by minority nationalities not only will experience great development in economic construction but must also have corresponding development in scientific and cultural spheres. As a social science that studies nationalities, ethnology serves the interests of the construction of socialism in many ways. Whether it is studying the contemporary practical problems in a minority region or carrying out an exploration of theory, it is serving the interests of the construction of socialism as long as its research results are conducive to the growth and prospering of the nationalities and to the development of the economy, politics, science, and culture of the areas where they reside. Ethnology circles may submit the results of their work in surveying, investigating, and research to the relevant departments of the party and government in the form of proposals and plans, and thereby provide scientific data as a basis for the formulation of policy and serve the resolution of practical problems in these minorities. They can also study theoretical problems and use the results of their research to propel forward Marxism. Furthermore, our country's ethnological studies as a field ought to step up to the international stage and play an active and proper role in the development of this field. All these are needed in the construction of socialism.

In recent years quite a few comrades have proposed very good ideas concerning the tasks that lie ahead for ethnology. Among the suggestions are such things as the continuation of the work of identifying and distinguishing nationalities, the continued study of the nature of minority societies, the launching of studies on social issues among the minority nationalities, determining how to study the socialist nation, studying the world's nationalities, studying ethnology as a discipline in other countries, establishing a museum of ethnology, drawing up maps of the distribution of nationalities and ethnic groups, developing ecological studies, making scientific documentary films to depict minorities' customs, etc. All these are undoubtedly projects that we urgently need to undertake. We must pay adequate attention to the restoration and development of the teaching apparatus and organization in ethnology, nurturing of the contingent of ethnological workers, compilation and writing of ethnology textbooks, and establishment of a theoretical system that undergirds the study of ethnology. Furthermore, we should stress that we do not aim merely to study the old and prior outlooks of the various nationalities; we will also stress the study of new conditions, the expression of their new outlooks, and revealing of their new problems. In regard to the study of the nationalities' past we have not done enough, but because the work has been suspended for many years many things are not yet done—and therefore the study must be picked up where we left off and continue into the future, and we must strive to recover and preserve material that is lost or on the verge of being lost. Still, given all this, we must not neglect the new topics being proposed for ethnologists in the various minority areas as they go through the process of realizing the four modernizations.

In the new period of socialism, the party and state have shifted the focus of their nationalities work to helping minority peoples to carry out economic and cultural construction, and to eliminating the de facto inequality that history has bequeathed them, so as to help them catch up with the development level of the Han nationality and thus achieve real equality. What inequalities actually exist among the nationalities? In what areas of life are these de facto inequalities concretely expressed in the 1980s and 1990s? What are the forms of expression of these inequalities among nationalities, which are in different forms and modes of society, live in different regions of the country, and possess different natural economic conditions? With regard to all these contradictions and gaps, what are the methods that the party, the government, cadres, and the masses have adopted or will adopt to resolve them in the process of construction? All these problems deserve to be investigated in a penetrating way by ethnological workers. If we investigate and analyze these problems in conjunction with the practice of nationalities work, it would be helpful for the thorough implementation of the party's policy and conducive to shortening the gaps that exist among the various nationalities in terms of economic and cultural development, and also promote solidarity among them.

The vast majority of our country's minority nationalities reside in border and hilly regions, and they are generally backward in economic and cultural development. In the past, the undertaking of reform and transformation of minority regions at different stages of social evolution opened up paths for developing productive forces. Today, China once more turns its attention to developing the economy and culture of the minorities. We anticipate that the various nationalities will enjoy common progress and prosperity on the broad avenue of socialism. In the large garden of the motherland, we are bound to see a splendid picture of many flowers blooming and many colors erupting forth simultaneously. The outlook of all the nationalities is bound to change continuously and be transformed. With modernized socialist industry, agriculture, and scientific culture, the level of political ideology among the masses will be greatly enhanced, and this will speed up the process of the forward development of the nationalities. However, the distinctions among them will not disappear, and their many different characteristics will continue to exist. Some national attributes will further develop while others may cease to exist. Their economic and cultural levels will gradually draw closer to one another, and this will forge an even closer relationship and stronger sense of commonality among them. The ethnological worker must study this process of change and explore the elements that are laws of the process. The study of ethnology may not produce a single new piece of equipment for the industrial or agricultural modernization of the minority regions, nor will it bring about higher yields in their agricultural crops, but it can faithfully express the new complexions of the minority people and reflect their problems during the process of socialist construction. These studies are needed in the four modernizations and in the development of scientific and cultural undertakings among the various nationalities.

In the last few years I have visited some minority regions, and from what I have learned, I think that there are many interesting phenomena that deserve to be studied. For example, slash-and-burn agriculture is a commonly cited phenomenon in ethnological books. In our country many minority nationalities reside in hilly areas, and for thousands of years they have carried on slash-and-burn agriculture. Even today, this backward agricultural method that has been passed down from primitive society has not undergone any basic change. In the past, no effective measure had been adopted to change this de facto inequality. Therefore, in the thirty years since Liberation, the nationalities residing in hilly areas have continued to burn the slopes and clear the ground for agriculture by cutting down trees. Not much improvement has taken place in their tools and techniques of production. Consequently, yields are low and the people's lives are poor and difficult. Besides, getting food by destroying forests and opening up land by defoliation destroys the ecological balance. The resolution of this problem is related to the question of how to build up the hilly areas in a modern fashion and affects the survival and development of the minority people residing there. This previously existing situation will have to be changed; unless it is changed we cannot even begin to speak of socialist modernization. Leadership at all levels in the minority regions and the broad masses of the people there are all striving to find an effective method to bring about development and prosperity for the minority nationalities and to do things in such a way that the conditions bestowed upon them by nature may be fully utilized while not violating the objective law of nature's metabolism. It is very meaningful to study this monumental transformation taking place before our very eyes.

It may appear as if the social systems that existed among the various nationalities prior to Liberation have become faded memories now that we have experienced democratic reform and undergone socialist transformation. In fact this is not so. In the period of socialism, we still can see the lingering effects and influences of the remnants of the old social systems. In many areas inhabited by minority nationalities, members of the masses and even some cadres that belong to the dominant nationality still use the expression "In the past we were the ones who controlled the area you are in" as an excuse to grab back the land cultivated by people of other nationalities, and to plunder the crops, thus leading to many disputes over land possession and forest possession among the nationalities, and even armed battles that cause casualties. There are many complex factors that give rise to new problems among the nationalities under the new situation, and the study of ethnology cannot ignore these practical issues.

The religious beliefs in minority regions may seem to have already been eliminated in the "great campaign" to "destroy the 'Four Olds,' " which itself followed the attacks on religion of several major political movements. Again we find this not to be the actual case. Religion is an ideological form; its genesis has a deep-seated social root that cannot be easily eradicated by adopting coercive measures. At present in some minority regions, religious activities are quite brisk and lively, and religious beliefs still play a big role in people's lives. With the development of economic and cultural construction and the enhancement of the levels of scientific knowledge, this situation will be changed. To change it, however, we must first study it thoroughly and earnestly.

Our Constitution stipulates that the freedom of choice of whether to maintain or reform mores and customs among the minority nationalities must be honored. The mores and customs of a nationality are the tradition of its social and cultural life that has been formed and molded in history; they are a concrete epitome of the characteristics of the nationality. In China today there is not a single discipline solely responsible for the study of the mores and customs of the various nationalities, nor have the party and government set up a special organization to study these. During the period when Lin Biao and the "Gang of Four" rode roughshod over the country, they indiscriminately considered the mores and customs of the various nationalities to be outmoded customs that ought to be eliminated. This, of course, was wrong. However, as to which of these customs and mores ought to be preserved and which ought to be reformed, naturally it is up to the masses of the individual nationality to decide, but we should have an academic field to record and study such developments.

Ethnology in our country ought to be developed, and there is a great deal of work to be done in this field. Let us allow the study of ethnology to make its proper contribution to the growth and prosperity of the various nationalities and to the scientific and cultural development of the Chinese people.

# Part VI

# Ethnolinguistics

FU MAOJI

# 14 Developments in the Scientific Study of Nationality Languages in the Thirty-five Years Since Our Nation Was Founded

IN THE OLD society, there were some minority nationality scholars who conducted investigations into their own and other nationalities' languages, publishing dictionaries, grammars, and orthographies. There were also some Han nationality scholars as well as foreign scholars who likewise conducted research on certain nationality languages and published dictionaries, grammars, and descriptive works. It was only after the founding of New China that universities started large-scale training of minority research workers for minority language and literature scientific research, including training many minority science and research workers; conducting large-scale general surveys on the minority languages of the whole country; proposing dialectal divisions for languages based on the results of their research and investigation; and helping to design writing systems for those nationalities that had requested such help. This work could only be done after the founding of the New China. The socialist system and the party's policies of nationality solidarity, nationality equality, and mutual development made possible the commencement and development of this work.

**Minority Nationality Languages Investigation and Survey**

Soon after Liberation, the Chinese Academy of Sciences established a Language Institute, and not long afterward, the Minority Languages

"Jian guo sanshiwu nian lai minzu yiuyen keyen gonzuode fazhan." Minzu yiuwen (Nationality language and literature) 5 (October 1984): 1–8.

Research Group was established within the institute. The Central Institute of Nationalities meanwhile was the first to set up a Department of Minority Nationality Languages. To train research workers to conduct minority language investigations and to encourage the development of research on nationality language and literature, the Nationalities Language Research Group of the Language Institute cooperated with the Central Institute of Nationality's nationalities language department in the two aspects of research and education. Both undertook the tasks of research as well as training cadres. In 1952, the Language Institute again entrusted Beijing University to set up special training courses in language to train cadres in language science research. At the same time, the Language Institute continued to send out small groups to conduct language surveys in Sichuan, Guangxi, Yunnan, Guizhou, and other provinces. The groups also helped resolve urgent problems in creating nationality writing systems. In 1955, the Language Institute together with the Central Institute of Nationalities and linguist cadres from the Inner Mongolian Autonomous Region and Xinjiang-Uygur Autonomous Region organized separate Mongol nationality languages and Xinjiang nationality languages investigative teams to explore conditions in the relevant nationality areas. In 1956, the five hundred current and recent graduates of the nationality language department of the Central Institute of Nationalities, graduates of Beijing University's language speciality program, and graduates of the nationality language departments of nationalities institutes of major regions as well as the research workers of minority language research institutes formed quite a considerable team. In 1956, to improve students' theoretical and technical abilities in conducting language investigation and research, the minority language research institutes and the Central Institute of Nationalities (including the South China Nationality Institute) got together to set up a language investigation training program. The training program played an important role in guaranteeing the quality of the language survey. After the completion of the program, under the leadership of the Central Nationalities Affairs Commission and the Chinese Academy of Sciences, seven large-scale work teams totaling seven hundred people were immediately organized as minority nationalities language investigative work teams to conduct separate surveys in the sixteen provinces and regions where minority nationality languages were prominent.

By 1959, comprehensive surveys had been done for the languages of forty-two nationalities, including the Zhuang, Buyi, Dong, Shui, Dai, Li,

Maonan, Yiaolao, Miao, Yiao, She, Tibetan, Qiang, Yi, Tujia, Bai, Hani, Lishu, Lagu, Naxi, Jingpo, Achang, Zhilao, Wa, Mongol, Dahure, Dongxiang, Tuzu, Baoan, Uygur, Kazakh, Kirghiz, Uzbek, Tartar, Sila, Yugu, Xibo, Hezhe, Owenk, Olunchun, Tajik, and Jing.

The investigation's accomplishments can be summed up in three main points:

1. A better understanding exists on how many languages are spoken within a nationality. For example, the Yugu nationality speaks two minority nationality languages. The language that the Yugu people living in the west part of Wugu Autonomous County in southern Gansu speak is the so-called West Yugu, which actually belongs to the Turkic language family. The language the Yugu in the eastern part of this autonomous county speak is the so-called East Yugu, which belongs to the Mongol language family. The language of communication between the people in the two parts is the Han language. For another example, the Yao speak three minority nationality languages. One is Mian Yao, which belongs to the Yao branch of the Miao-Yao language. Another is Bunu, which belongs to the Miao branch of the Miao-Yao language, and the third one is Lajia, which belongs to the Shui branch of the Zhuang-Dong language family. The three parts of the Yao people communicate with each other in the Han language.

2. Certain languages should be divided into dialects if that is indeed what is being spoken. For example, the Zhuang language is divided into two dialects, north and south. Mongolian is divided into three dialects: middle, west, and east. The Uygur language is divided into the central, Hetian, and Luobu dialects; Tibetan is divided into Lhasa, Kang, and Anduo dialects; Miao is divided into Xiangxi, Qiandong, and Chuanqiandian dialects; Wa is divided into Baraoke, Wa, and Awa dialects; Bai is divided into southern, middle, and northern dialects; Li is divided into Xiao, Ti, Bendi, Meifu, and Jiamao dialects; and Yi is divided into the north, east, south, west, middle, and southeast six dialects.

3. Not only was the language itself investigated, but also language usage and whether or not a written script exists. Before the general survey, it was mistakenly thought that the She nationality had converted to Han language use. Only in the general survey did it come out that in Guangdong Province's Boluo, Zengcheng, Huidong, Haifeng, and some other counties, the She nationality speaks a language that belongs to the Miao-Yao language family. For the nationalities that had requested the

creation of a written script, scientific symposia were held where the nationality's representatives got together with language experts to discuss the report of the language survey team, which made suggestions on choosing standard dialects and standard pronunciation, and on a draft of new script design. If the nationality already had a written script but still requested changes, the design of the team's script reform suggestions was brought up for discussion at the scientific symposium. Since the survey team members included a certain percentage of minority nationalities, these members not only participated in their own language's survey, but also participated in the planning for their own script. The draft script proposal drawn up by the survey team usually passed without major changes. I myself attended all these scientific symposiums, and when I saw how, immediately after the new script was approved, the minority nationality representatives wrote poems in the new script to welcome it, my feelings were profoundly stirred!

In 1960 the Altaic language family language survey team finished its general work. After the Tibeto-Burman, Zhuang-Dong, Miao-Yao, and South Asian language families survey teams finished their general surveys, they continued working in their districts and provinces for a period of time before their return. After this, except during the Cultural Revolution when work was impossible, the supplementary surveys never stopped.... The last four or five years have seen the supplementary survey works commence again. The Mongols in Henan Mongol Autonomous County of Qinghai Province lost connections with other Mongols at the beginning of the seventeenth century. Investigations done in 1983 found that Mongolian herdsmen living along the north bank of the Yellow River still use the Mongolian language. According to research, although the Mongol language in that area has many peculiarities, it clearly belongs to the western dialect. This is the first time this has been disclosed to Mongolian language academic circles. In 1979, Qu Aitang and Tan Kerang went to conduct language investigations in the previously unresearched Ali region. Their research reveals that Ali Tibetan mainly belongs to the Weizang dialect....

Although at the present circumstances prevent us from making an on-the-spot investigation of Taiwan's Gaoshan languages, nevertheless there still are Gaoshan nationality teachers and Han nationality cadres who cooperate on researching the Ameisi, Paiwan, and Bunong language. According to the investigations of Dong Tongshu, Li Renkui, and other Taiwanese scholars, the Gaoshan nationalities in Taiwan Province speak Paiwan, Ameisi, Buhong, Lukai, Saixia, Bainan, Shao, Ataizhie, Saide, Zou, Sha, Kayemei, and other languages; there are in addition some languages already extinct and some on the verge of extinction.

The number of known languages already totals more than eighty.

## The Task of Devising Scripts

When work began on creating new scripts, there was a general agreement that a phonetic script was the best way to proceed. The next question to be decided was what type of alphabet to use. In 1956 a conference was held in Guiyang to discuss this question. A consensus was reached at the meeting on two questions. First, the Roman alphabet should be used; second, when pronunciation is similar between a minority nationality language and Han Putonghua [Mandarin] language, it is preferable to use the standard alphabet of the Chinese Phonetic Alphabet [pinyin]. However, at that time, even though it was agreed to use the pinyin system, there was still the question of which letter to use to represent which sound. Due to the urgent demands of some minority nationalities for a new script, the only way to get immediate results was to devise temporarily a conversion table based on transcribing the symbols of the international phonetic system into the preferred Roman alphabets, and to use this as a reference in formulating the minority nationalities' scripts. In 1957, the Institute of Minority Nationality Languages first proposed "Some Principles of Formulating Minority Nationalities' Scripts" to the Chinese Writing System Reform Committee, and after discussion there it was examined and approved by the State Council. Five rules were examined, modified, approved, and passed in the council meeting presided over by Premier Zhou. The main thrust of these five rules was that the foundation of formulating writing systems for minority nationalities should be the Roman alphabet. If the original script is undergoing reform, and during the period of transition in adopting a new writing system, as great an effort as possible should be put into making the new Latin script the preferred one. Second, when the sound in the minority nationality's language is similar to the Han standard pronunciation, it should be written as close as possible to the corresponding symbol in pinyin. Third, when the sound in the minority nationality's language is not the standard Han sound, and if it is difficult to use one Roman letter to represent one sound, according to the concrete language conditions the problem can be met in the following ways: using two letters to represent one sound, creating new letters, or using other suitable letters from other alphabets. Under certain situations, one can also place additional symbols on top of the letter. Guided by the above rules, Zhuang, Miao, Buyi, Dong, Li, Hani, Naxi, Wa, Lisu, Tu, Bai, and eleven other nationalities had writing systems formulated.

From the very beginning of our work in creating scripts there were some comrades who thought that devising scripts for minority nationalities would hinder the study of Chinese characters. My opinions are as follows:

1. When nationalities have their own phonetic alphabets, not only is there no obstacle for the study of the Han language and writing, but it could also help people study spoken and written Han. When the Zhuang nationality was in the midst of promoting the Zhuang script, an experiment was conducted in the elementary school. The students in class A studied the new Zhuang script first and then studied Han characters later; class B was taught Han characters directly. The results of the examination showed that the class A students did not do worse but in general did even better than the students in class B. This is because when people study their own phonetic alphabetic they can quickly pick it up, and later when they study Han characters it is far easier for them to make pronunciation and meaning notes and thus easier for them to understand and remember. From this point of view, formulating writing systems not only does not hamper the study of Han characters, it also improves Han language and script study. In the past, the Yi language work team conducted similar experiments with adults in the Yi-speaking area and had similar results. People who had first studied their own nationality language's writing system would reach a degree of cultural competence, and so when they then studied other scripts, naturally it was relatively easy. More of this kind of experiment should be done in the future.

Minority nationalities are rich in intelligence and wisdom; they are also very reasonable. Their demands for the use of their scripts do not exceed their practical needs. When minority nationalities have their own writing system, they do not demand that all university courses use textbooks in their own nationality script. For some fraternal nationalities, this is not practical, and it is not beneficial to their study. Everyone understands that, aside from language and literature classes, it is impossible to teach all other classes using their own nationality script textbooks and reference books. If, because this was impossible to do, one was to then assume that minority nationality scripts were useless, this would also be incorrect. The use of a nationality's script in the schools at whatever level is determined by that nationality's concrete conditions.

2. Each nationality without a written script still has its own orally transmitted literature. They have folk tales, maxims and proverbs, and poems and songs of varying lengths. Some nationalities also have their own national dramatic forms. Not only are these part of the common national fortune of all our country's nationalities, but they are furthermore part of one of the world's Eastern treasure-houses of oral literature. Each nationality's script can record, transmit, research, and develop these oral literary arts. The nationality's own language is especially suited to record its own songs, drama, and scripts. In addition, you can use the nationality's script to write dramas with socialist content. This can be of great use in the development of fraternal nationalities' socialist culture.

3. An important aspect of all this is that the rapid development of a minority nationality district broadcasting industry could help conscientiously propagandize the party's policies and the country's laws, raise the nationality area's scientific and cultural levels, and quicken the pace of the nationality district's construction of the four modernizations. Today in some nationality districts, especially in the Southwest Border Region, broadcasting time in nationality languages is too short, the content is too boring, and as such the service will never catch up with the needs of the border districts for economic and cultural development. A major factor in creating this situation is the lack of spoken and written language tools which the local masses would understand and which would enable materials to be translated and only then broadcast. This problem would be solved if a phonetic script were devised that represented the local people's commonly used speech. If we do not set up the writing system first but instead use phonetic symbols, the result will be the same. Phonetic symbols are the best tool to use in spreading education because they do not require standard pronunciations; how the native speaks is how it is written, and this makes it the easiest for the masses to understand. Linguistic workers who understand the local language can undertake the task of setting up a system of phonetic symbols for broadcasting. With phonetic symbols, training broadcasting personnel becomes easy. Of course, this kind of broadcaster has to have been trained to a certain level of knowledge, to enable him to translate news or some popular technical knowledge. I made this suggestion at our institute a few years ago, arguing that we should take up the task of designing this type of broadcasting symbol, but it has yet to be carried

out. I still resolutely stand by this recommendation even today. Only if we have this type of phonetic symbol, and the broadcasting personnel to use it, can the party's voice and socialist culture's technical knowledge quickly spread to the border areas where the Han language is little understood by minority languages. These broadcasting personnel should raise their professional and work standards through study at local nationality institutes.

As we can see, totally solving the nationalities' script problems will require great efforts. We must conduct more investigations and indeed carry out some experiments. Of course we shouldn't overdo this script-creating business; some fraternal nationalities want to study Han script or find other scripts suitable, and they should be supported in this and helped to study Han characters or phonetic symbols. Our country's constitution stipulates that "each nationality has the freedom to use and develop its own language and writing system," so we should conscientiously study the import of this rule, to be able to advance a step in helping minority nationalities lacking scripts to achieve a compatible writing system.

## Special Works and Dictionaries on Language Structure

[This section contains an annotated list of the major publications by Chinese language scholars on minority language grammar, pronunciation, and vocabulary from pre-Liberation to the 1980s. It is omitted here.]

## Miscellaneous Research Papers and Works on Ancient Scripts and Documents

In the 1950s and 1960s minority nationality language research papers were restricted to being published mostly in *Zhongguo yuwen* (Chinese language and literature). Thanks to the strenuous efforts of the Chinese Academy of Social Sciences, the Nationalities Publishing House, and the Nationalities Press, a national scientific and research publication, *Minzu yuyen* (Nationality languages) was created in February 1979. Quarterly the first three years, the journal became a bimonthly in 1982. In 1981 the Language Institute of the Central China Institute of Technology started publishing *Yuyen yanjiu* (Language research). In 1983, the Chinese Linguistics Society set up the *Zhongguo yuyen xuebao* (China language bulletin). Research papers concerning nationality languages are now frequently published by national nationality institutes and schools as well as by the local branches of the Academy of Social Sciences Nationalities and Language institutes and by provincial and district higher educational institutions. *Zhonguo yuwen* has continued to publish this kind of paper. The range of published nationality language research papers is growing broader. These are the glory days for minority nationality languages research work, and the daily increase in the number of articles is one reason. First in *Zhongguo yuwen* and then in *Yuyen yanjiu*, from 1954 until now, forty-five articles have been written describing the varied circumstances of the minority nationality languages, including pieces on the Gaoshan nationality languages of Taiwan and the Zhuang, Miao, Yao, Shiala, Qiang, Tajik, Yi, Li, Tibetan, Mongol, Bai, Jingpo, Tujia, Olunchun, Dongxiang, Dong, Dahure, Shui, Loba, Hani, Yibo, Dulong, Wa, Kazakh, Naxi, Pumi, Jino, Baoan, Jingpo, Zaiwa, Chilo, Kerekezi, Korean, Tu, West Yugu, Jing, Bulong, Achang, Lisu, Benglong, Owenke, Jiarong, Lagu, and Lai languages. This type of general research paper, which covers the phonetic system, vocabulary structure, and key grammatical features of each language, can be very helpful in giving research workers in linguistics, ethnology, and nationality work a beneficial introduction to our country's multilinguistic nature.

These specialized research papers are quite colorful, penetrating, and rewarding. Within the past five years, the number of articles has increased as well. By Comrade Gao Baozhen's count, aside from the 102 books that came out between 1980 and 1983, more than 800 articles were published.

Let us now give some examples of these papers, beginning with those dealing with descriptions of modern language structure. This type of paper makes up the largest number of articles. Some discuss pronunciation while others discuss consonants, vowels, the whole consonant system, the vowel system, or the problem of vowel harmony. Some articles discuss tonal adjustment and classification, some are reports on the results of computer tone research. Regarding grammar, some articles describe the structure and function of grammatical categories; for example, imperative verbs, verb tense, and directional verbs. Some deal only with possession, while others discuss all kinds of verb grammatical categories. Regarding sentence structure, some articles discuss declarative tones, while some are about definite and indefinite tones. Others discuss inquisitive tones, some single and complex sentences, and still others deal with the parts of speech and their functions. Research papers on vocabulary and descriptive pieces on etymological structure are far fewer than papers on phonetics and grammar. Some of the former discuss homonyms, polysemants, synonyms, words of similar meaning, and antonyms. Others discuss homophonic combinations, alliterative words, or conjunctions, while still others discuss word formation or foreign loan-words.

There are also some comparative history articles. For example, there are articles about the subjective structuring of the initial consonant and (single or compound) vowels in the ancient Miao-Yao language. There are also some articles about research on ancient languages of the Zhuang-Dong language family. Some articles explore a common source for the Zhuang-Dong and Miao-Yiao language families and Han Chinese. Some discuss Miao-Han linguistic proximity in terms of grammar, and some deal with the common origins of languages in the Altaic language family. As far as we are concerned, these articles represent the earliest stage of research, and we hope that more articles will be forthcoming in these areas. We must continuously raise the quality of our academic argument. As for research, there are many ideas on whether the Bai languages belong to the Yi language branch. Some comrades suggest we set up a Qiang language branch, while others suggest we establish a Burmo-Yi branch instead.

In addition to the above, other research directions have been pursued. Work has been done on the question of a standard dialect and pronunciation for nationality languages, on vocabulary standards, and on the standardization of the writing and pronunciation of foreign loan words. Today there are more articles on sociolinguistics, with articles on the influence of social structure on kinship terminology an example.

[A section listing work done on ancient languages and script has been deleted here.]

## On the Prospects for Future Work

1. On-the-spot language investigation is a growing part of our modern language research work, and we absolutely cannot slacken. Every kind of modern language has to undergo an unceasing investigation to continually deepen our understanding of it and make progress in our studies. Since Liberation, conditions have been quite favorable to the study of nationality languages in our country. First of all, one can go anywhere one wants to conduct research; second, one always gets enthusiastic help

from the local cadres and masses. But we have to be careful and humble and assume an attitude of study. We should make sure to collect and understand documents in the nationality language. For comrades doing research on ancient language, it is best to investigate one or two modern languages that are possibly closely related to the ancient language being studied or have historical relations. This will prove beneficial to the ancient language research. Plans to investigate little-understood languages should be made. If those places in our country where we are still unclear about the language situation could be investigated within three of four years, we could then answer the question of how many languages exist in our country. This could also help us to find the descendants of some ancient words that we have trouble understanding.

2. We should contribute to solving the problem of those nationalities who have a spoken language but are without a written script. We should find out what types of nationalities are still without scripts and investigate their situation, and learn what ideas different strata of the masses and cadres may have. This is a very complicated and sensitive problem. I believe the best thing to do is to bring up this question but not to raise it directly. One should humbly listen to the local masses and cadres' opinions without showing one's own opinion. This is a problem that should be solved by the nationality itself. This problem should not only be settled without delay, it must be settled immediately. We especially need to help those nationalities that have little understanding of the Han or a neighboring nationality's language and writing system, in order to solve the problem as soon as possible. If this work is done well, it can quicken local economic and cultural development and thus speed up the four modernizations in these nationality areas. This problem should be linked to sociolinguistic research.

3. Strengthen comparative language classification research and deepen the discussion of the rules of linguistic contact. Our country's languages are so many and so varied; not only are there different language families, branches, and sub-branches among the languages, but these differences also exist between different dialects of the same language. My use of the term "classification" is a broad one, with any structural difference in pronunciation, grammar, vocabulary, or meaning potentially a cause to make this type of comparative classification. These classifications are not created ex nihilo and of course could be related to the genetic relationships of these languages. But such linguistic classification belongs to another branch of study. Research into how languages

mutually affect one another has the closest relationship to classification research. In the past, we overemphasized the effect Han Chinese has had on minority nationality languages. This of course should be studied, but other research should not be overlooked. In the future we shall conduct research on how minority nationality languages have affected Han Chinese, as well as how nationality languages affect each other. Languages affect each other not only as regards type, but also in other areas as well.

4. The transcription, interpretation, and study of minority nationality language documents and ancient writing systems should be promoted effectively. We have had great achievements in this area in the past, and we should move forward yet another step in the future. Many of our country's precious scriptures, documents, and ancient-inscription-bearing implements have been transferred to foreign countries, so that we ourselves do not have them any more; we should ask all manner of experts both at home and abroad to edit lists or charts of these items. For domestic lists, the current location of the real item should be listed, while the foreign catalogues should list the country and institutional custodians of the object. If the situation abroad is not now perfect, there can be substantial yet gradual improvements in the future. Copies reprinted abroad exist in our country and should be placed in the original location. Current paleographic research has made great achievements in research into the structures of several writing systems. For certain scripts it is very difficult to decipher their structure. In the future we should make every effort to find out the language background of a number of ancient scripts. If this point can be resolved, we can take a big step forward.

5. Historical comparisons of languages should be improved gradually. In the past we did not emphasize this enough. Now we have a better grasp on the modern nationality languages of our country; we are making unceasing progress in the study, transcription, and translation of nationality scripts and of ancient documents, and conditions to continue research in these areas are improving as well. Some high-quality papers have already been published. Step by step we must continue to move forward.

Under the guidance of Marxism-Leninism and Mao Zedong Thought, we must work on the above five points as well as other related practices, so as to be able to raise unceasingly the level of our linguistic theory.

MA XUELIANG AND DAI QINGXIA

# 15 | Language and Nationality

WHEN PEOPLE speak of language, they often link it to ethnicity; we believe that language is an important attribute that forms the identity of a nationality, and its development and evolution are contingent upon the development and evolution of that group. At the same time, when we speak of nationality, we also always think about language; we feel that a nationality cannot be considered apart from its language, and that the nature of a language influences the development of a nationality. Therefore, when linguists and ethnologists study the subjects of languages and nationalities, they very often encounter problems of how they are to understand the relationship between language and nationality, and they all feel that it is necessary to clarify the relationship between these two areas, from the standpoint of both theory and practice. While working on our country's nationalities work (including nationalities language work), we, too, often encounter questions that involve the relationship between language and nationality; furthermore, we have also seen some mistakes in the work caused by insufficient clarity over the relationship between these two.

Indeed, there is an intimate relationship of mutual dependence between language and nationality. Nonetheless, this relationship is very complex and not easily understood. This is particularly true of our country with its long history and multinationality flavor. Because the various nationalities, through the many ages of prolonged historical development, have continuously separated from one another at times and at other times blended and assimilated with one another, the relationship between languages and nationalities has presented many complex phenomena. Therefore, if we are to understand scientifically the relationship between languages and the nationalities in our country, we must proceed

"Yuyan he minzu." *Minzu yanjiu* (Nationality studies) 1 (1983): 614.

from the realities of the nationalities in our country and do quite a bit of earnest and careful analysis and research.

If we can clarify the relationship between language and nationality, it can be of great help in our scientific understanding of the special attributes of languages and nationalities, and in our attempt to formulate correct nationalities policies in our country (including policies regarding nationality languages). This essay will attempt to employ extant materials on our nationalities and their languages to discuss the relationship between language and nationality in response to three problems.

## Status of Language among the Various Attributes of a Nationality

Generally speaking, language and nationality are distinguishable from each other and yet at the same time connected to each other. As for their distinctiveness, language and nationality have their own characteristics and own laws of development. Language is the most important tool of social communication and interaction in human society, and it bears the responsibility for the mutual interaction and exchange of ideas among people. It is made up of three major components, namely, phonetics, syntax, and vocabulary. It is intricately related to human thought. Nationality, on the other hand, refers to the type of stable commonality that human beings form in the course of history. In it, common attributes and characteristics among people are expressed in the areas of language, resident territory, economic life, state of mind, etc. The development of language is manifested primarily in the changes that occur in the various components within the language, whereas the development of a nationality group is chiefly manifested in the changes of the attributes or characteristics of the nationality. Also, language and nationality were not produced at the same time. Language appeared somewhat earlier. As soon as there were human beings there was language, but nationality did not exist at the very beginning of human society. Rather, it was a product of the development of human society when it reached a certain stage, and therefore it appeared somewhat later than language. Because language and nationality have their own characteristics and laws of development, from the perspective of targets of study, they are therefore two different objects: the study of language is known as linguistics, whereas the study of nationalities is known as ethnology.

Nonetheless, ever since human society took the shape of nationalities, language has born the branding mark of these nationalities and therefore has come into an inextricable relationship with nationality. From that time on, languages belonged to each specific nationality and became an important attribute of these nationalities. For example, the common language of the Han nationality came to be known as the Han language, the language that commonly belongs to the people in the Uygur nationality came to be known as the Uygur language, and so on. From that time on, a language that did not belong to any particular nationality no longer existed; rather, each language came to bear the emblem of nationality. After language became an attribute of nationality, the two, in the course of development, became mutually affecting and mutually dependent. On the one hand, the development and transformation of languages came to be influenced and controlled by the development of nationalities; on the other hand, languages influenced the development of nationalities. The history of a language is therefore always closely linked to the history of a nationality. Thus, it is impossible to study languages apart from the study of the nationalities and, vice versa, the study of nationalities cannot be done in isolation from the study of languages.

It is important to recognize that language is one of the chief attributes of nationality. But this in itself is not enough; we must further understand its relationship with the other attributes of the nationality, and the status of language among the various attributes of a nationality. Stalin provided the concept of nationality with a scientific definition: A nationality is a "stable commonality formed through the course of history of people that have a common language, hold a common region or territory, lead a common life, and possess common mental qualities that are expressed in terms of a common culture." He thus identified four principal attributes of a nationality and placed the attribute of language ahead of the others. Stalin's insightful argument provides us with a major theoretical foundation for an in-depth exploration of the relationship between language and nationality. When we examine the relationship between language and nationality we can see that although language is just one of the attributes of a nationality, in comparison with the other attributes, it has many different and special characteristics, and therefore, among the various attributes of nationality, it occupies a special status. Generally speaking, it is the most important attribute of nationality. Why do we say that?

1. Language can more comprehensively and profoundly epitomize and embody the attributes of a nationality. This is something that other

attributes cannot do. We know that the characteristic nature of language itself is that it is a social phenomenon. Its sphere of activity is very broad and encompassing, and it has an intimate and intricate relationship with almost every other human activity. Furthermore, language is intimately connected to thought. People's understanding of the objective world has to be carried out through language and can be consolidated only through language. Therefore, such things as the characteristics of society, people's way of life, and the characteristics of their natural environment are bound to be reflected in language. Different nationalities, owing to difference in the circumstances of their socioeconomic development and differences in the stages of culture that they have experienced, also have differences in the characteristics of the development of their languages. In this sense, language becomes like a mirror from which the various characteristics and attributes of different nationalities can be faithfully reflected; in other words, from the "kaleidoscope" of language we can see the various attributes in different areas and facets of a nationality. In particular, in the vocabulary of a language, we can find the most sensitive and rapid reflections of the attributes of a nationality. Each ethnic language has its own special characteristics in terms of its vocabulary, particularly in the contents and quantity of the vocabulary and in the permutations of the meanings of words and phrases. For example, among the nationalities in the northern part of our country, which are primarily engaged in animal husbandry and herding, there is a vocabulary in which we can find an entire set of words and phrases that reflect the nomenclature and actions of animal husbandry and breeding. Moreover, in this vocabulary the meanings of words and phrases related to this category are very finely distinguished and detailed, and there are things that the nationalities of southern China, who are primarily engaged in agriculture, cannot fully comprehend. On the other hand, among some southern nationalities there is a relatively abundant word stock of names of grain crops and vegetables that grow in the wild, and this is something that is not matched in the languages of the nationalities of the North that are engaged in animal husbandry and herding.

The several other nationality characteristics that are not language-related still have to be reflected and expressed through the medium of language. Take, for, instance, the attribute of "a common mental quality." It has to be communicated through language and is sustained—among the members of the group—by language. Without a language that is of common understanding and reflects the common feelings and emotions, it would be difficult for a common mental quality or state of mind to exist. We have often seen how people of the same nationality who do not know each other as individuals get to know each other very quickly once they begin to communicate in a common language, and indeed begin to converse with congeniality and warmth. What is the basis of this? It is the communicating of the mental quality that is common between the two parties through the use of their common language. A person who lives in a foreign country feels particularly comforted and touched when he hears his native tongue being spoken. This, too, is evidence that a common language among people transmits their common national feelings and emotions. Not only that, but language itself to a certain degree can also be expressive of the special characteristics of the national mentality. For example, when Kazakh herdsmen speak with one another, they have a taboo against using the words for "wolf" ("qasqer" or "bori"), and instead like to use a combination of the words for "dog" ("ijt") and for "bird" ("qus") to make up the word "ijtqus," which expresses the meaning of "wolf." This evidently is related to their hate of wolves, a consequence of their long-term involvement with the mode of production of animal husbandry and breeding.

Furthermore, language can also reflect the attributes of the economic life common to members of a particular nationality. For every nationality, material life is always the most basic and most frequent subject of activity. When people have over a very long time experienced a common type of economic life and been in contact with the same objective things, this cannot but leave a number of special features and characteristics in their common language. In another sense, a common economic life also needs to be held together by a common language. Without a common language it would be impossible to coordinate the common economic life of the group. For example, the Jingpo nationality lives in a mountainous region. Prior to Liberation, they had a slash-and-burn mode of production. For that reason, in the Jingpo language, there are many phrases, words, and expressions that reflect the reality of slash-and-burn. For example: khjen$^{31}$lu?$^{31}$khjen$^{31}$sha$^{35}$ stands for "blade earth-turning fire planting," and therefore the meaning of "slash-and-burn." Similarly, the phrase ji?$^{55}$khu$^{55}$ stands for "land that is abandoned to fallow for one year after slash-and-burn"; ji?$^{55}$fa$^{55}$zi$^{55}$ stands for "ripened-burned fallow land"; jit$^{31}$ta$^{55}$ stands for "abandoned dry land"; khzuan$^{33}$ stands for "twigs and firebrands left behind from slash-and-burning"; and khzuan$^{33}$ji?$^{55}$ stands for "slash-and-burned land." Because in their productive and everyday life the people of the Jingpo nationality could not do without the knife, they have in their language a particular abundance of terms and phrases that stand for the names given to different types of knives and the actions involved in their use. For example: ka$^{31}$tham$^{31}$ stands for "chop"; kzan$^{33}$ stands for "cutting down"; phzang$^{31}$ means "cutting and paring"; tha$^{31}$ means "chopping firewood"; katong$^{33}$ stands for "cutting into short sections"; toi$^{33}$ stands for "a level cut"; khjen$^{31}$ stands for "a horizontal cut"; tum$^{31}$phjot$^{55}$ stands for a "slanted cut"; a$^{31}$tai$^{33}$ stands for "cutting at the root"; and so on. Among the Kazakh people, when a woman gives birth to a child, if the child is a male it is called "qojsher," meaning "a person who tends sheep"; if it is a female, then it is called "dzerlqersher," meaning "someone with a horse." The idea here is that if one gives birth to a boy, that would mean later there would be a person to tend the sheep, and if one gives birth to a girl there would be in the future someone to exchange for horses. The characteristics of these terms and phrases are evidently reflections of the economic life of the Kazakh people in the past.

2. Language not only reflects the contemporary characteristics of a nationality, but also reflects its historical characteristics. Even from the modern and contemporary language of a nation it is possible to see traces of the characteristics of the society of various periods gone by. Certain characteristics, even of a society of the remote past, may to a larger or lesser degree leave traces of itself in modern-day languages. For example, among the people of the Naxi nationality in such places as Lijiang and Weixi, prior to Liberation, there had been formed the system of individual families that revolve around the core of the husband's authority. In that society women belonged to their husbands and were of a low social status. Today, however, in the contemporary Naxi language, some phrases and words remain that reflect an ancient matrilineal society and its social characteristics of "women being superior to men." For example, in the language the idea of a "husband and wife" relationship is expressed as ni$^{33}$nv$^{31}$ (wife) er$^{33}$ka$^{31}$zi$^{33}$ (husband); that is, placing the "wife" before the "husband." Similarly, the idea of "male and female" is expressed as mi$^{55}$ (female) zo$^{33}$ (male); i.e., putting the word for female ahead of the word for male. In addition, the word for "mother" has the same meaning as the word for "big," and the word for "man" has the same meaning as the word for "small." Thus the term for "big tree" is "ndzer$^{31}$ (tree) mer$^{33}$(mother)," whereas the term for "small tree" is

ndzer$^{31}$ (tree) zo$^{33}$ (male).[1] This is because there is an element of heredity in the development of language. Language is not the product of just one age, but is something formed through the gradual accumulation and development of many ages and periods. It is because a language can at the same time synthetically reflect the characteristics of several different ages that it is especially rich in flavor of nationality. When different members of a nationality employ their common nationality language, the feelings and emotions that flow and are exchanged among them are particularly rich. These convey the attributes of the nationality at the present time as well as traditional national attributes; some reflect mental culture, others epitomize social customs and mores. All these converge to blend into a very special national sentiment.

3. Among the various attributes of nationality, language is the more stable one and also changes most slowly. This is because language is a tool for social interaction and therefore cannot change too rapidly. Still less can it be changed arbitrarily and at random. Rather, it must maintain relative stability and historical continuity; otherwise, the social interaction among people will be hindered. Language can transcend the confines of time and be passed on from generation to generation, and it can also break through the boundaries of space and, following the shifting and moving of peoples and nationalities, move from one region to another. In the history of our nation, the shifting of peoples has occurred with frequency, and there has been continuous changes in the distribution of peoples. Each change, however, does not and did not immediately lead to a change in language. Although the changes in languages are indeed controlled and affected by social conditions, they are slower, and it takes a fairly long time before relatively obvious changes in language can be discerned. Therefore, under many conditions, even when society has been separated and people's places of residence have been separated, their language may remain unified. For example, the people of the Hani nationality on the two banks of the Hong River and the people of the Hani nationality in Xishuangbanna live far apart from each other, and there is already an absence of [physical and social] connections between the two groups.

[1]He Zhiwu, "Cong xiangxingwen dongba jing kan naixizu shehui lishi fazhan de jige wenti" (A view of several questions about the sociohistorical development of the Naxi nationality from the perspective of the Dongba hieroglyphic classics), *Zhongyang minzu xueyuan xuebao* (Bulletin of the Central Institute of Nationalities) 2 (1980).

Yet they continue to use the same unified language and belong to the same dialect group. The Tai nationality is primarily distributed in two areas, one in the Dehong Autonomous Prefecture in Yunnan Province, and the other in the Xishuangbanna Autonomous Prefecture. Owing to a very extended period of separation, the social developments in these two places have been very uneven. Even before Liberation, the Tai people in Dehong had already made the transition from a feudalistic overlord economy to a landlord economy, whereas the feudalistic overlord economy has been retained relatively intact in the Xishuangbanna region. However, the people in these two regions continue to use two different dialects of the same language—the Dehong dialect and the Xishuangbanna dialect of the Tai language. The differences in socioeconomic formation have not made the dialects develop separately into different languages.

Under certain conditions, such attributes as social customs and mores, religion and beliefs can change more easily and rapidly than language does. Some nationalities, owing to protracted cohabitation with other nationalities, have seen major changes in their way of dressing; indeed, they may even have fundamentally adopted the dress of other nationalities. And yet in terms of language they have continued to retain their own national language (naturally there may be a certain influence there as well). For example, among the Achang nationality in the area of Longchuan, because they have cohabited with the Tai people for a long time, the Achang women have basically adopted the costumes of the women of the Tai nationality. There has been no change in language, however; they still use the Achang language.

Historically, there have been many changes in the religion and beliefs of the Mongol nationality. It has in the past believed in Shamanism, Lamaism, etc. But its language has remained Mongolic all along. The chief belief of the Lisu nationality in the past has been polytheistic; since the mid-nineteenth century some of its members have been converted to Protestant Christianity and Catholicism, but there has not been much transformation of the language.

4. Language is one of the attributes of nationality and at the same time a tool on which the development of a nationality must depend. Without a language of common understanding for the members of a nationality, that nationality cannot develop. Every nationality's language reflects to a certain degree the level of understanding of objective things that the members of the nationality have, and it represents a

congealing of people's knowledge through a long period of practice. The process by which people learn and use their own nationality's language is also a process by which they learn, inherit, and exchange their national culture. It is only when people have a common language that the history, culture, and science of the nationality can be enhanced and developed continuously and passed on from one generation to another. In the long process of historical development of our country, the various nationalities have commonly contributed to the creation of a splendid and glorious historical culture for the motherland, and each has, through a different nationality language and system of writing, retained a large and precious cultural legacy, including literature, art, astronomy, the calendar, and medicine. The influence of language on the development of a nationality is great beyond measure.

In short, language occupies a special status among the various attributes of nationality. When people use their own nationality language, they inject into it the deepest emotions of the nationality and make the language sparkle with the brilliance of the attributes of the nationality. On the part of the listener, too, there is also an abundance of national feelings, emotions, folklore, and knowledge in the comprehension of the language. It is precisely because there is such an intimate link between language and emotions that the question of how to deal with a language is always linked with the question of nationality. The common attitude among people is that to discriminate against a language is to discriminate against the nationality; to harm the language is tantamount to damaging the nationality. During the period when the "Gang of Four" was rampant, some nationality schools in regions inhabited by the Tai people were forced to suspend the use of their nationality language, and the masses of the Tai nationality became furious and called the schools "their schools." After the "Gang of Four" was crushed, the use of the nationality language was restored and the masses began to call the schools "our schools." From this we can see that discrimination against a language is bound to lead to contradictions among nationalities, whereas respecting the various nationality languages will be conducive to the unity of the nationalities. Marxism upholds the principle of equality among the languages and advocates that regardless of whether they are used by a larger or smaller population, all nationality languages are equal. This is precisely because it perceives the special status and influence of language as an attribute of nationality.

## Relationship Between the Boundaries of Language and the Boundaries of Nationality

Because language is one of the attributes of nationality, under most circumstances the boundaries of a language are consistent with the boundaries of the nationality. In other words, people of the same nationality employ the same language, and people of different nationalities employ different languages. For example, people of the Tibetan nationality use the Tibetan language; people of the Miao nationality use the Miao language, and people of the Korean nationality employ the Korean language. Nonetheless, because language and nationality have their own laws of development and characteristics, it is not possible for them to develop in exactly the same ways and stay abreast of each other all the time. Therefore, under certain conditions there will be circumstances in which the boundaries of language are inconsistent with the boundaries of nationality. In general, we say that languages differ in accordance with the differentiation and division of society and also merge and unite in accordance with the unity of society. However, this is in reference to the overall trend of development of language, and is not to suggest that at every movement language is reflecting changes in society. Changes in language often come more slowly than do social changes in the nationality. When divisions occur in a nationality, language may not follow immediately. Similarly, when nations merge and become assimilated, their languages do not immediately follow suit. Therefore, it is by no means accidental that the condition of inconsistency between the boundaries of language and the boundaries of nationality should appear. Rather, this is something that has its causes in social history and is in conformity with the laws of the development of language. When we examine the relationship between language and nationality, we must explore the reasons and characteristics of the emergence of such a phenomenon.

From the viewpoint of the conditions of the nationality languages in our country, the majority of cases are those in which there is consistency between the boundaries of language and the boundaries of nationality. However, in addition to this basic mode, there are the following conditions:

1. Where one nationality uses more than one language. In some cases, these [polylinguistic nationalities] employ two languages, in some cases even three. In some cases the different languages belong to different branches of a language group; in other cases they belong to a totally

different language branch. For example, the Yao nationality uses three languages: the Mian language belongs to a branch of the Yao language group; the Bunu language is closer to the Miao language; and the Lajia comes close to the Tong language of the Zhuang-Tong language branch. The Jingpo nationality uses two languages: the Jingpo language belongs to the Jingpo branch of languages in the Tibeto-Burman language family, and the Zaiwa language belongs to the Burmese (Mian) branch of languages in the Tibeto-Burman language family. Similarly, the Yugu nationality also uses two languages: the Eastern Yugu language belongs to the Mongol language branch (also known as Engeer language), whereas the Western Yugu language belongs to the Turkic language branch (also known as the Yaofuer language).

Among the people of the nationalities mentioned above that use more than one language, there is generally an obvious consistency on matters involving other nationality attributes. The differences between them lie primarily in the area of language. For instance, the Jingpo people who use the Jingpo language and the Jingpo people who use the Zaiwa language all live together in the region of the Dehong Autonomous Prefecture in Yunnan. They lead a similar economic life and share the same attributes in terms of manner of dress and customs. Moreover, over the centuries they have interacted with each other amiably and frequently intermarried. They share a common ethnic or national mentality and a common understanding that although they may not have the same language they are nonetheless one nationality. This demonstrates that the difference in language does not necessarily inhibit the formation of a united nationality; people speaking different languages can still form a united nationality.

What is worth further study is the question of how, when people of a nationality use more than one language, they resolve the problem of internal communication and exchange. When several languages are used side by side, how do they affect one another? From the use and development of the Jingpo languages we can see that the Jingpo people mainly resolve the problem of communication by way of bilingualism. In the region inhabited by the Jingpo nationality, many people understand both the Jingpo language and the Zaiwa language. Especially in the areas where people commingle and cohabit, the number of those able to speak both languages is particularly large. What is most interesting and amusing is that when, as in many families, the people of the older generation do not all use the same language, the two languages are used together over the long run. The father and mother may each speak his or her language, but they can understand each other; the children, on the other hand, know both languages, and when they converse with their parents they learn to use them separately. In the areas where there is a concentration of people using only one language, there is a trend toward a gradual increase in bilingualism. Naturally, we also can see where differences in the languages used can bring about certain difficulties in the internal communications and interactions within a nationality. Furthermore, we must acknowledge that this very real and practical contradiction is something that cannot be resolved in a short time. From the viewpoint of the development of languages, however, there is a trend toward their mutual influencing, each absorbing from the other elements that it needs to enrich itself, resulting in the gradual increase in common and overlapping elements.

Such a developmental trend tends to be more obviously and clearly reflected in the area of vocabulary. The Zaiwa language borrows more words and expressions from the Jingpo language than the other way around; this includes words and phrases in the areas of politics, economics, and culture. For example, in the Zaiwa language, the words $ning^{31}po^{55}$ (leader), $zap^{31}za^{55}$ (equality), $khjing^{31}$ (costume), $tso?^{31}si^{31}$ (key), $phun^{55}thau^{55}$ (cutting board), $ka^{31}pu^{55}$ (happy), $la^{31}van^{55}$ (fast), $san^{31}seng^{55}$ (clean), $la^{31}kon^{31}$ (lazy), etc. [are borrowed from the Jingpo language]. From the above-mentioned phenomena, we can see that the Jingpo language and the Zaiwa language are moving in a direction conducive to their becoming unified. Whether or not these two languages can eventually blend into one is still hard to say. Even if it is possible, it will probably be a very long process of historical evolution.

Eastern Yugu and Western Yugu are also two languages of such substantial differences that the two are hardly mutually communicable. Nonetheless, there is no question that the people speaking these two languages are of one nationality as they have many common national attributes. For example, they are commonly distributed in the Yugu Minority Autonomous County in southern Gansu, and in terms of economic life, way of dress, and manner of salutation, they maintain similar characteristics. As for the matter of interaction and communication within the nationality, they resolve it by two methods: One is that a few of them are conversant in both languages; the other is that quite a few of them use the Han language as the common tool for communication.

2. Different nationalities using the same language. For example, in

our country the Hui and the Manchus both use the Han language, and some members of the She nationality and the Tuchia nationality also use the Han language. For different nationalities to employ a common language is a situation determined by social conditions. The primary factor is that diverse nationalities have lived together in the same place over a long period and have developed a close relationship with one another in regard to politics, economy, and culture. Without such a condition it would be impossible for them to use the same language. When a language is used by different nationalities, often the various usages may carry with them some different characteristics, but usually these differences are negligible and do not affect the basic attributes of the language.

The Hui in China are a national group made up of a variety of nationalities of Central Asian, Persian, and Arabian origins that successively and gradually moved to China from the mid-seventh century onward. Not only are their points of origin diverse and complex, the languages they originally used were also diverse. They had separately used such languages as Persian, Arabic, etc. Due to various factors that governed their historic migrations and other social factors, the majority of the Hui people are distributed over many different regions in our country and are mingled in with other nationalities, especially the Han. Their distribution is marked by the characteristic of being scattered broadly in relatively small concentrations. Changes in the environment of the language determined the changes in the use of the language. Over a fairly long period of time, the Hui people have gradually shifted to using the Han language and adopting it as their own national tongue. The Han language is not only the tool for communication between the Hui and other nationalities but also the tool for the same purpose among the Hui people themselves. It is through the Han language as a communication medium that the Hui people accumulate and exchange their culture, express their national feelings and psychological attributes, and develop their common economic life. Using the Han language is a national attribute of the Hui people, and the Han language has already become the common communication tool for members of the Hui nationality. The primary cause of the Hui people's use of the Han language is their long-term cohabitation with the Han. Second, it may also have something to do with the overdiversity of languages used in the past.

Nonetheless, in some regions the Han language used by the Hui carries interesting features. Mainly this is expressed in the mingling in of a small amount of words and phrases (mostly religious) of Persian and Arabic origin. For example, they call a friend "duositi," as in the sentence "Duositi, you have given me too much help." The word "duositi" comes from the Persian. They call the "Holy Land" "Hanzhi," and express the idea of pilgrimage as "going to pay homage to Hanzhi." The word "Hanzhi" comes from Arabic. Furthermore, they use the following phrases that come from Persian: "Duhetaier" (little girl), "mietie" (intention), "duozihai" (hell), "naimazi" (worship). The following words and phrases are of Arabic origin: "Dunya" (the world), "ergabu" (condemned by God), "nikahan" (marriage), "baiheilai" (stingy), and "saiwabu" (thank you). Naturally, by using some "imported" words and phrases they have not actually transformed the character of the language; what they speak is still essentially the Han language, except with a little exotic flavor.

According to some investigative material, even today, the Hui nationality people residing in Ya County on Hainan Island still use a unique language different from either the Han language or the language of any local minorities. They use this language for communication within the nationality community but use the local Han language when communicating and socializing with the Han. This is something special.[2]

The She nationality uses both the She language and the Han language. Those using the She language are small in number—no more than one to two thousand—and account for less than 1 percent of the total She population. This language belongs to the Miao language branch of the Miao-Yao subfamily of languages in the Sino-Tibetan language family. On the other hand, over 99 percent of the She population have taken to using the Hakka dialect of the Han language. The adoption of the Han language by the She is closely related to their [historical] migration and distribution. Before the Sui and Tang dynasties, the She people already resided in the mountainous region bordering the three provinces of Fujian, Guangdong, and Guangxi. From the fourteenth century onward, they began gradually migrating toward eastern Fujian and southern Zhejiang, and their migratory patterns resulted in their being widely dispersed but in small concentrations. The majority of the She commingled with the Han people. Over the centuries, the She nationality and its Han nationality neighbors have formed an intimate relationship in terms

[2]Zheng Yiqing, "Hainan dao ya xiande hui zu ji qi yuyan" (The Hui nationality of Ya County on Hainan Island and its language), *Minzu yanjiu* (Nationality studies) 6 (1981).

of economic life and mutual intersection of culture. They have come to share many common habits and customs and celebrate similar days and festivals. All these are social conditions contributing to the She adoption of the Han language.

The Hakka dialect of the Han language used by the She people is different from that used by the Han people. There are differences in phonetics, grammar, and vocabulary. For example, there are some words different from the original Hakka dialect, such as $pi^{35}$ (meat), $hau^{31}$ (brightness), $kuai^{33}$ (this), $lau^{33}khoe^{31}$ (spider), $khiu^{33}$ (centipede), etc. In some cases these words and phrases are closer to those used in the Bunu language of the Yao nationality and the Boluo She language of Guangdong.[3]

The above refers to situations where either a nationality as a whole or the vast majority of the members of a nationality use the language of another nationality. If we stretch it to cover cases where part of a nationality uses the language of another nationality then we would have to multiply the number of instances. In our country many minority nationalities include some people that to a degree have shifted to using the Han language or the language of some other nationality such as the Mongols, the Zhuang, the Bai, or the Yi nationality. This phenomenon is inseparable from our country's characteristic as a multinationality country with the Han people as the mainstream.

3. Where the difference between languages or dialects used internally by the same nationality is greater than the difference between any one of the languages or dialects and the language of another nationality. For instance, the difference between the Jingpo language and the Zaiwa language is greater than that between the Zaiwa language and the Achang language. In concrete terms, there are, between the Jingpo language and the Zaiwa language, relatively few terms that have the same linguistic origin, and there is only a loose phonetic correspondence. Few homologous words or phrases exist. On the other hand, there are more words and phrases that came from the same source between the Zaiwa language and such languages as the Achang and Hani, and the patterns of phonetic correspondence between these are also more regular and complete, with many homologous terms and phrases.

[3]Mao Zongwu and Meng Chaoji, "Boluo she yu gaishu" (A general discussion of the She language of Buluo), *Minzu yuwen* (Nationality language and literature) 1 (1982); Luo Meizhen, "Shezu suoshuode kejiahua" (The Hakka language spoken by the She nationality), *Zhongyang minzu xueyuan xuebao* 1 (1980).

Also, the difference between the northern and southern dialects in the Zhuang language is greater than the difference between the northern dialect itself and the Buyi language. The formation of such circumstances has in each case specific historical and developmental reasons behind it: Either it is because after different and previously separate communities blended to form a new nationality, languages of the previous parts have yet to be unified and therefore have retained their original differences; or it may be that as a result of the division of the parts of a previous unified community, part of the population of a nationality has become separated from the original body, and thus its dialect has become a language.

**Studying Languages from the Angle of Nationality**

Because such an intimate relationship exists between language and nationality, it is inevitable that from the realms of linguistics and ethnology there will be, by subdivision, the emergence of two new disciplines. The study of the attributes and developmental processes of languages through the angle of nationality is called "ethnolinguistics," and the study of the attributes and developmental processes of a nationality from a linguistic perspective is called "linguistic ethnology." In the essay "On Linguistic Ethnology" the authors have made an attempt to discuss, on the basis of the intimate relationship between language and nationality, the special significance and particular methodology of studying nationalities from a linguistic perspective; here, let us take a further step and explore the questions of the content and methodology of studying languages through the angle of nationality.[4]

The influence of nationality on language is multifaceted and complex. In general, the development and transformation of a nationality has a controlling influence over the development and evolution of its language. These determine and stipulate the general direction in which the language may develop. However, when we take a special segment of time, within that frame the transformation and evolution of the nationality may not necessarily lead to immediate changes in the language. Therefore, when we study language from the angle of nationality, we must observe not only the aspect in which nationality influences and controls language, but also the peculiarities of the language's independent development. In general, therefore, when we study language from the angle of nationality,

[4]Ma Xueliang and Dai Qingxia, "Lun yuyan minzu xue" (On linguistic ethnology), *Minzuxue yanjiu* (Studies in ethnology) 1 (1981).

we should pay attention to the following aspects:

1. We should look at the formation of a nationality's language from the perspective of the formation of the nationality. The nationality's formation determines the formation of the nationality's language. Only when there is a nationality community can there be a common nationality language. When we study the question related to the formation of a nationality language, we can understand the question clearly only if and when we examine it in connection with the social history of the nationality and verify linguistic material in light of the material of social history. For example, the formation of the various languages in the Mongolian family—including Mongol, Dongxiang, and Dawoer languages—took place around the turn of the sixteenth century. This is connected to the collapse of the Mongol empire and the division and dissipation of the once united Mongol nationality. When we relate this to the history of the division of the Mongol nationality, it would not be difficult to explain the relationships among the various languages in the family of Mongol languages.

In our country, for the moment it is still difficult to resolve some problems related to the categorical and family connections of certain languages. This is related to the fact that the problems of the origin of the nationalities with which these languages are connected have not yet been fully clarified. For example, there is, as of now, no complete consensus on the classification of the language of the Bai nationality, even after much discussion of the subject. Some people believe that it belongs to the Yi language branch of the Tibeto-Burman language family; others believe that it is itself an independent branch of the Tibeto-Burman family. As for the origin of the Bai nationality, there are even more differences of opinion. Some people even think that it was a nationality formed by the merging of several historical nationalities, that it was a confluence of nationalities of different sources. If a scientific solution can be found regarding the origins of the Bai nationality, it would certainly help to resolve the problem of the identity of the language.

2. We should look at the division and unification of languages from the perspective of the division and unification of nationalities. Historically speaking, the division and migration of a nationality often leads to the division of language; indeed, even to the adoption by a part of its population of another language. On the other hand, when nationalities move in the direction of unification, their language will also correspondingly move toward a trend of unified development. To understand clearly the condi-

tions of national division and unification will be conducive to understanding the evolution of languages. In our country, the division of dialects among many of the languages of minority nationalities is intimately related to the division of branches of the nationality; very often the lines of demarcation in each area correspond to one another. In some cases, each branch represents a dialect, in other cases, two or three branches share the same dialect. Therefore we can use the material indicating the division of branches of a nationality as a point of reference for the division between dialects, or even to draw conclusions verifying the division of dialects; this is a relatively dependable and simple method. Let us take a look, for instance, at the relations between the division of dialects in the Hani language and the division of branches of the nationality:

**Hani Language**

1. Haya dialects (Hani, Yani branches)
   a. Hani subdialect (Hani branch)
   b. Yani subdialect (Yani branch)

2. Bika dialect (Biyue, Kaduo, and Onu branches)
   a. Biyue local dialect (Biyue branch)
   b. Kaduo local dialect (Kaduo branch)
   c. Onu local dialect (Onu branch)

3. Haobai dialect (Haoni, Baihong branches)
   a. Haoni local dialect (Haoni branch)
   b. Baihong local dialect (Baihong branch)

The distribution of different dialects within a nationality language is intimately related to the natural divisions and boundaries of valleys and rivers. For example, the Naxi language is divided into two dialects, the western and the eastern, and the line of separation between these two dialects is, generally speaking, made up of rivers. The eastern Naxi dialect is located to the east of the Wuliang and Jinshajiang rivers and to the north of the Wulang River; the western Naxi dialect lies to the west of the Wuliang and Jinshajiang rivers and to the south of the Wulang River. The division of location between the northern and southern dialects of the Zhuang language is marked by the north-south distinction of the Yongjiang River.

3. We should look at the characteristics of language from the perspective of a nationality's social characteristics. The various characteristics of a language are primarily determined by the different internal laws of development of different languages. However, the characteristics of a nationality's social development can affect the development of a language and cause it to possess different characteristics. If we study a language in conjunction with the characteristics of its society, we can gain a deeper comprehension of the language.

Prior to Liberation, our country's various nationalities' social development was quite uneven; the nationalities belonged to different socioeconomic modes. Some nationalities (such as the Zhuang, Miao, Korean, and Bai) had moved, in the way that the Han nationality already had, into the phase of a feudal society; others were still in the slavery stage (such as the Yi nationality of Sichuan); and some retained to some degree the remnant characteristics of primitive society (such as the Dulong, Jingpo, and Wa nationalities). The question of what effects differences in socioeconomic mode may have on the development of language is one deserving of study. From the viewpoint of the overall situation, the various minority nationalities in our country are mostly in the precapitalist stage of history, a stage in which the circulation, formation, and development of a standard language are subject to a certain set of restraints. In many cases, the languages of these nationalities have not yet taken shape as unified standard languages. For example, in the cases of the Yi, Miao, and Hani languages, the divergences among the dialects within the languages themselves are relatively great, and a unified standard language has yet not been formed. When our party and government took up the task of resolving problems related to the languages of these nationalities after Liberation, they came up against the problem of how to establish a standard language for each of these nationalities. The solution to this problem must be sought in conjunction with consideration for the social characteristics of these nationalities.

Another problem that deserves to be studied is the problem of the development of "cross-boundaries" languages. By this we mean languages that remain the same but are distributed in different countries. The majority of the languages of our country's minority nationalities are distributed in the border regions, and quite a few "cross boundaries," such as the languages of the Kazakh, Kirghiz, Lisu, Lagu, and Jingpo nationalities. When the same language is distributed in different countries, owing perhaps to differences in social system or to variations in historical tradition, natural environment, habitation, etc., different characteristics may also appear in the ways in which the language develops. For example, besides being in our own country, there are also people using the Jingpo language in Burma, our neighbor. The Jingpo language used in these two countries is basically the same in fundamental characteristics, with only minor variations. Nonetheless, owing to the difference in the environment there are certain different characteristics in each case. One of these characteristics is that the Jingpo language in our country is influenced more by the language of the mainstream nationality—the Han—whereas the Jingpo language in Burma is more deeply influenced by the major nationality language of that country, the Burmese language. What are the characteristics of the laws of development of cross-boundary languages? What would be the correct way of handling the relationship between the various parts of the language as they are located in different countries? These are problems that have yet to be thoroughly studied.

In general, with regard to studying language from the perspective of nationality, the social conditions of a nationality can only provide some evidence for the study of language and thereby help us to understand linguistic phenomena. However, under some conditions, to determine the nature of a certain linguistic phenomenon we must in the main rely on understanding the social conditions of the nationality. For example, in determining whether the difference between some languages is actually a difference between languages or a difference between dialects, we must rely chiefly on the nationality composition of the subjects to make the distinction, and in this case, the characteristics of language are not the more important. The Kazakh language and the Kirghiz language are two different languages, and yet the difference between them is really minor. People who use one of the two languages can understand the other language. On the other hand, the differences between the various dialects of the Yi language are much greater, and yet they are differences of dialects. In these cases, the magnitude of differences in terms of linguistic characteristics is not a determining factor; rather, it is the nationality composition that plays the major role. In the former case, there are two nationalities, whereas in the latter case, there is just one nationality. In people's minds, generally, when there are some differences between the languages spoken by different nationalities, they should be considered as different languages, whereas when there are differences of magnitude in the ways in which people of the same nationality speak (naturally there are certain boundaries and parameters), they should be considered as different dialects of the same language. In addition, the degree of mutual influence between nationality languages is often determined by the nationalities' relationship. When the relations between nationalities are congenial, the mutual influence between their languages may be greater. The magnitude of the mutual influence between languages is determined mainly by social conditions; it is only from social factors that we can find relatively reliable answers. For example, the Gelao language influence from the Han language has been relatively great; its basic vocabulary is already more than two-fifths Han loan words, since most of the new vocabulary items introduced since Liberation are technical terms borrowed from the Han language. In the case of many concepts, a term from the vocabulary of the nationality's own original language and a term borrowed from the Han language coexist and are used interchangeably or together. The Gelao language, moreover, has absorbed many abstract terms from the Han language, and its grammar has also been to some degree transformed as a result of the influence of the Han language. The reason that the Gelao language can be thus multifacetedly and deeply influenced by the Han language is that the Gelao nationality has remained in close interaction with the Han people for a very long time; in general, the Gelao people also know and are conversant in the Han language, and there is a tradition of learning and using the Han written language.[5]

4. We must look at the development of the phenomenon of bilingualism from the perspective of a nationality's characteristics. The phenomenon of bilingualism is a worldwide question. Among every nationality in the world there is, to a certain degree, a problem of bilingualism. Today, owing to the continuous development of science and culture, to the increasing convenience of communications and transportation, there are more and more people who use more than one language in all the nationalities of the world. The manner and degree to which the question of bilingualism is resolved has a direct impact on the development of the nationality's cultural and educational enterprise and on the nationality's own prosperity and growth. The development of bilingualism has its own objective internal law, and this law is primarily controlled by the nationality's social conditions. In our country, owing to the fact that the development of the various nationalities is uneven,

[5]Zheng Guoqiao, "Shi lun hanyu dui gelaoyude yingxiang" (A tentative discussion of the impact of the Han language on the Gelao language), *Zhongyang minzu xueyuan xuebao* 4 (1980).

and because different nationalities have many different characteristics, the bilingualism of different nationalities also differs. For example, the characteristics of bilingualism may differ from one nationality to another according to the size of population. For populous nationalities such as the Uygurs, Tibetans, and others, nationality languages are spoken over wide areas and in a broad pattern of uses, and thus the number of people who use two languages in these nationalities will be smaller. On the other hand, with nationalities that have a smaller population, such as the Xibo, Achang, and Ji'nuo nationalities, the area where the nationality language is used is relatively small; add to that the fact that their people have more frequent interaction with people of other nationalities, and they consequently have more people who use two languages. Take the Xibo nationality in Xinjiang Province: many of its members, in addition to using the Xibo language, are also fairly conversant in the Han language and the Uygur language. Similarly, many people of the Achang nationality in Yunnan can use the Han language and the Tai language in addition to their native tongue. Furthermore, there are variations between regions where people of one nationality are concentrated and regions where they commingle with other nationalities, between nationalities that have a written language and those that do not, and between nationalities that have a higher standard of economy and culture and those that have lower standards. In a multinationality country, the conditions of the relations among the nationalities have a tremendous influence on the development of bilingualism. Where the unity of the nationalities is well-promoted there will be a more conducive atmosphere for people of different nationalities to learn each other's languages and more people will be bilingual. On the other hand, where there are problems in the relations among the nationalities, bilingualism is often obstructed. Owing to the continuous strengthening of nationality unity since Liberation, there has been an equally continuous development and growth among the people of the various nationalities in our country to learn languages from each other; nothing from before Liberation can match this. The study of the laws of development of bilingualism in conjunction with the social characteristics of the nationalities is an important topic for linguistic studies.

# Index

Achang nationality, 179, 185, 196, 203, 210
Alphabet. *See* written scripts
Altaic language family, 180
American Museum of Natural History, 99
An Zhimin, 24, 136
*Ancient Society*, 15
Andersson, Johann, 7
Animal husbandry, 192, 193
Anthropological linguistics. *See* Linguistics and anthropology
Anthropological sciences, definition of, 3
Anthropology: in academia, 4, 25, 55; application of, 8, 18, 28, 41, 52–53; in China, 6, 8–9, 28, 47, 53; and the CPC, 8–9; definition of, ix, 3, 10, 19, 23, 24, 33, 42–46, 48; foreign influence in, x; and historical materialism, 40, 51; and Marxism 38–40; 1980s' rebirth of, 8–20, 24–27; and other disciplines, 36–37, 47, 49–54; sinification of, 26–28, 39–41; and the Soviet model, 9–10; subfields of, 38–39, 44–46, 48, 51, 54, 96; theoretical schools in, 39; in United States, 5. *See also* Archaeology; Ethnology; Linguistics; Paleontology; Physical Anthropology; United States, anthropology in
Anthropometry, x, 4, 13, 121–26
Anthroposociogenesis, theory of, 39–40, 51
Applied anthropology, 35
Arabs, 201, 202,
Archaeology, 12; in academia, 4, 10, 47, 69; application of, 18; in China, 5, 10, 17, 21–22, 59–61, 71; definition of, ix, 24, 48, 61–63, 67, 167; as a discipline, 5, 62–65, 68–69, 70–71; foreign influence on, 7, 15; goals of, 65, 70–72; and history, 61–63, 65–68; in the 1980s, 22, 51, 55; origins of, 59–60; and other disciplines, 36, 45, 64–65, 68–69, 93–94, 167; sinification of, 27, 69–70; subfields of, 69, 94–95
Archaeology Institute (CASS). *See* Institute of Archaeology, CASS
Archeometry, 47
Australia, 48, 50, 97–98, 102–4
Australian National University, 48, 50

Bai nationality, 179, 182, 185, 186, 203, 205, 207
Banpo, 16, 75, 77, 84, 85, 95
Baoan nationality, 179, 185
Behavioral science, 112
Beijing, importance of, 5, 116
Beijing Museum of Natural History, 47
Beijing University, xii, 9, 23, 69, 178
Benglong, 185
Bilingualism, 199–200, 209–10
Binford, Lewis, x
Biology and archaeology, 69
Birharis, 103, 104
Bishop Museum of Hawaii, 95
Black, Davidson, 6, 7
Bloomfield, Leonard, 7
Boas, Franz 8
Botswana, 99
Brazil, 98
Britain. *See* Great Britain
Bulong nationality, 185
Bunu nationality, 199, 203
Burma, 208
Burmese languages, 186, 199, 208
Bushmen, 99–100, 102–4
Buyi nationality, 199, 178, 182, 204
Byzantine Empire, 95

Cai Yuanpei, 6, 24

Cenozoic Research Laboratory, 4
Central Asia, 201
Central Institute of Nationalities (CIN), xii, 5, 9, 14, 19, 23, 48, 149, 161, 178
Chao Yuanren, 7
Cheboksarov, Nikolai, 14–15, 26
Chen Guoqiang, ix, 8, 19, 24
Chen Yongling, 27
Chie Nakane, 49
Chilo nationality, 185
Chinese Academy of Sciences (CAS), 12, 20
Chinese Academy of Social Sciences (CASS), 20
Chinese Anthropological Society, 19
Chinese characters, xi, 182, 184
Chinese Communist Party. *See* Communist Party of China
Chinese Linguistics Society, 184
Choukoutien. *See* Peking man; Zhoukoudian site
Christianity, 196
Chronology, definition of, 112
*Cihai*, 149
Cishan-Peiligang culture, 77, 83, 87
Class struggle, 13
Communist Party of China (CPC). and academia, 9, 11, 37, 53–54, 142, 168; and the minority nationalities, 143, 153, 159, 170, 177, 183, 184, 207. *See also* Historical materialism; Marx, Karl; Marxism; Marxism-Leninism
Congress of Anthropological and Ethnological Sciences (CAES), 53
Cultural anthropology, 34–35, 44, 45, 47, 49, 52.
Cultural Revolution, 16–18, 23, 150, 159, 180. *See also* "Gang of Four"
*Current Anthropology*, 18

Dahure nationality, 179, 185
Dai Qingxia, xi
Dai nationality, 178
Darwin, Charles 68
*Das Kapital*, 64
Dawenkou culture, 78, 80, 83, 86, 87
*Daxue congshu*, 44
Democratic reform, 146, 148, 172

Dialectical materialism, 39, 51,
Dialects, 11, 179, 186, 187, 196, 203, 204, 206–9
Diffusionism, 6
Dingcun site, 136–37
Dong nationality, 178, 182, 185
Dongxiang nationality, 179, 185
Dulong nationality, 185, 207

Eastern coastal region, 86
Engels, Friedrich, ix, 12, 15, 16, 21, 39, 43, 52, 63, 66, 151, 164
English language, use in anthropology of, 18, 19
Erlitou culture, 86, 87
Ethnic groups. *See* Ethnology; Minority nationalities; Nationality; *names of specific nationalities*
Ethnoarchaeology, 24; definition of, 91–92, 103; examples of, 94–96, 97–100, 103–6; function of, 96–101; methodology of, 101–5; origins of, 92–93; and other disciplines, 100–101, 105–6; in the West, 91–92, 97
Ethnography, 21, 45–46, 52
Ethnolinguistics, 204. *See also* Minority nationalities
Ethnology, 51; in academia, 4, 47, 149, 161; application of 10–11, 145, 169, 172; bourgeois, 157, 162–64; in China, 6, 14, 142, 144–45, 148–49, 153, 160–61, 163–65, 169; cross-cultural study of, 155–56; definition of, 21, 24–28, 48, 149, 152, 165–66, 190; goals of, 153–61, 169; and the Han nationality, 155; and historical materialism, 164; in Japan, 166; linguistic, 204; and Marxism, 142, 160, 162–64, 168, 169; methodology of, 11–12, 145, 165; 1980s' reemergence, 19, 150; and other disciplines, 34–36, 152, 165–68; and politics, 37, 149–50, 162–63, 168; scope of, 5, 21, 141, 152, 165; sinification of, 160, 165; and socialism, 168–69; and the Soviet Union, 160, 166; and the West, 144–45, 156, 158,

Ethnology (*continued*): 160, 166; *See also* Cultural anthropology; Nationality studies
Ethnology, Museum of, 169
Eugenics, 52, 116, 118
Europeans, 6, 152
Evolution, 6, 8, 21, 112; human, 37, 111, 121; social, 148, 154–57, 170, 171

Fei Xiatong (Fei Hsiao-t'ung), 6–9, 25
Feng Hanqi, 105
*Feuerbach and the End of German Classical Philosophy*, 66
Folklore, 35–36, 47, 106, 155, 183
Forensic medicine, 126
Fossils, 111–12
Four modernizations, 41, 52, 53; and anthropology, 51, 55; and ethnology, 153, 160; and national minorities, 168–69, 171, 183, 187; and physical anthropology, 119–20, 122; and population planning, 116
France, 9, 23, 122
Fu Maoji, xi, 23
Fudan University, 4, 10, 47, 149
Fujian Province, 4, 123, 202. *See also* Xiamen University
Functionalism, 6, 8, 9

"Gang of Four," 51, 53, 141, 150, 152, 159, 172, 197. *See also* Cultural Revolution
Gansu Province, 84, 85, 129, 132, 200
Gaoshan nationalities, 180, 185
Gelao nationality, 209
Gelek, 4
Genetics, human, 4, 117, 118
Geography and ethnology, 159
Geology and archaeology, 68
Great Britain and the anthropological sciences, 6–8, 9, 35, 44, 61, 101, 122
Great Leap Forward, 11, 13, 16
Greece, 59
Guangdong Institute of Nationalities, xii
*Guangdong Minzu Xueyuan*, xii
Guandong Province, 88, 123, 154, 179, 202, 203. *See also* Guangzhou; Zhongshan University
Guangxi Zhuang Autonomous Region, 106, 123, 129, 144, 178, 202
Guangzhou, 123, 124
Guiyang, 37
Guizhou Province, 123, 129, 130, 135, 144, 154, 178
Guomindang (GMD), 143

Hainan Island, 154
Hakka, 202–3
Han dynasty, Western, 105
Han nationality, 10–11, 145, 148, 155, 177, 180, 202, 207, 209; culture of, 22; definition of, xi; languages of, xi, 179, 181, 182, 184, 186, 188, 191, 200, 201–3, 209, 210; script of, 11, 182, 184
Hani nationality, 179, 182, 185, 195–96, 203, 206, 207
Harvard University, 99, 100
Hebei Province, 129
Heilongjiang Province, 82, 129
Hemudu culture, 75, 77, 86, 87, 105
Henan Province, 84, 85, 87, 129, 180
Hezhe nationality, 179
Historical linguistics, 188, 205–6. *See also* Language; Linguistics
Historical materialism, 40, 51, 151–52, 164
Historical particularism, 6, 8
History and ethnology, 166–67. *See also* Archaeology, and history
*Holy Family, The*, 63
Homo erectus pekinensis, 127–28. *See also* Peking Man; Zhoukoudian
Hong Kong, 49
Horticulture, 77, 98, 171, 193–94
Huang Shumin, 50
Huang Shuping, xi
Huang Xinmei, x
Huaqiao, 155
Hubei Province, 84, 87, 89, 129
Hui nationality, 142, 201–3
Human variation, 113. *See also* Physical anthropology
Hunan Province, 89

India, 144
Inner Mongolia, 81, 82, 84, 134

# 214  INDEX

Institute of Archaeology, CASS, xii, 10, 17, 46, 185
Institute of Languages, CAS, 177, 178
Institute of Minority Nationality Languages, CAS, 9, 181
Institute of Nationalities Studies, CASS, xii, 9–10, 20, 46, 48, 115, 147, 158, 185
Institute of Sociology, CASS, 53
Institute of Vertebrate Paleontology and Paleoanthropology (IVPP), CASS, xii, 4, 10, 17, 24, 46
Interdisciplinary studies, 166-68

Japan, 6, 8, 19, 49, 61, 122
Japan University, 49
Java Man, 128
Jia Lanpo, 7, 24
Jiangsu Province, 87, 129
Jiarong nationality, 185
Jilin Province, 129, 132
Jing nationality, 179, 185
Jingpo nationality, 179, 185, 193–94, 199, 200, 203, 207, 208
Jino nationality, 185
*Jinruigaku senkan*, 49
Jinuo nationality, 144, 210

*Kaogu*, 18
Kazakh nationality, 179, 185, 193–94, 207, 208
Kerekezi nationality, 185
Kirghiz nationality, 179, 207, 208
Korean nationality, 185, 198, 207
Kroeber, Alfred, 8
Kuomintang (KMT), 143

Lagu nationality, 179, 185, 207
Lai nationality, 185
Lajia language, 199
Lamaism, 196
Language: aspects of, 190; and boundaries, 198–204, 207–9; changes in 195–96, 198–200; and emotions 192–93, 195, 197; journals on, 184–86; and Marxism, 197; and nationality, 189–210; origins of, 190–91; and society, 193–94, 197, 207, 209; surveys, 178, 179
Language Institute (CAS), 177–78

Lassal University, 48
Latin America, 145
Law, 51
Lenin, Vladimir I., xi, 15
Levi-Strauss, Claude, 37
Li nationality, 178, 182, 185
Li Jie and Peking Man, 137
Li Fanggui (Li Fangkwei), 7
Li Youyi, 9
Liang Zhaotao, ix, x, 7, 19, 24, 26
Liaoning Province, 129, 130, 132
Lin Biao (Lin Piao), 150, 152, 159, 172
Lin Huixiang, 7, 19, 24, 44–45, 47, 105
Lin Yaohua, x-xi, 7, 9, 26, 144, 145
Ling Chunsheng, 7, 8
Lingnan University, 7. *See also* Zhongshan University
*Lingua franca*, 100, 179
Linguistics, 6, 9; American, 7, 23; and anthropology, xi, 25, 36–37, 48; definition of, 190; and minority identification, 144; in the 1980s, 23; and Stalin, 15. *See also* Anthropology; Minority nationalities, language studies on
Lishu nationality, 179, 185, 196, 207
Liu Han, 7
Loba, 185
London University, 45
Longshan Culture, 22, 77, 78, 80, 85–88
Lowie, Robert H., 8
Luoba nationality, 144
Luo Changpei, 7

Ma Xueliang, xi, 23
Maba Man, 77
Majiabang Culture, 75, 77, 78, 83, 85–86
Malinowski Bronislaw, 6, 7, 8, 43
Manchus, 201
Mandarin. *See* Han language
Mao Zedong (Mao Tse-tung), xi, 11
Mao Zedong Thought, 55, 157. *See also* Communist Party of China; Marxism-Leninism
Maonan nationality, 179
Maps of minorities, 159–60, 169
Marriage, 114–17
Marx, Karl, xi, 15, 16, 39–40, 63, 64, 151, 164

Marxism, 14; and anthropology, 53, 55; and archaeology 65–66, 69–72; and ethnology, xi, 10, 16, 142, 153; and language, 188, 197; and nationalities theories, 151, 153, 156–57, 164; and stages of history, 34; in universities, 12
*Marxism and the Problem of Linguistics*, 156
Marxism-Leninism and the anthropological sciences, 15–16, 20–23, 26–27
May 7 Cadre Schools, 17
Mead, Margaret, 14
Menba nationality, 144
Mental retardation, 116
Mesolithic, 74
Miao language, 199
Miao nationality, 119, 154, 179, 182, 185, 198, 199, 202, 207
Miaodigou culture, 83–85
Miao-Yao languages, 11, 179, 180, 186, 202
Microlithic cultures, 81–83, 88, 134, 137
Ming dynasty, 94
Minority nationalities: identification of, 11, 142–45, 154, 169; language studies on, 5–6, 8–9, 10, 11, 177, 178, 184–86; policies toward, 146, 148, 170, 171; studies of, 142–43, 145–46, 155, 157, 186–88
Minority Nationalities Languages Institute (CAS), 9, 181
*Minzu fangwen tuan*, 10–12
*Minzu wenti wu zhong congshu*, 158
*Minzu xueyuan*, 5, 20
*Minzu yuyan*, 18, 184
Mongol: language, 179, 180, 185, 199, 205; nationality, 142, 178, 179, 180, 196, 203, 205
Mongolian Autonomous Region, 178
Mongoloid race, 74
Morgan, Lewis Henry, 15, 21, 164
Moscow University, 14, 69
Museums, 47, 159
Mythology, 52

Nationalities Affairs Commission, 46, 47, 178
Nationality: aspects of, 190; boundaries of, 198; definition of, 15, 21, 26, 191; and languages, 189–210. *See also* Language and nationality; Minority nationalities
Nationality Institute, CASS. *See* Institute of Nationalities Studies, CASS
Nationality relations, 10–11
Nationality studies: in China, 14, 18; and the four modernizations, 38. *See also* Minority nationalities, studies of
National People's Congress, 11
National Twelve-Year Plan for Scientific Research, 147
*Natural Dialectics*, 43, 52
Naxi nationality, 115, 179, 182, 185, 194–95, 206
Neoanthropology, definition of, x, 112–13
Neolithic, x, 16, 73–90, 92, 98; analysis of, 79–90; aspects of, 75–79; in China, 22, 38, 73, 75, 79–80
*Netherlands Bulletin*, 18
New archaeology, 23, 65
Ningxia-Hui Autonomous Region, 81, 82, 84, 85, 134
North China Plain, 84
Northeast China, 123
Northwestern University, 50

Olunchun nationality, 179, 185
Oral literature. *See* Folklore
*Origin of the Family, Private Property and the State*, 12, 15, 39–40, 151, 164
*Origin of Species*, 68
Overseas Chinese, 155
Owenk nationality, 179, 185

Pacific basin, 95
Pacific Lutheran University, xi
Paleoanthropology, 12; in China, 18, 22, 46; definition of, 34, 42, 111; and other disciplines, x, 111, 135–37; and sinification, 27; Soviet influence on, 15
Paleography. *See* Written scripts
Paleolithic: aspects of, 78, 81, 135–37; in China, 129–30, 132–35;

Paleolithic (*continued*): cultures, 73–75, 127–37; tools used 130–35
Paleontology and archaeology, 68. *See also* Paleoanthropology
Pan Guangdan, 7, 9, 12
Peiligang culture, 22, 77
Pei Wenzhong, 7, 24, 127, 137
Peking Man, x, 4, 7, 115, 127–28, 135–36. *See also* Zhoukoudian site
People's Liberation Army, 28
Persia, 201, 202
Philippines, 48, 50
Physical anthropology, 10, 76, 117–19; applied, 115, 119–20; definition of, 4, 34, 48, 114; scope of, 47, 49. *See also* Paleoanthropology
Pinyin system. *See* Written scripts
Political campaigns, 11–14, 16–18, 20, 172
Polynesia, 95
Prehistoric stages of culture, 72–73
Primatology, 4, 104, 111–13
Primitive societies. *See* Ethnology
Pumi language, 185

Qiang nationality, 179, 185, 186
Qijia culture, 77, 83
Qinghai Province, 84, 85, 180
Qinghua University, 7, 8, 9
Qujialing culture, 78, 83

Race, study of, 47, 158
Radcliffe-Brown, A. R., 6, 8, 14
Red Guards, 8, 16–17
Religious studies, 51, 172, 196
*Renleixue xuebao*, 18
Rh factor, 118–19
Roman Empire, 95
Ruey I-fu, 8
Russian language, 18–19

Sapir, Edward, 7
Shirokogorov, Sergei, 6, 24
Shaanxi Province, 83, 84, 85, 129, 132
Shandong Province, 87
Shang Dynasty, 22, 78, 80
Shanxi Province, 84, 85, 129, 132, 134
She nationality, 179, 201–3
Shi Zhenmin, 48
Shiala nationality, 185

Shoshone people, 104
Shui nationality, 178, 185
Sichuan Province, 87, 88, 123, 129, 144, 154, 178
Sila nationality, 179
Sima Qian, 163
Sinanthropus pekinensis. *See* Peking Man; Zhoukoudian
Sinification of anthropology, 20–21. *See also* Archaeology; Ethnology, in China, Physical anthropology
Sino-Japanese War, 8
Sino-Soviet split, 16
Sino-Tibetan language family, 11, 202
Slash-and-burn agriculture, 77, 98, 171, 193–94
Social History Research Project, 11, 12–14, 16, 21, 47, 147–48, 158
Socialism: and anthropology, 114; and ethnology, 163, 168; and minority nationalities, 146, 157, 168, 172
Sociolinguistics, 186, 187
Sociology, 5, 7, 8, 9, 46, 51, 53–54; and anthropology, 45, 49–50, 53, 54; contrast with archaeology, 66; definition of, 54; and historical materialism, 54, 151
South Asian language family, 180
South China, 81, 88–89
South China Nationality Institute, 178
Southwest Region, 89–90
Soviet model, 4, 20, 23, 25, 27; and anthropology, ix, 14–16, 44; and other anthropological sciences, 26, 63–64, 69, 122, 153, 163; and the use of Russian, 18–19
Soviet Union, nationalities in, 144, 155
Stalin, Joseph, xi, 15, 21, 26, 156, 191
Stanford University, 48
State Council, 9, 46, 144, 181
Sun Yat-sen University. *See* Zhongshan University

Tai nationality, 196, 197, 210
Taiwan, 8, 10, 49, 154, 180, 185
Tajik nationality, 179, 185
Tatar nationality, 119, 179
Teilhard de Chardin, Pierre, 7
Thought Reform, 12, 14, 20
Tibetan nationality, 4, 89, 130, 144, 154, 179, 180, 185, 198, 210

Tibeto-Burman language family, 180, 199, 205
"Two Civilizations," x, 114, 116, 119, 165
Tu nationality, 182, 185
Tujia nationality, 179, 185, 201
Turkic language family, 179, 199
Tuzu nationality, 179

UNESCO, 158
United States, 9, 50, 104; anthropology in, ix, x, 3, 4, 27, 28, 35, 44, 48, 50; anthropometry in, 122; archaeology in, 61, 65; ethnoaracheology in, 101, 102; Indian languages of, 7; influences on China, 6–8. *See also* Western model
University of California at Los Angeles, 96, 103
University of Hawaii, 97
University of Manila, 7
University of Maryland, 48
Uygur nationality, 179, 191, 210
Uzbek nationality, 119, 179

Venezuela, 98, 99

Wa nationality, 179, 182, 185, 207
Wang Kang, 54
Warring States period, 101
Wei Huilin, 8
*Wenhau renleixue*, 44
Western model, 6–8, 14, 26
Wissler, Clark, 43
Written scripts, 178–84, 187, 188
Wu Dingliang, 7, 24
Wu Rukang, x, 18, 24, 136
Wu Wenzao, 7, 12
Wu Zelin, 12

Xia dynasty, 86
Xia Nai, 21–22
Xiamen University, xii, 4, 5, 7, 8, 19, 24, 44–45, 47, 48, 50, 149
*Xiandai renleixue*, 45
Xibo nationality, 179, 210
Xinjiang-Uygur Autonomous Region, 81, 82, 178, 210
Xiqiaoshan site, 77

Yan'an period, 142

Yanomamo, 98–99
Yang Chengzhi, 7, 13, 24
Yang Kun, 7, 37
Yang Zhongjian, 137
Yangshao culture, 16, 77, 78, 80, 83–86, 87
Yangzi River Valley, 16, 22, 77–79, 86–88, 89
Yanjing University, 7, 9
Yao nationality, 185, 199, 203
Yellow River Basin, 22, 75, 77–82, 86, 88, 134, 180
Yi nationality, 144, 179, 182, 185, 186, 203, 205, 207, 208
Yiao nationality, 179
Yiaolao nationality, 179
Yibo nationality, 185
Yuanmou Ape-Man, 37, 136
Yue cultural group, 101
Yugu nationality, 179, 185, 199, 200
Yunnan Province, 4, 89, 95, 96, 105, 115, 123, 129, 144–46, 154, 178, 195–96, 199, 210
Yunnan University, 149
*Yuyen yanjiu*, 184, 185

Zaiwa language, 185, 199, 200, 203
Zeng Qi, x
Zhang Liyuan, 45
Zhang Shouqi, 26
Zhang Zhenbiao, x
Zhejiang Province, 105, 202
Zhilao nationality, 179
*Zhonggu yuwen*, 184–85
*Zhongguo yuyen xuebao*, 184
Zhongshan University, xi, 8, 9, 18, 19, 24; academic majors at, 5, 47; and American model, 4; and ethnology, 149
Zhou dynasty, 78, 80
Zhou Enlai, 148, 181
Zhoukoudian site, 17, 115, 127, 133, 136. *See also* Peking Man
Zhuang nationality, 178, 182, 185, 203, 204, 206, 207
Zhuang-Dong language family, 179, 180, 186, 199